转喻在新闻语篇中的组织功能

Functions of Metonymy in News Text Organization

戴理敏 著

山东大学出版社

图书在版编目(CIP)数据

转喻在新闻语篇中的组织功能/戴理敏著. —济南:山东大学出版社,2016.6

ISBN 978-7-5607-5555-7

Ⅰ.①转… Ⅱ.①戴… Ⅲ.①英语-语言学-研究
Ⅳ.①H31

中国版本图书馆 CIP 数据核字(2016)第 140987 号

责任策划:张申华
责任编辑:张申华
封面设计:张 荔

出版发行:山东大学出版社
社 址 山东省济南市山大南路 20 号
邮 编 250100
电 话 市场部(0531)88364466
经 销:山东省新华书店
印 刷:山东省英华印刷厂
规 格:720 毫米×1000 毫米 1/16
13.75 印张 254 千字
版 次:2016 年 6 月第 1 版
印 次:2016 年 6 月第 1 次印刷
定 价:26.00 元

前 言

近年来,随着认知语言学的发展,转喻已经逐渐被作为一种基本的认知与语言现象而引起关注。人们已经突破传统修辞学对转喻研究的限制,不再仅把转喻看作为词汇间的相互替代。转喻表达被广泛应用于日常交际,越来越多的研究试图揭示转喻在人类的认知与概念化中发挥的作用。目前,关于转喻的研究主要集中在揭示转喻的认知本质上,如转喻的定义、分类、与隐喻的关系以及在语用推理中的作用等,且几乎都是在词汇及句法层面展开的,很少涉及语法层面,而在语篇层面进行的转喻研究则更罕见。总之,转喻的语篇功能及其产生的语境效果等问题亟须深入研究。

本研究选择新闻语篇作为语料是基于以下两种考虑:首先,新闻语篇属于正式书面文体,研究转喻在新闻语篇中的组织功能可以揭示转喻在其他书面文体中的组织功能;其次,新闻语篇读者广泛且众多,是人们获取信息的重要途径,也是英语学习者重要的阅读材料来源。所以,本研究选择新闻语篇作为研究载体来研究转喻的语篇功能。研究语料主要选自英美主要新闻媒体网站,包括《纽约时报》、《华盛顿邮报》、有线电视新闻网(CNN)、《华尔街日报》、《卫报》、《观察家报》、英国广播电视公司(BBC)及《路透社》;新闻报道的内容涉及突发事件、外交、科技、经济、环境、政治、娱乐、体育等各个领域。

本研究综合了认知语言学对转喻研究的理论成果,认为语言的本质是转喻性的。本研究认为尽管转喻存在于语言形式、概念及真实世界的实体三个域,但语篇是概念世界的表征、不涉及真实世界中的实体,并在此之上提出转喻的“语言形式—概念”模式,将转喻涉及的三个域简化为两个,语言形式作为源域对目标概念提供心理通道。基于转喻表征的两个基本原则——邻近原则及因果原则,本研究将转喻分为整体—部分转喻及原因—结果转喻两类,并分别讨论两种类型的转喻如何影响语篇组织。

研究发现，转喻的“语言形式—概念”模式能够对词汇及语法衔接手段提供认知解释：相同的语言形式激活不同的目标概念、不同的语言形式激活相同的目标概念、不同的语言形式激活的概念存在包含关系或者邻近关系都可以产生衔接力。整体—部分转喻与原因—结果转喻对应两种语篇组织模式：整体—部分模式及原因—结果模式。两种转喻各作用于语篇的不同层面，包括词汇、语法以及语篇；两种模式往往相互结合共同作用于语篇组织。新闻各组成部分之间的关系也存在整体—部分及原因—结果的转喻关系：新闻标题往往选择新闻事件认知模型中最重要的部分作为载体激活整个事件；导语是对标题的详述或补充，与标题激活的概念存在部分—整体或者部分—部分关系；标题与导语组成的摘要部分则与主要事件存在部分—整体关系；背景及后果与主要事件之间存在原因—结果关系。

本研究对真实语料进行分析，将转喻在词汇及句法层面的研究延伸到语篇层面，结合功能语言学与认知语言学的研究方法，扩展了研究领域。本研究从转喻角度建立了一个较为综合全面的分析框架对新闻语篇进行分析，不仅对新闻语篇分析具有重要意义，对书面语篇分析也有重要贡献。本研究之成果不仅可以弥补以往研究的不足，而且可以在对揭露语言奥秘感兴趣的语言研究者及学者中引起讨论。总之，研究转喻在新闻语篇中的组织功能无论在理论层面还是在实际应用层面都具有重要意义。

戴理敏

2016 年 1 月

List of Abbreviations

BBC	British Broadcasting Corporation
CDA	Critical Discourse Analysis
CG	Cognitive Grammar
CxG	Construction Grammar
CL	Cognitive Linguistics
CNN	Cable News Network
ICM	Idealized Cognitive Model
ISA	Indirect Speech Act
NYT	New York Times
NP	nominal phrase
RST	Rhetorical Structure Theory
SFL	Systemic Functional Linguistics
SAM	Speech Act Metonymy
SoA Scenario	State-of-Affair Scenario
VP	verbal phrase
WP	Washington Post
WSJ	Wall Street Journal

List of Tables

List of Figures

Contents

Chapter 1
Introduction

Metonymy has been recognized as a fundamental cognitive and linguistic phenomenon which is pervasive both in spoken and written language. People have come to realize that metonymy is not just a process of substitution among words, as the majority of classical rhetorical works perceive it to be. However, most of the existing studies on metonymy are restricted to lexical and syntactical levels and little has been done to explore the roles of metonymy at the discourse level. In other words, textual functions of metonymy have been a much neglected area so far. This chapter introduces the research background, rationale for the study, research objectives and significance of the study, as well as organization of the study.

1.1 Research Background

Like metaphor, metonymy has been traditionally treated as a figure of speech realized through "the transfer of the name of a thing to something else that is closely associated with it" (Bredin, 1984: 46). With cognitive linguistics gaining increasing attention in recent years, people have come to realize that metonymy is not just a process of substitution among words as most of the classical rhetorical works perceive it to be, but is a fundamental cognitive and linguistic phenomenon pervasive both in spoken and written language. Recent studies in cognitive linguistics not only differentiate metonymy from metaphor and treat them as two distinct phenomena, but also elevate its status to one of the cognitive processes, a property of conceptual structure, a relation among concepts and not merely among words (Lakoff & Johnson, 1980), a way people conceptualize the world (Panther & Radden, 1999) and a mode of thinking "used automatically, effortlessly, and without conscious awareness" (Lakoff & Turner, 1989: 104).

Influenced by the rhetoric tradition which treated metonymy as a process of substitution, research on metonymy has been largely focused on its referential functions. Besides, metonymic expressions have been analyzed mainly at the lexical level, focusing on such issues as the role of metonymy in word formation and metonymy-motivated non-prototypical lexical meaning.

As metonymic expressions are so widely used in daily communication, more and more emphases have been put on the roles of metonymy as a conceptualizing capacity of human beings. In particular, most of the cognitive researches on metonymy have been focused on revealing the cognitive nature of metonymy, setting up definitional and typological criteria, studying the relationship between metonymy and metaphor and the roles of metonymy in semantic extension and pragmatic inferencing. Most of the researches on metonymy have been confined to analysis at the conceptual level, whereas the study of the potential impact of metonymy on linguistic structure has been largely neglected.

Jakobson (2003: 42) claims that "the development of a discourse may take place along two different semantic lines: one topic may lead to another either through their similarity or through their contiguity". The former is the metaphoric way and the latter is the metonymic way. Both metaphor and metonymy are fundamental cognitive processes, and metonymy may be more fundamental than metaphor (Radden, 2000). Yet compared to the detailed investigations that metaphor undergoes, the functions of metonymy in organizing discourse are a much neglected area waiting to be explored.

1.2 Rationales for the Study

Based on actual language data, this study combines both the cognitive and functional approaches to study the textual functions of metonymy with the ultimate goal to show that metonymy is far more than just a figure of speech applied only in the literary world but is an omnipresent everyday phenomenon in texts of any kind.

Traditional approach treats metonymy as a rhetorical trope while cognitive approach treats it as a conceptual and pragmatic phenomenon which is deeply rooted in human cognition (Panther & Radden, 2005). Both approaches focus on how metonymy affects the senses of words but cognitive linguists put more emphasis on the role of metonymy in affecting grammatical constructions. Recent studies have also paid increasing attention on the role of metonymy in pragmatic inferencing. Lots of outstanding works have come out concerning the roles of metonymy in indirect speech acts and functions of metonymy in utterance interpretation. It can be noticed that the focus of metonymy research has been shifted from the lexical level to the grammatical level. The textual roles of metonymy have already caught attention of some researchers, but a systematic study of metonymy at the textual level has not been shaped yet.

One of the most important textual functions of metonymy is to enhance cohesion and coherence, because two topical concepts are referred to by means of one linguistic form (Brdar & Brdar-Szabó, 2009). Revealing the functions of metonymy in achieving text coherence in terms of cohesion and organizational patterns is of great importance to reveal how metonymy organizes our language and makes a piece of news text a "meaningful whole".

The text of the news media embraces two key components: the news story and the process involved in producing the texts (Cotter, 2001). The first dimension has been one of the major concerns of a range of academic areas, such as media research, cultural studies, CDA, semiotics, and rhetoric studies. Most of them focus on one of the following aspects: linguistic function or the impact of news media on shaping ideology. However, the second dimension, about the process involved in producing the texts or aspects of the production of news texts, has been drawing increasing interests but few significant works have come out. Focuses of these studies are confined to the syntactic structures or the semantic structures of news text and few of them have attempted to reveal the deep structures of media language or the cognitive mechanisms behind the production of news texts. Therefore, this study provides a theoretical framework both for news text production and for interpretation.

News texts are one of the most familiar genres of language with distinct characteristics. There are lots of metonymic expressions in news texts, which makes the language of news text concise and economic. Exploring the functions of metonymy in news text organization is not merely an important contribution to the analysis of news texts but also help us understand the organization of written text in general. In modern times, news reporting has become an inseparable part in people's life and an important way of acquiring information about the world around. It is possible for people not to read novels or essays, but impossible for people not to read, hear or watch news reports of any kind, such as newspapers, online news reporting, or television and radio news broadcast. It can be said that news texts have a larger audience than texts of any other genre. Besides, lots of English learners use news texts as a source of reading materials. Therefore, an integrated analytical framework for news text analysis will also facilitate news text comprehension.

1.3 Research Objectives

Given the fact that text organization is multifaceted, and it is beyond the possibility to research into all the related aspects in one study, so the focus of the study falls upon the roles of metonymy in organizing clauses into larger units of language, such as passages or even the whole text, to show that metonymy is far more than just a figure of speech applied only in the literary world but is an omnipresent everyday phenomenon in texts of any kind. Therefore, the study is devoted to answering the following two questions:

(1) How does metonymy function to organize news texts in terms of text cohesion?

Much of the current research has agreed that text cohesion refers to the connections which have their manifestation in the text while coherence is a characteristic of the mental representation of the text rather than of the text itself.

To put it simply, coherence occurs in the readers or listeners' mind based on knowledge outside the text. If metonymy is a conceptual operation where one entity stands for another but both are activated or at least partially activated across the ontological realms of form and concept, then metonymy would be an efficient way to enhance text cohesion in the realm of form and coherence in the realm of concept. Halliday and Hasan (1976) distinguish two categories of cohesion: lexical cohesion and grammatical cohesion. Thus, the first objective of the study is to show how metonymy functions or what roles metonymy plays in lexical and grammatical cohesion in news texts.

(2) What patterns does metonymy demonstrate in organizing news text?

As a basic cognitive tool, metonymy functions at all levels of language use. The functions of metonymy in organizing news texts through cohesion may be regarded as functions of metonymy at the local level, and therefore, another question this research attempts to solve is how metonymy functions at the global level, i. e. what patterns metonymy demonstrates in news text organization. Cognitive linguistics argues that cognition determines our language which in turn is a reflection of our cognition. If metonymic relations are organized by contiguity and causality, then texts should be organized in Whole-Part patterns and Cause-Effect patterns, given the fact that contiguity is the guiding principle behind Whole-Part metonymy and causality is the guiding principle behind Cause-Effect metonymy.

1.4 Significance of the Study

The cognitive perspective holds that language is part of the human cognitive system which comprises perception, categorization, abstraction processes, and reasoning. All these cognitive abilities interact with language and are influenced by language. Thus, the perspective on language offered by Cognitive Linguistics emphasizes the effect of human experience of the world, the unique way humans perceive and conceptualize that experience, and how these are in turn reflected in the structure of language itself. As a cognitive process which is firmly rooted in our experience (Lakoff & Johnson, 1980), to reveal the functions of metonymy in news text organization is of great significance both theoretically and practically.

In the first place, this study aims to expand the study on metonymy from the lexical and syntactical levels to the textual level. Although the past few decades have witnessed an increasing interest in the roles of metonymy as a conceptualizing capacity of human beings, the textual functions of metonymy are still an area waiting to be explored.

In the second place, this study is expected to open up a new prospect for discourse analysis. Although it is not new to apply cognitive methods in discourse studies, to study text organization from the perspective of metonymy is quite a new area. Based on actual language use, this research is another attempt to show how functional and cognitive linguistic approaches can complement each other in discourse studies.

In the third place, this study attempts to offer a relatively comprehensive and integrated framework for news texts production and interpretation from the perspective of metonymy.

1.5 Organization of the Study

This study consists of 9 chapters. Chapter 1 introduces the research background, rationales, objectives and significance of the study as well as the organization of this study.

Chapter 2 reviews the related studies accomplished by both foreign and domestic linguists, starting with an overview of the cognitive-functional approach to discourse studies, then a review of studies on news text organization and discourse studies from the perspective of metonymy, with the aim to highlight the potential academic contributions of the present study.

Chapter 3 starts with an elaboration of the theoretical foundations on which this research is based and then proposes a Form-Concept model of metonymy for analyzing the textual functions of metonymy. This chapter also elaborates on the theoretical framework for the study.

Chapter 4 elaborates on the methodology of the study, including the data sources, data collection and procedure of analysis.

Chapter 5 attempts to answer the question of how metonymy functions to organize news text in terms of text cohesion to reveal the roles of metonymy in contributing to the continuity of text. The discussion starts with an explicit exploration of how metonymy contributes to lexical cohesion and then moves on to an investigation into its contributions to grammatical cohesion.

Chapters 6 and 7 are devoted to revealing the metonymic patterns of news text organization, focusing on how metonymy functions to organize sentences into larger units of language. Chapter 6 discusses the patterns demonstrated by Whole-Part metonymy and Chapter 7 discusses the patterns demonstrated by Cause-Effect metonymy in news text organization.

Chapter 8 explores the functions of metonymy in structuring news schemata, with a detailed discussion on how metonymic thinking organizes Headline, Lead, Main Events, Background and Consequences.

Chapter 9 concludes the Study by summarizing the major findings, discussing implications and limitations of the study and providing suggestions for future studies.

Chapter 2
Literature Review

This chapter starts with an overview of the cognitive-functional approach to discourse studies, and then moves on to review previous studies on news text organization and studies on metonymy at the textual level accomplished by both foreign and domestic linguists, with the aim to highlight the potential academic contributions of the present study.

2.1 An Overview of the Cognitive and Functional Approaches to Text Studies

There have been increasing interests in the discussion of the similarities and differences between different varieties of functionalism (Croft, 1995; Butler, 2003a, 2003b, 2006) and between functional and cognitive approaches (Tomasello, 1998, 2003; Horie & Comrie, 2000; Nuyts, 2005).

The functional approach to text studies pays special attention to the functional properties of language and its use, including issues such as the analysis of topic, comment, foregrounding, and focus. It also stresses the social and cultural functions of text from the sociology perspective (Billig, 1987; Gee, 1996; Halliday & Hasan, 1985; van Dijk, 1997). The most prominent theory within the functional approach is SFL (Halliday, 1985). Other functional approaches, represented by the functional grammar (Dik, 1978, 1989) and the Cardiff

Grammar (Fawcett, 2008), may have differences in some details but share almost all of the major theoretical assumptions of SFL.

The systemic functional approach provides a very useful descriptive and interpretive framework for viewing language as a strategic, meaning-making resource. Systemic functional theory views language as a social semiotic, a resource people use to accomplish their purpose by expressing meanings in context and sees texts as authentic products of social interaction. SFL recognizes not only ideational and interpersonal meaning, but also textual meaning, and has been increasingly recognized as the mainstream model of functional approach. Its framework has been the basis of a great deal of current research work, widely adopted by the major approaches in analyzing both oral and written texts.

In one word, the functional approach to text studies deals with grammatical and other functional relations of textual structures or strategies, which analyzes the functional relations between these textual structures and various structures of the context (van Dijk, 1977).

Cognitive linguistics (hereinafter CL) aims to reveal how cognitive processes influence the text production and interpretation. The cognitive approach concerns the problem of how people construct meaning in thought and language as the priority of language research. It is cross-disciplinary by nature and the most closely related fields are psychology, neurophysiology, computer science and general cognitive science. CL is better described as a paradigm which subsumes a number of theories and programs.

The most prominent theories within the cognitive paradigm include: conceptual metaphor theory (Lakoff, 1987; Lakoff & Johnson, 1980, 1999; Lakoff & Turner, 1989), blending theory (Fauconnier, 1998; Fauconnier & Turner, 1998, 2002), cognitive grammar (Langacker, 1987, 1991, 2009), frame semantics (Fillmore, 1977, 1982, 1985; Fillmore & Atkins, 1992, 1994) and construction grammar (Goldberg, 1995, 2003; Croft, 2001; Fried & Östman, 2004). Most of the cognitive researches have focused on such issues as conceptual categories, metaphor, semantic change, prototype effects, blending, mental spaces and embodiment.

It can be said that the most important difference between cognitive linguistics and functional linguistics lies in their focus of research. For functionalists the stress is on the social-communicative functions of language, while for cognitive linguists, the stress is on the conceptual and psychological aspects (Brdar, 2007). However, it is never a clear-cut matter. An increasing number of scholars have been trying to bridge the gap and blur the contrast between the functional and cognitive approaches (van Dijk & Kintsch, 1977, 1983; Croft, 2001; Bybee, 2003; Nuyts, 2005).

A lot of researchers from the functional school put emphasis on the cognitive functions of texts, and the relations between texts structures and their contexts or even argue that meaning, or the semantic functions, have cognitive basis (van Dijk & Kintsch, 1977, 1983; Kintsch & van Dijk ,1978; Givón, 1992, 1995, 2002; Wierzbicka, 1992; Chafe, 1994; Halliday & Matthiessen, 1999).

Linguists from the cognitive school also try to combine these two approaches in investigating into the roles of cognitive devices in affecting language use. For instance, the Conceptual Metaphor theory has been employed by many researchers in exploitation of cognitive tools in realizing text coherence (Kövecses, 2002). Studies have also been done to explore the roles of metaphor in shaping ideology (Lakoff, 1996, 2002, 2004; Charteris-Black, 2004; Billig & Macmillan, 2005; Ahrens, 2010). Heyvaert (2003) studies nominalization in English from a perspective of combining SFL and the theory of prototype effect and offers a synthesized framework for the study of nominalization. The work of Langacker (2009) presents a substantial range of recent researches in cognitive grammar, covering fundamentals of CG and analysis of various grammatical phenomena, such as constructions, grounding, clause structure and complex sentences.

The functional approach and cognitive approach complement each other in many ways. As Nuyts (2005: 69) claims, these two approaches are "two brothers in arms". Cognitive models accept the functionalist premise that language structures cannot be productively analyzed independently of language uses, while many functionalists recognize the necessity to discover the properties of our cognitive systems underlying the production and interpretation of language. To summarize, we should manage to combine the insights from these two approaches to achieve a " full-fledged account of language as a cognitive system for communication" (Nuyts, 2005: 71).

2.2 Studies on News Text Organization

Text organization is one of the central issues in text studies. Studies on text organization focus on relations between the units of text as well as between the units and the whole text (Goutsos, 1997). Thus, researches into text organization have been largely focused on the issues of cohesion, coherence and text genres. News texts, as a genre with distinctive organizational features, have been a focus of interest for many researchers from various academic fields.

2.2.1 Studies on Text Organization

The issue of cohesion has been put into the spotlight and drawn remarkable attention of linguists from different perspectives, such as semantics, pragmatics, psychology, cognitive studies and computer science, ever since Halliday and Hasan published *Cohesion in English* in 1976. And since then, an abundance of books, studies and articles focusing on various aspects of cohesion and coherence have been published and a great number of models of analysis have been introduced, showing how cohesion and coherence are manifested in different types of spoken and written text. This section tries to provide an overview of the theories and models of both functional and cognitive approach on the issue of text organization with emphasis on text cohesion and textual patterns.

Text studies before the Hallidayan approach, especially in the 1960s and early 1970s, were mainly influenced by formal linguistics, which were confined to surface-level features of language. Much of the research during that time focused on features of lexis and grammar in texts of particular disciplines and most of these studies were done by linguists in applied linguistics.

With the booming of the interdisciplinary approach in text study in the 1970s and 1980s, many theoretical frameworks concerning the study of text coherence were put forth. The most distinctive theories including cohesion and register consistency theory (Halliday & Hasan, 1976), the macrostructure theory (van

Dijk, 1977a, 1980a), the rhetorical structure theory (Grimes, 1975; Meyer, 1975; Mann & Thompson, 1987, 1988; Matthiessen & Thompson, 1988), the mental framework theory (Brown & Yule, 1983), and the theme-rheme theory (Danes, 1974; Fries, 1983; Eiler, 1986; Francis, 1989).

Cohesion, lexical cohesion in particular, contributes a great deal to a text's organization (Hoey, 1991), but much less attention has been devoted to lexis than grammar in functional linguistics and other discourse analysis approaches as well. Halliday and Hasan proposed a model of analyzing lexical cohesion in *Cohesion in English*, but they devoted only about twenty pages to lexical cohesion, which by no means parallels its importance in realizing discourse cohesion. Halliday and Hasan's (1976) model of cohesion also has aroused lots of debates and many linguists, including Halliday and Hasan themselves, have tried to improve this model. For instance, Martin's (1992) model of lexical cohesion offers a redefinition of Halliday and Hasan's (1976) model. According to Martin, cohesion relations can be divided into three main categories: taxonomic, nuclear and activity sequence relations. The taxonomic relations are almost identical with the general relations of Hasan (1984) or the synonymy relations of Halliday (1985). In spite of all the debates and criticisms, Halliday and Hasan's (1976) model of cohesion is still the most widely adopted model in analyzing text cohesion.

Contrastive studies have shown that lexical cohesion occurs in nearly all forms of text, but the distribution of cohesive devices vary dramatically from one genre to another (Thompson, 1994; Campell, 1995; Louwerse et al., 2004; Tanskanen, 2006; Yankova, 2006). Buitkiene (2005) examines the frequency and distribution of cohesive devices across registers and finds out that lexical cohesive devices prevail in the texts belonging to different registers while grammatical cohesive devices are register-dependent. Verikaite's (2005) research verifies the generally acknowledged argument that substitution and ellipsis are more regular in spoken discourse than written texts while conjunction is a preferred cohesive link in academic discourse. Some computational linguistic studies try to reveal lexical patterns through analyzing large corpora utilizing computational tools (Conrad, 2002; Stokes, 2004).

Entering the 1990s, more researchers came to put emphasis on the study of the patterning in text organization. Studies on organizational patterns of written text aroused interests in the analysis of larger units of text.

There are three rather distinct stages in the development of discourse analysis: stages of "textualization of lexico-grammar", "organization of discourse" and "contextualization of discourse" (Bhatia, 2004: 4). According to Bhatia, the first stage focuses on patterns of information organization; the second focuses on general text organization patterns without any reference to functional variation; and the third focuses on text patterns across academic and professional genres.

With respect to the issue of text organization, there are also three views. The first view holds that there is no organization of text at all, which has been rejected by most linguists; the second view holds that text has some organization, but this organization does not permit one to make predictive statements about the data under examination; and the third view holds that text organization does permit of full structural description (Hoey, 1991). According to Hoey, the third view is the view held by most linguists (van Dijk, 1972; Grimes, 1975; Pike & Pike, 1977; Longacre, 1983; Graustein & Thiele, 1987). Some other linguists also support the third view but with focus on text structure from the perspective of genre (Halliday & Hasan, 1985; Martin, 1985; Ventola, 1987). Although Hoey is not in full support of the third view, he still believes that text is patterned and much of his research has been devoted to describing text patterns (Hoey, 1983a, 1983b, 1986a, 1986b, 1988, 1991).

Dickson et al. (1995) study the relationship between text organization and reading comprehension of textbooks and argue that text organization includes the physical presentation of text and text structures: physical presentation of text includes visual textual cues such as headings and subheadings, signal words, and location of main idea sentences; text structures are more abstract, less visual presentations of text that involve organizational patterns of text written to convey a purpose, such as to persuade, describe, compare/contrast or entertain with a story.

Influenced by SFL, a lot of Chinese scholars have also made great endeavor in perfecting the cohesion and coherence theory. Hu Zhuanglin (1994) employs the framework of SFL in examining cohesion and coherence in both English and Chinese texts. He distinguishes four types of cohesion in Chinese texts, referential cohesion, structural cohesion, logical cohesion and lexical cohesion, in terms of the structural features of Chinese. Zhang Delu is another Chinese scholar, whose research has greatly promoted the theory of cohesion and coherence (1992, 1999, 2000, 2001a, 2001b). Zhang Delu and Liu Rushan (2003) study coherence in terms of the relationship between coherence and the context of situation, semantics and form. Zhu Yongsheng, Zheng Lixin and Miao Xingwei (2001) provide a detailed comparative study on cohesive devices between Chinese and English texts and explain why certain cohesive devices are preferred over others in Chinese texts. Some other scholars, such as Huang Guowen (1988), Zhu Yongsheng (1996, 1997), and Miao Xingwei (1998, 1999) have also made great contributions to the development of cohesion and coherence theory.

2.2.2 Studies on News Texts

News texts, either in print or in digital form, are handy repositories of language data, and media language, for its omnipresence and easy accessibility in modern societies, turns out to be a natural data source for linguists interested in the study of language and other researchers interested in the influence of language on culture as well as for foreign language learners. There are three main approaches to the study of media text: 1) discourse analytic, 2) sociolinguistic, and 3) "non-linguistic", and researchers tend to blend aspects of these three approaches in a cross-disciplinary manner no matter which approach they take, and the methods they take can be critical, pragmatic, stylistic, comparative, or cognitive (Cotter, 2001).

The discourse of the news media embraces two key components: the news story and the process involved in producing the texts (Cotter, 2001). The first dimension has been one of the major concerns of a range of academic areas, such as media research, cultural studies, CDA, semiotics, and rhetoric studies. Most of them focus on one of the following aspects: linguistic function or the impact of news media on shaping ideology. However, the second dimension, about the process involved in producing the texts or aspects of the production of news texts, has been drawing increasing interests during the past several years, but few significant works has been completed (Cotter, 2001).

Fairclough (1995) provides a survey on the approaches for the study of media discourse and summarizes the following approaches: linguistics, sociolinguistics, CA, CDA, semiotics, critical linguistics, van Dijk's "social-cognitive" model and the cultural generic approach.

The stylistic approach to media discourse study focuses on the superficial structure of news texts, concerning such issues as novelty lexical items and expressions and rhetorical devices (Crystal & Davy, 1979; Wang Zuoliang & Ding Wangdao, 1987).

Current news studies usually take a sociological perspective, focusing on the institutional, professional and cultural context of news production from the macro level or journalistic routines, practical rules and news values or ideologies from the micro level (van Dijk, 1985c). CDA regards news as a social practice, like any other discourse, constructed by the social and political world on which it reports (van Dijk, 1989, 1991, 1995; Fowler, 1991). What is said or written in a piece of news is articulated from a particular ideological position, "because the institutions of news reporting and presentation are socially, economically and politically situated, all news is always reported from some particular angle" (Fowler, 1991: 10).

Many researchers have tried to reveal how news texts are organized. News reporting has typical structures, which are called by van Dijk the global organization of news, thematic structures or schematic structures (van Dijk, 1985b). van Dijk (1985c, 1986, 1988) exploits the notion of *schemata* to describe the overall form of a discourse. According to van Dijk, each type of text has a fixed, conventional and culturally variable schema and news text also has a "news schema". The organization of a news text is a top-to-bottom mapping of the underlying semantic macrostructure. The highest or most important topic is expressed in the headline, the top of the complete macrostructure of text is formulated in the lead, and the initial sentences or paragraphs of the text express lower level of macrostructure, featuring important details about time, location, participants, cause/reasons or consequences of the main events.

It has been widely agreed that the organization of discourse is multifaceted. Given the complexity of news types, many researchers have tried to reveal the organizational patterns of different journalist genres. Some studies focus on the organization of narratives in news writing (Green, 1979), the organizational and textual structures of radio news text (Al-Shabab, 1988), the interactional organization of news interviews (Clayman, 1988), or the aspects of topical organization in news interviews (Greatbatch, 1986). With the development of information technology and the internationalization of communication across the world, researchers began to study how the network has changed text types. For instance, Kornetzki (2012) makes a contrastive study on news text types in Russian, British and American business online and print media. Studies have also been carried out in China to find out the features of specific news types (Ju Yumei, 2004); Liao studies the relationship between headlines and news stories through investigating the textual functions of metaphor (Liao Meizhen, 2007). Efforts also have been made on the study of metaphor in political discourses within the paradigm of CDA by Chinese scholars (Xin Bin, 2007; Zhang Hui & Jiang Long, 2008).

To summarize, focuses of these studies are confined to the syntactic structures or the semantic structures of news texts and few of them have attempted to reveal the deep structures of media language or the cognitive mechanisms behind the production of news texts.

2.3 Metonymy in Text Studies

Cognitive studies have shown that many aspects of language use are closely connected to people's everyday conceptual systems and much of our ordinary cognition is constituted by metaphor, metonymy, and other figurative modes of thinking (Gibbs, 1994a, 1994b, 1999; Johnson, 1987; Lakoff, 1987; Turner, 1987). Metonymy has been studied for over 2,000 years by rhetoricians but only about 30 years by cognitive linguists. Moreover, most of the researches on metonymy have been devoted to revealing its cognitive nature, setting up definitional and typological criteria (Croft, 1993; Kövecses & Radden, 1998; Radden & Kövecses, 1999; Seto, 1999), studying the relationship between metonymy and metaphor (Barcelona, 2000a, 2000c, 2002; Radden, 2000; Ruiz de Mendoza, 2000; Barnden, 2010) and the roles of metonymy in pragmatic inferencing (Ruiz de Mendoza, 1997; Thornburg & Panther, 1997; Panther & Thornburg, 1998, 1999, 2003a; Ruiz de Mendoza, 1997; Ruiz de Mendoza & Hernandez, 2001). Most of the researches on metonymy have been confined to analysis at the conceptual level, whereas the study of the potential impact of metonymy on linguistic structure has been largely neglected.

Like metaphor, metonymy has been traditionally treated as a figure of speech realized through "the transfer of the name of a thing to something else that is closely associated with it" (Bredin, 1984: 46). Influenced by this rhetoric tradition, researches on metonymy have been largely focused on its referential functions and metonymic expressions have been analyzed mainly at the lexical level (Nunberg, 1995; Dirven, 1999; Warren, 2002, 2004). Issues such as the role of metonymy in word formation (Panther & Thornburg, 2001, 2002; Basilio, 2009) and metonymy-motivated non-prototypical lexical meaning (Barcelona, 2009; Brdar & Brdar-Szabó, 2009) have been a focus of metonymy study.

Before metonymy's impact on grammar attracted interests of western scholars in the early 21st century, a Chinese scholar, Shen Jiaxuan, had proposed the notion of *grammatical metonymy* in his research (Shen Jiaxuan, 1999). He claimed that this transferred designation of *de* constructions in Mandarin Chinese, such as *kai che de* (开车的, people who drive), is in essence a kind of grammatical metonymy.

Studies on metonymy in relation to grammar have been carried out from the perspective of semantics and have mainly focused on grammatical areas in which metonymy has a motivating role (Sweetser, 1990; Traugott, 1985; Traugott & König, 1991; Bybee et al., 1994; Heine, 1995; Geeraerts, 1997; Goosens, 1999, 2000; Goldberg, 1995, 2003; Barcelona 2003, 2004; Panther, et al., 2009). For instance, Nikiforidou (1999) observes that there is a systematic ambiguity in nominalizations in English. Panther and Thornburg (2000) study stative predicates such as "know" and "love" in constructions that require action verbs and find that the conceptual shift is motivated by the RESULT-for-ACTION metonymy. Panther and Thornbury (2001) claims that metonymic coercion plays a role in the interpretation of non-finite clauses that involve the problem of "control".

Most researchers agree with the claim that relationship between metonymy and grammar is a two-way traffic relationship (Brdar, 2007; Brdar & Brdar-Szabó, 2009; Panther et al., 2009). Ruiz de Mendoza and his collaborators have been exploring into the interactive relationship between metonymy and grammar and believe that metonymy is under some grammatical structures which in turn influence the metonymic operation (Ruiz de Mendoza & Hernandez, 2001, 2003; Ruiz de Mendoza & Otal, 2002).

Compared to the investigation into metonymy at the lexical level and grammatical level, fewer works have been done to explore its functions at the discourse level. The first research into the nature of discourse from the perspective of metonymy can be credited to Jakobson (2003), who proposed a theory in which the nature of discourse is defined as either metaphoric or metonymic, and claimed metonymy rather than metaphor structures the sequence of events, occurring as a structural element of discourse as well as a one-word substitution based on semantic principles.

Jakobson's notion on metonymy raised a lot of debates on the functions of metonymy in discourse. Researchers started to find out how metonymy influences the creation of subtexts and its function in structuring events in fictional narratives (Riffaterre, 1990; Steen, 1994, 2005), as well as the roles of metonymy in meaning construction at discourse level (Thornburg & Panther, 1997; Panther & Thornburg 1998; Barcelona, 2007).

Lakoff and Turner (1989) were among the first linguists who related metonymy to the pragmatic phenomenon of deixis. Following their studies, an increasing number of researchers started to explore functions of referential metonymy in anaphoric pronouns (Stallard, 1993; Nunberg, 1995; Ruiz de Mendoza, 2000; Ruiz de Mendoza & Diez, 2002; Warren, 2002, 2004).

Stallard (1993) sees metonymy as a phenomenon of semantic coercion and distinguishes between referential metonymy and predicative metonymy. In referential metonymy, the referent of the NP is shifted; while in predicative metonymy, the referent of the NP is not shifted but the argument place of the predicate is shifted. Referential metonymy indicates indirect referent, for instance, "the ham sandwich is waiting for his check". The intra-sentential anaphora agrees with the target referent of the NP, and therefore, the pronoun "his" anaphorically refers back to the implicit target entity "people who ordered ham sandwich". In predicative metonymy, the intended referent is the same with the source entity, but the predicate is coerced, which can be exemplified by "which airlines fly from Boston to Denver?" The argument structure of the verb is shifted so as to make the source entity an argument.

Nunberg (1995) sees metonymy as a mechanism of meaning transfer and distinguishes between deferred reference and predicate transfer when accounting for anaphora. Deferred reference is exemplified by "this is parked out back" uttered by the owner of a car when handing over his car key. Predicate transfer is exemplified by "I am parked out back". In deferred reference, the antecedent will be the target entity; in predicate transfer, the antecedent will be the source entity. The problem with Nunberg's solution is that it is hard to distinguish a predicate transfer from a reference transfer because the boundary between them seems unclear.

Ruiz de Mendoza (2000) claims that there is a matrix and subdomain relationship between the source entity and the target entity in a metonymic relationship and argues that only the matrix domain can be used as antecedent. If the source entity is a subdomain of the target entity, then the target entity will be the antecedent; if the source entity is a matrix domain of the target entity, then the source entity will be the antecedent. The problem of this explanation is similar with Nunberg's (1995) solution: it is hard to tell which domain is the matrix domain and which one is the subdomain.

Warren (2004) regards metonymy as a focusing construction and claims that referential metonymy occurs because the speaker is focusing on an attribute of some entity rather than on the entity itself although both the attribute and the entity are mentally activated. He argues that the two utterances, "the laces of the boots were neatly tied" and "the boots were neatly tied" express the same proposition but their focuses are different. The former focuses on the laces while the latter on the boots. Thus, the pronoun used as an anaphor should agree with the entity which is in focus.

In addition to the studies discussed above, some other researchers (Gibbs, 1994b) also emphasize the role of metonymy as a cohesive device especially in anaphora. It is due to the nature of metonymy as a conceptual operation where one entity stands for another but both are activated or at least partially activated. Brdar (2007) argues that metonymy necessarily enhances the cohesion of the utterance because two or more topical concepts may be referred to by means of a single label.

These studies provide us invaluable inspiration in investigating into text organizaiton from the perspective of metonymy. However, most of these studies are heavily dependent on intuition and lack of corpus support.

It can be argued that corpus-linguistic methods are not enough when it comes to categorizing metonymic mappings and frequency analyses are better complemented by other methods which take the structure of the target and vehicle concepts into account. Therefore, studies into metonymy are either entirely theoretical (Radden & Kövecses, 1999; Barcelona 2003, 2004; Peirsman & Geeraerts, 2006) or restricted to only a few lexical items or mappings (Hilpert, 2006a).

Al-Sharafi (2004: 1) defines metonymy as "a process of REPRESENTATION in which one word or concept or object stands for another by contiguity or causality". He further claims that the crucial relation that underlies the process of metonymy is that of "representation" and deems metonymy as "a process of signification in which the signifier represents a signified which is associated with it in some way" (Al-Sharafi, 2004: 105). Al-Sharafi's (2004) research investigates the textual potential of metonymy, breaking through the confinement of traditional research on metonymy as just a trope. His textual model has been adopted by many researchers to explore the text functions of metonymy (Wei Zaijiang, 2007a, 2007b; Li Yongzhong, 2008).

Many Chinese researchers have also tried to explore the functions of metonymy at the discourse level. Some of their works focus on the application of conceptual metonymy in generating and interpreting narrative (Yang Xuemin, 2004; Lu Weizhong & Liu Yuhua, 2009). A few studies have been carried out to explore the functions of metonymy in realizing discourse coherence (Li Yongzhong, 2004a; Lu Weizhong & Lu Yun, 2006; Sun Zhinong, 2007; Wei Zaijiang, 2007b; Chen Xianglan & Zhou Liuxi, 2007; Chen Xianglan & Shen Tujing, 2008; Chen Xianglan & Shen Dan, 2009) and in pragmatic inferencing (Chen Xianglan, 2006).

Wang Yin (2006) discusses the relationship between CL and SFL and exploits some cognitive theories, including Salience/Prominence, conceptual metaphor theory, iconicity, ICM, cognitive reference point, current discourse space, prototype and categorization, in analyzing discourse coherence. Apparently, metonymy's textual functions have not drawn enough attention which parallels its significance as a fundamental cognitive tool.

Although many important insights and observations concerning the textual functions of metonymy have come out, such issues as the cohesive function and the organization patterns of conceptual metonymy in natural language discourse, especially written discourse, still remain uninvestigated. Research on metonymy's textual functions, especially its contribution to text organization is a much neglected area waiting to be explored.

Chapter 3
Theoretical Framework

This chapter firstly elaborates on the theoretical foundations on which this research is based, and then proposes a Form-Concept model of metonymy and an analytical framework for exploring the functions of metonymy in news text organization, with the aim to enrich both the theoretical and analytical framework of news text studies from the perspective of metonymy.

3.1 Theoretical Foundations

The study is based on the following two theoretical sources: one is the cohesion theory of Halliday and Hasan (1976) and the other is the conceptual metonymy theory, precisely, a set of notions about conceptual metonymy in cognitive linguistics, in particular, Radden and Kövecses' (1999) theory of metonymy, Panther and Thornburg's (1998, 1999; Thornburg & Panther, 1997) SAM theory and Al-Sharafi's (2004) model of textual metonymy.

3.1.1 Halliday and Hasan's Theory of Cohesion

SFL distinguishes three main kinds of meanings or metafunctions of language which work simultaneously: the ideational, interpersonal, and textual meanings or metafunctions. The textual function is largely realized through cohesion. The publication of *Cohesion in English* by Halliday and Hasan in 1976 ushered in a new era for discourse studies and aroused fierce debates at the same time. The notion of *cohesion* refers to "the relations of meaning that exist within a text, and that define it as a text" and "cohesion occurs when the interpretation of some element in the discourse is dependent on that of another" (Halliday & Hasan, 1976: 4).

In Halliday and Hasan's (1976) model of cohesion, when two elements in a text are related to each other, they form a *cohesive tie*, contributing to the unity of the text; grammatical and lexical elements become cohesive only when they are interpreted through their relation to some other element in the text (Halliday & Hasan 1976: 31-33). The various cohesive relations are specified into two major categories: *lexical cohesion* and *grammatical cohesion.*

Lexical cohesion is the category of cohesion that concerns connectivity between lexical items in the text, representing relations between meaning and concept, which can be further distinguished into *reiteration* and *collocation.*

Reiteration is "a form of lexical cohesion which involves the repetition of a lexical item, at one end of the scale; the use of a general word to refer back to a lexical item, at the other end of the scale and a number of things in between—the use of a synonym, near-synonym, or superordinate" (Halliday & Hasan, 1976: 278). In other words, a reiterated item may be a direct repetition, a synonym or near-synonym, a superordinate, or a general word.

Collocation is "cohesion that is achieved through the association of lexical items that regularly co-occur" (Halliday & Hasan, 1976: 284). In other words, collocation is a kind of lexical cohesion depending on a particular association between the items in question.

Grammatical cohesion represents a feature of grammatical dependency, and the grammatical links are classified into four broad types, namely *reference*, *substitution*, *ellipsis* and *conjunction.*

Reference refers to the "set of grammatical resources that allow the speaker to indicate whether something is being repeated from somewhere earlier in the text or whether it has not yet appeared in the text" (Thompson, 2008: 180). This term is particular to Halliday and Hasan, and other researchers may have different names; for instance, Brown and Yule (1983) substitute the term *co-reference* for it.

Figure 3.1 shows Halliday and Hasan's (1976: 33) categorization of the reference items.

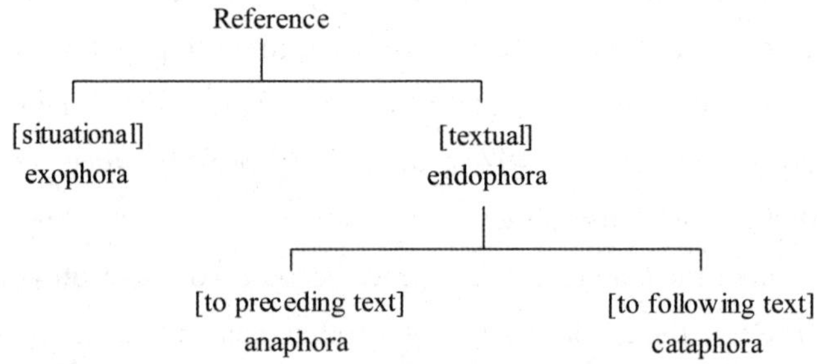

Figure 3.1 Reference in Halliday and Hasan's model of cohesion

According to Halliday and Hasan (1976), situational reference, also referred to as EXOPHORA, or EXOPHORIC reference, does not point to a meaning earlier or later in the text, but out into the world, and therefore it does not contribute to the texture of a text, since it does not bind two elements together into a text. *Textual reference*, referred to as *endophora* or *endophoric reference*, also includes two subcategories: *anaphora* and *cataphora*. Anaphora refers to "a relation between two linguistic elements, wherein the interpretation of one (called an anaphor) is in some way determined by the interpretation of the other (called an antecedent)" (Huang 1994: 1). To put it simply, anaphora is a concept in which a word or an expression can be used to refer back to another word or expression in the same text (Quirk et al., 1985).

Substitution is the second subcategory of grammatical cohesion. Some other researchers treat it as a kind of lexical cohesion because substitution items function in a way very similar to lexical repetitions (Hoey, 1991). Halliday and Hasan hold that substitution is a grammatical relation in the wording rather than in the meaning, so the types of substitution are defined grammatically rather than semantically. However, they also emphasize that "all distinctions in types of cohesion are not clear-cut" (Halliday & Hasan, 1976: 88). Therefore, sometimes it is hard to say what type of cohesion ties a relationship belongs to.

Ellipsis refers to the cohesive device in which full repetition of a clause or clause element is avoided. Ellipsis has been dealt with as a category of grammatical cohesion and a kind of substitution by zero. In this respect, it is difficult to separate ellipsis and substitution as ellipsis is simply "substitution by zero" (Quirk et al., 1972; Halliday & Hasan, 1976; Halliday, 1994).

Conjunction is the fourth type of grammatical cohesion. Unlike the other three types of grammatical cohesive ties, it also includes lexical features. Conjunctive elements are able to relate linguistic elements to each other "that occur in succession but are not related by other, structural means" (Halliday & Hasan, 1994: 227). Conjunctions usually structure a discourse in a precise way and bring the explicitly presented elements into a logical order.

3.1.2 Theories of Metonymy within the Cognitive Paradigm

The publication of the seminal work of Lakoff and Johnson in 1980, *Metaphors We Live by*, not only led to an academic revolution in the study on metaphor but also brought metonymy to the spotlight. Ever since then, studies on metonymy have no longer been confined to the field of rhetoric. Moreover, it has been recognized as "a cognitive phenomenon underlying much of our ordinary thinking and that the use of metonymy in language is a reflection of its conceptual status" (Panther & Radden, 1999: 2). Even though it has been attracting increasing academic attention, there is still no systematic theory concerning the nature, the mechanism, as well as a unanimously accepted definition or categorization of metonymy.

Most of the studies on metonymy within cognitive linguistics are found in a number of collective volumes (Panther & Radden, 1999; Barcelona, 2000; Dirven & Pörings, 2002; Panther & Thornburg, 2003, 2006; Panther et al., 2009). A few monographs have also been coming out (Ruiz de Mendoza & Campo, 2002; Al-Sharafi, 2004). This subsection elaborates on some of the prominent theories or viewpoints which have shed light on the theoretical framework of the study, specifically, Radden and Kövecses' (1999) theory of metonymy, Panther and Thornburg's (1998, 1999; Thornburg & Panther, 1997) SAM theory and Al-Sharafi's (2004) model of textual metonymy.

3.1.2.1 Radden and Kövecses' Theory of Metonymy

Radden and Kövecses (1999) were among the first linguists who tried to propose an integrated theory toward metonymy from the cognitive perspective. Their theory contributes to metonymy research mainly in the following ways: it proposes the most widely accepted definition of metonymy, identifies three ontological realms in which metonymy may occur, classifies various metonymy-producing relationships into two configurations, and distinguishes several principles that guide the selection of preferred vehicles.

The definition given by Radden and Kövecses (1999: 21) has been regarded as the most widely accepted definition of metonymy:

> Metonymy is a cognitive process in which one conceptual entity, the vehicle, provides mental access to another conceptual entity, the target, within the same idealized cognitive model.

One of the reasons why this definition has been preferred to other definitions is that it is based on the idea of *reference point* proposed by Langacker (1984, 1993, 2004, 2009); and another reason is that this definition takes the notion of *idealized cognitive model* as the knowledge structure within which metonymic processes take place.

Langacker argues that "the entity that is normally designated by a metonymic expression serves as a reference point affording mental access to the desired target (that is, the entity actually being referred to)" (Langacker, 1993: 30). According to Langacker (1999), the notion which functions as a reference point must be salient and easily activated before being established as the entity serving as a reference point. Thus, in a metonymic expression, a salient entity can easily provide a mental access to a target that is less salient or harder to describe by language.

The term *idealized cognitive model* (hereinafter ICM) put forth by Lakoff (1987) is adopted in Radden and Kövecses' (1999) definition because this notion brings all the other notions, such as *frames* (Minsky, 1975; Fillmore, 1975, 1977, 1982, 1985; Fillmore & Atkins, 1992, 1994), *scripts* (Abelson, 1976; Hoey, 2001), *domain/domain matrix* (Lakoff, 1987; Langacker, 1987; Clausner & Croft, 1999; Peirsman & Geeraerts, 2006; Taylor, 2002; Ruiz de Mendoza &

Campo, 2002), *schema* and *scenarios* (Panther & Thornburg, 1998, 2003; Thornburg & Panther, 1997), under one unified term, in describing the human knowledge structure underlying the metonymic processes.

Many researchers accept Lakoff's notion of ICM as the best framework to describe the nature of metonymic process (Radden & Kövecses, 1999; Gibbs, 1994a, 1994b) on the ground that "the notion of ICM is meant to include not only people's encyclopedic knowledge of a particular domain but also the cultural models they are part of" (Radden & Kövecses, 1999: 20). In addition, the notion of ICMs, as Radden and Kövecses (1999) argue, is "not restricted to either the world of reality, the world of conceptualization, or the world of language but... may cut across these ontological realms" (p. 20). Gibbs further argues that "ICMs make some sense, given that ICMs are idealized and do not fit actual situations in a one-to-one correspondence but relate many concepts that are inferentially connected to one another in a single conceptual structure that is experientially meaningful as a whole" (Gibbs, 1994b: 58).

In Radden and Kövecses' (1999) model of metonymy, there are three ontological realms: the world of *concepts*, the world of *forms* (in particular, forms of language), and the world of extralinguistic entities (things or events in the real world), corresponding to the three entities that comprise the semiotic triangle of *thought*, *symbol* and *referent*. Metonymy occurs not only between concepts, but also between word forms and referents in the real-world. Figure 3.2 illustrates Radden and Kövecses' (1999: 23) model of metonymy.

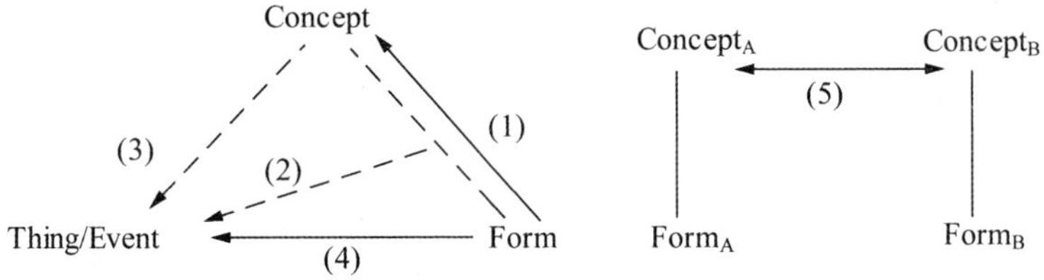

Figure 3.2 Sign, reference and concept metonymies

According to Radden and Kövecses (1999), the pairing of a *concept* and a *form* establishes a *sign* and may be described as "*sign ICM*" and the metonymies aroused in sign ICMs are described as "*sign metonymy*" (e. g. the relation between the form *house* and the concept HOUSE); the pairing of a *thing/event* and a *sign*, a *form* or a *concept* establishes a referential situation and may be described as "*reference ICM*" and the metonymies aroused in reference ICMs are described as "*reference metonymy*" (e. g. the relation between the form *house* or the concept HOUSE and the actual referent, i. e. a concrete house or the set of houses). ICMs of different semiotic units within the same ontological realm or realms involving concepts are referred to as "*concept ICMs*" and the relation between one sign and another sign are described as *concept metonymy* (e. g. bus-BUS standing for *bus driver*-BUS DRIVER). As illustrated in Figure 3. 2, the semiotic relationships lead to one type of sign metonymy (1), three types of referent metonymies (2), (3), (4), and one type of concept metonymy (5); and the arrows indicate the direction of the metonymic mapping.

In Radden and Kövecses' theory of metonymy, an ICM can be metaphorically viewed as a whole constituted by parts, which are conceptual entities or elements. From this perspective, metonymies may occur in two ways: between the whole and its parts, or between different parts within the same whole. Thus, the various types of metonymy-producing relationships can be subsumed under two general conceptual configurations:

(1) Whole ICM and its Part(s)

(2) Part(s) of an ICM

The first configuration may produce WHOLE-for-PART and PART-for-WHOLE metonymies and the second may lead to PART-for-PART metonymies, in which a part may be accessed via another part within the same ICM. These two kinds of relationships give rise to metonymies that occur frequently in language.

Kövecses (2002: 150-151) modifies these two configurations somewhat and uses Figure 3. 3 to explain the relationships between Whole ICM and its Parts in two configurations.

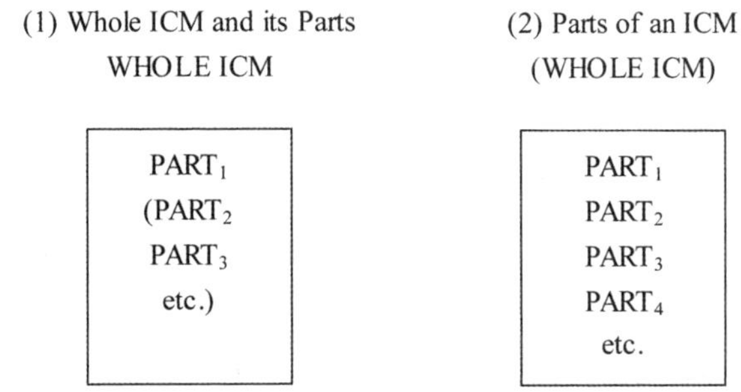

Figure 3.3 Two configurations of metonymic ICMs

According to Kövecses, the parentheses around the various parts in Configuration (1) indicate that metonymy emerges between the Whole and a Part of it instead of between a PART and another PART, but other PART(s) are still present in the background. The parentheses around the WHOLE ICM in Configuration (2) indicate that metonymy emerges between a PART and another PART instead of between a PART and the WHOLE but the WHOLE is still present in the background.

Radden and Kövecses also distinguish some principles that guide the selection of preferred vehicles. They categorize these various principles into: (1) cognitive principles of relative salience, which are related to three general determinants of conceptual organization: human experience, perceptual selectivity, and cultural preference; and (2) communicative principles, which determine the default selection of a metonymic vehicle: the principle of clarity and the principle of relevance.

Radden and Kövecses' theory of metonymy not only acknowledges metonymy in the world of concepts but also in the world of linguistic forms as well as the world of extralinguistic things and events, which means that metonymy not only occurs between concepts but also between linguistic forms as well as the things in the real world.

3.1.2.2 Panther and Thornburg's SAM Theory

In a series of publications (Thornburg & Panther 1997; Panther & Thornburg, 1998, 1999, 2003b, 2003c), Panther and Thornburg propose that indirect speech acts can be accounted for by speech act scenarios, which are essentially ICMs of conventional activities, which include not only the event involved, but also knowledge about the preconditions, results and consequences of this event.

Thornburg and Panther's research into metonymy finds that metonymy does not occur only on the referential level but also on the propositional and illocutionary levels. Based on their findings, they classified metonymy from the pragmatic perspective into *propositional metonymy* and *illocutionary metonymy* (or *speech act metonymy*); more specifically, the former includes *referential metonymy* and *predicational metonymy*, as Figure 3.4 shows.

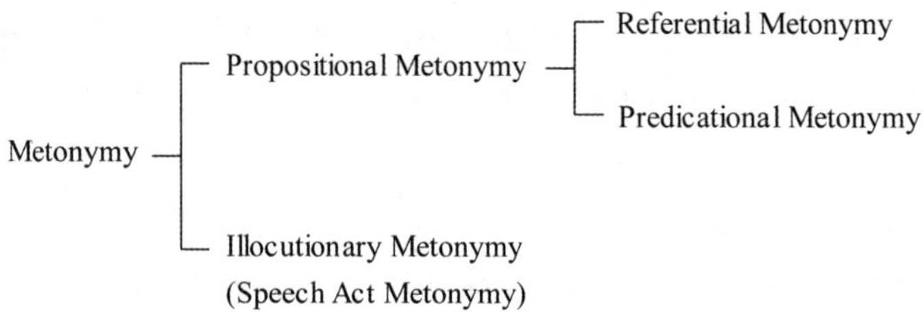

Figure 3.4 Panther and Thornburg's classification of metonymy

Referential metonymy refers to noun phrases used referentially, typically used for indirect referring; for example, the "White House" is conventionally used to refer indirectly to the executive branch of the government of the United States, a spokesperson for that branch, or even the president of the U.S.

Predicational metonymy refers to metonymy used in the predicational part of a proposition; as in "she is just a pretty face", the nominal phrase "a pretty face" is used predicatively. Another case of predicational metonymy can be found in "General Motors had to stop production", where the obligation to stop production stands for the actual event of stopping production. A potential event, the ability, possibility, permission, obligation to undertake an action is linked metonymically to its actual occurrence. By mentioning one of them and the whole event or other part of the Event ICM will be triggered. Panther and Thornburg label this kind of metonymy as POTENTIALITY-for-ACTUALITY metonymy (Panther & Thornburg, 1999, 2003a). The sentence is also a propositional metonymy because "General Motors" metonymically refers to the executive officers of the company in this case.

Illocutionary metonymy (or *speech act metonymy*) refers to the cases in which one illocutionary act stands for or has the same illocutionary force as another illocutionary act, as in "I don't know where the bath soap is". When heard by native English-speakers, it would be interpreted as "Where is the bath soap?" Illocutionary metonymies are well illustrated by the conventionalized indirect speech acts, where the expression of one speech act metonymically evokes another.

According to Panther and Thornburg(2003b), an attribute of a speech act can stand for the speech act in the same way that an attribute of a person can stand for the person. The request scenario would include the following parts:

BEFORE:	H can do A. S wants H to do A.
CORE:	S puts H under a (more or less strong) obligation to do A.
RESULT:	H is under an obligation to do A.
AFTER:	H will do A.

The BEFORE component states preconditions and motivations for performing a request. The CORE defines the essential features of the request. The RESULT shows the immediate pragmatic outcome of a felicitous performance of a request. The AFTER component describes the intended consequences of a request. For instance, the cognitive model for a "giving" event may include the core idea of an act of giving, but also various peripheral ideas, such as the hearer is able and willing to perform that act, the speaker wants something the hearer has. By referring to any part of the model, such as "can you give me that book" or "I want that book", the speaker can access the core of the scenario or the whole scenario.

Panther and Thornburg's (1999: 337) scenario approach into metonymy distinguishes a State-of-Affair Scenario (hereinafter SoA), which displays the following structure:

a	the BEFORE:	necessary preconditions: motivations, potentialities, capabilities, abilities, dispositions, etc., which can bring about the SoA
b	the CORE:	the existing/true SoA
	the EFFECTS:	necessary consequences immediately following from the SoA
c	the AFTER:	non-necessary consequences of the SoA

According to Panther and Thornburg (1999), each element can be exploited as a trigger which provides access to the whole scenario, or other element(s) of the same scenario.

To put it simply, a scenario consists of several parts, and each part in this scenario can be used as a vehicle to provide access to the whole scenario or some other parts within the same scenario. Panther and Thornburg (1998: 761-768) further argue that:

(1) the more distant a speech act scenario component is from the CORE, the weaker is its ability to evoke the scenario metonymically;

(2) the more components of a scenario present in a discourse, the easier it is to identify the scenario and the more likely even a relatively peripheral component can stand metonymically for the scenario.

SAM theory pushed metonymy research from the semantic field into the pragmatic field. The basic insight of Panther and Thornburg's approach is that a cognitive model integrating a speech act scenario and an event schema can serve as the conceptual basis for interpreting and producing a wide variety of indirect speech acts because an utterance that refers to any aspect of the model can metonymically evoke the whole model.

3.1.2.3 Al-Sharafi's Model of Textual Metonymy

Al-Sharafi (2004: 1) defines metonymy as "a process of REPRESENTATION in which one word or concept or object stands for another by contiguity or causality". He further claims that the crucial relation that underlies the process of metonymy is that of "representation" and deems metonymy as "a process of signification in which the signifier represents a signified which is associated with it in some way" (Al-Sharafi, 2004: 105).

According to Al-Sharafi, the representational nature of metonymy is realized through two major relations: contiguity and causality, with the former realized through part-for-whole and whole-for-part metonymies and the latter through cause-for-effect and effect-for-cause metonymies. Figure 3.5 (Al-Sharafi, 2004: 105) shows the representational nature of metonymy.

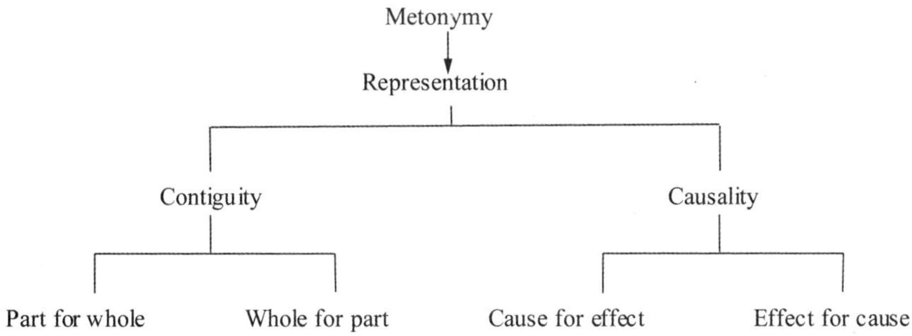

Figure 3.5 Relational model of metonymic signification

These four relations account for the interrelations between form, cognition and context. On this basis, Al-Sharafi further proposes a textual model of metonymy and applies this textual model to identify their formal connectedness and their cognitive connectedness, i. e., cohesion and coherence. His model (Al-Sharafi, 2004: 107) is fundamentally based on the conception of metonymy as representation, as Figure 3.6 shows.

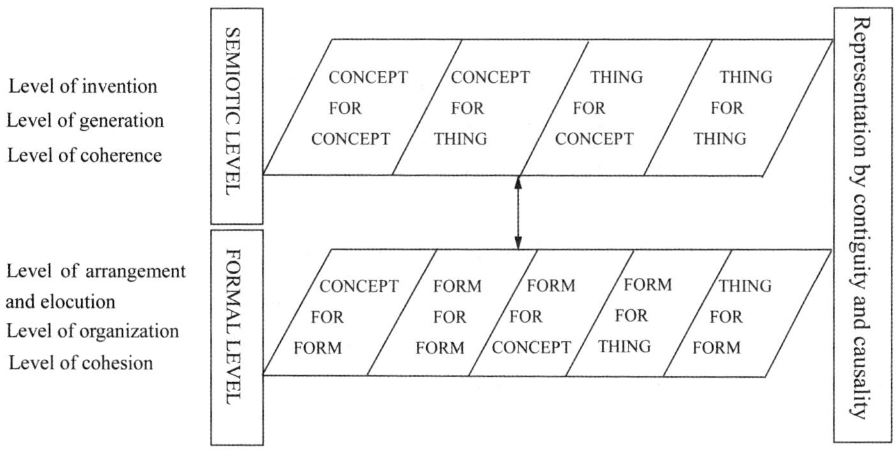

Figure 3.6 A model of textual metonymy

The model is divided into two levels. The first level is about the level of formal signification in text, which involves five metonymic relations:

(a) CONCEPT FOR FORM;

(b) FORM FOR FORM;

(c) FORM FOR CONCEPT;

(d) FORM FOR THING;

(e) THING FOR FORM.

At this level the three realms of language, mind and reality interact but the interaction is led by language and thus form has primacy. Al-Sharafi (2004) also emphasizes that the model is interactionist in nature and it also incorporates ideas from rhetoric. The formal level corresponds to the parts of classical rhetoric, known as *arrangement* and *elocution*, which is termed by Al-Sharafi as *the level of text organization* and *the level of text cohesion.*

The second is the level of cognition, which is represented by the following relations:

(a) CONCEPT FOR CONCEPT;

(b) CONCEPT FOR THING;

(c) THING FOR THING;

(d) THING FOR CONCEPT.

The second level corresponds to the classical term *invention* and gives an idea about where the ideas and the forms in the text come from and can be termed *the level of text generation* and *the level of text coherence.*

According to Al-Sharafi, this textual model of metonymy is interactive in nature, which captures the textual potentialities of metonymy because in text there is always dynamic interaction between forms, concepts and contexts. Forms play a major role as triggers to these cognitive and contextual processes.

Al-Sharafi's (2004) model of textual metonymy proposes a theoretical framework combining rhetoric, figurative theory and textlinguistics. It regards a text as representing the cognitive processes underlying it and argues that the formal text stands in metonymic representational relation of part for whole to the cognitive text, and any formal text is just one way of encoding social experience.

3.2 A Form-Concept Model of Metonymy

Since metonymy came into the spotlight on the cognitive arena, lots of researchers have attempted to define it in a way capable of revealing its cognitive nature. Generally, metonymy is treated within cognitive linguistics as a domain internal mapping, a reference point phenomenon, a figure/ground effect, meaning expansion or reduction, or meaning elaboration, but each and every of them is problematic in one way or another. By far, the most widely accepted definition of metonymy is given by Radden and Kövecses (1999: 21), and the present study also adopts this definition:

> Metonymy is a cognitive process in which one conceptual entity, the vehicle, provides mental access to another conceptual entity, the target, within the same idealized cognitive model.

To put it simply, the *source entity* (*vehicle*) directs attention, or provides mental access to the *target entity*. This definition clearly shows that metonymy serves as a reference point affording mental access to the desired target and the notion of *mental access* subsumes *mapping*, *highlighting*, *activation* as well as *meaning expansion*, *reduction* or *elaboration*, satisfactorily revealing the cognitive nature of metonymy.

Thus, in this research, the term *metonymy* is used in a broad way; that is to say, linguistic phenomena involving metonymic thinking, such as synecdoche and metonymy-based metaphor, are all subsumed under the umbrella name of metonymy. In the present study, *entity* may refer to a linguistic form, an event or action, as well as a concept (Seto, 1999).

The fact that metonymy is conceptual in nature does not mean that metonymy occurs only between concepts, that is, between two conceptual entities within the same conceptual domain. Metonymic relationships can also be found between word forms and real-world (nonlinguistic) referents and between word forms and corresponding concepts. Metonymy exists in our knowledge of the world as well as our knowledge of words, so metonymy is a problem between language and the extra-linguistic world ICM, which may be a conceptual, an extra-linguistic or intra-linguistic relationship (Radden & Kövecses, 1999; Al-Sharafi, 2004). However, in linguistics and cognitive theory, we do not deal with things, actions or events in the real world, but with their counterparts in our conceptualized world. Words, sentences and whole discourse are not interpreted relative to the world, but to the way we believe the world to be. Thus, the present study focuses on metonymic process in two of these three worlds, the world of form and the world of concept.

Based on Radden and Kövecses's (1999) theory of metonymy and Al-Sharafi's (2004) textual model, the study proposes a Form-Concept model of metonymy, in which the *source entity* may be formal or conceptual. That is, a vehicle may be a linguistic form or a concept activated by a linguistic form, depending on the nature of the metonymic mapping; and similarly, the *target entity* may also be formal or conceptual. This model is consistent with the semiotic nature of language: as long as language is concerned, there are always forms and corresponding concepts involved. There are four kinds of possibilities in this Form-Concept model of metonymy, which can be diagramed in Figure 3.7.

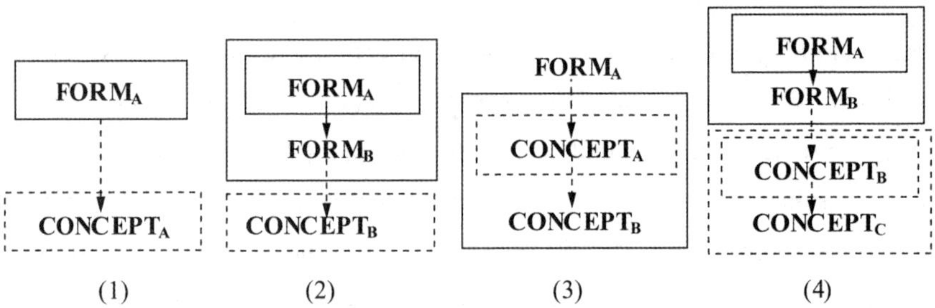

Figure 3.7 Four possibilities in the Form-Concept model of metonymy

In all of these four figures in Figure 3.7, CONCEPTs are enclosed in dashed boxes because concepts, as well as ICMs, may vary among cultures or even among people from the same culture, and there may not be a clear boundary for a specific concept or ICM. The dashed arrow indicates the mental path from a form to a concept or from a concept to another concept, which is also variable among language users. On the other hand, the boundary for a linguistic form is clear, so forms are enclosed in solid line boxes and solid arrows are used to indicate the stand-for relationship between two forms.

Each of the four figures in Figure 3.7 represents one possibility of metonymic relation in the Form-Concept model. Figure (1) represents a *sign metonymy* in Radden and Kövecses' (1999) terminology (e.g. the form "the United States" provides access to the concept of "the country of the United States of America").

It shows that the very nature of language is metonymic, i. e., a linguistic form provides mental access to a concept. Lakoff and Turner (1989) describe this FORM-for-CONCEPT metonymy as WORDS STAND FOR THE CONCEPTS THEY EXPRESS.

Figure (2) shows that metonymic shift may occur in the world of forms, in which one FORM is used to stand for another FORM and both forms provide access to the same CONCEPT (e. g. "U. S." stands for "the United States", both of these two forms provide access to the concept of "the country of the United State of America"). Usually $FORM_A$, the source entity, is an abbreviated form of $FORM_B$, constituting a PART-for-WHOLE relationship, which can be labeled as PART OF A FORM-for-WHOLE FORM metonymy (Bierwiaczonek, 2007).

Figure (3) indicates that there are two kinds of metonymic shifts: the first occurs between a FORM and a CONCEPT, constituting a sign metonymy; the second occurs between two CONCEPTs, constituting a concept metonymy in Radden and Kövecses' (1999) terminology (e. g., the FORM, "White House", provides access to $CONCEPT_A$, "the white building where the government of U. S. is located", which further provides access to $CONCEPT_B$, "the government of the U. S. which is located in the white building"). In figure (3), $CONCEPT_A$ is included in $CONCEPT_B$, but it does not mean that $CONCEPT_B$ should be more inclusive than $CONCEPT_A$ because there are no clear boundaries for concepts and sometimes it is hard to tell which one is more inclusive than another.

Figure (4) depicts the most complicated metonymic transfer, in which $FORM_A$ is used to stand for $FORM_B$. Both forms provide access to $CONCEPT_B$ which provides access to $CONCEPT_C$. For instance, the form, "U. S.", ($FORM_A$, the source entity), may give rise to the following target entities: the form, "United States" ($FORM_B$), the concept of "the country of the United of States of America" ($CONCEPT_B$), or the concept of "the government of or the person who represents the country" ($CONCEPT_C$).

3.3 Theoretical Framework of the Study

The study attempts to incorporate both the functional and cognitive approaches to explore the textual functions of metonymy in news text organization to show that our cognition is fundamentally metonymic and that textual knowledge is also metonymically constructed and metonymically interpreted. Figure 3.8 shows the theoretical framework for the study.

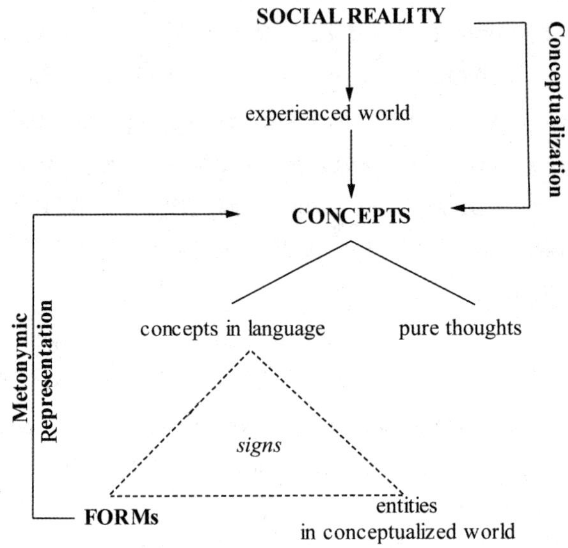

Figure 3.8 A proposed theoretical framework

In Figure 3.8, SOCIAL REALITY, CONCEPTs and FORMs are interlinked and marked by capital letters and bold type to highlight their importance in the model. CONCEPTs are mental representation, or people's ideas about something in the real world. Any concept is ultimately based on a person's experience of social reality. Language is motivated by and grounded in the CONCEPTs stored in the human mind, which are the underlying principles operating at the conceptual level of language. FORMs, specifically, the linguistic forms, are the actual realization of these underlying cognitive principles. The representational view of the language holds that what language actually stands for is a concept in the mind.

According to Dirven and Vespoor (2004), conceptualization gives rise to *concepts in language* and *pure thoughts*. Thoughts and language do not necessarily match as there are thoughts in our mind that language does not have the corresponding forms to refer to. A sign consists of a form and a concept, which is ultimately based on people's conceptualization and their experience of the world; the concepts also relate to entities in the conceptualized world, which shows that it is possible that different people may conceptualize the same entity in the real world of social reality differently. This is in line with what is suggested by cognitive linguistics that language is an integral part of human cognition as a whole, rather than a separate and unique faculty (Langacker, 1987).

Chapter 4
Methodology

This study is a basically qualitative study based on the analysis of actual language data with the aim to reveal the functions of metonymy in news text organization, specifically, its functions to organize news text in terms of text cohesion and the metonymic patterns of news text organization. This chapter elaborates on data sources, data collection and procedure of analysis.

4.1 Data Sources

Although this research is largely theory-driven, the examples were drawn from a rather extensive database. The data collected were in digital form for their easy accessibility and convenience in analysis, mainly from the following sources with their websites listed below: The New York Times (NYT), The Washington Post (WP), Cable News Network (CNN), The Wall Street Journal (WSJ), The Guardian and The Observer, British Broadcasting Corporation (BBC), and Reuters.

NYT	http://www.nytimes.com/
WP	http://www.washingtonpost.com/
CNN	http://www.cnn.com/
WSJ	http://www.wsj.com/

The Guardian	http://www.guardian.co.uk/
The Observer	http://observer.guardian.co.uk/
BBC	http://www.bbc.com/
Reuters	http://www.reuters.com/

These websites were chosen basically because of their popularity and comprehensive international news coverage. The NYT, WP, CNN and WSJ are headquartered in U.S., and the other four in U.K. All of these news websites are popular news websites with broad news coverage, though some of them have preference in their reporting. For instance, the WP has a particular emphasis on national politics and the WSJ primarily covers American economic and international business and financial news and issues.

4.2 Data Collection

A total number of over 500 articles published from January, 2009 to December, 2012 were collected, with numbers of articles and average length listed in Table 4.1:

Table 4.1 Data collected for the study

News Websites	Number of Articles	Average Article Length (words)
NYT	150	863
WP	150	927
CNN	50	805
WSJ	50	798
The Guardian	40	934
The Observer	20	837
BBC	20	907
Reuters	20	932

The articles for the data were selected from the news websites listed above based on two major considerations: firstly, most of these articles are "front page" news, i.e., most of the articles collected are news stories that were highlighted on the news websites, including both hard news reporting and soft news reporting, issues covering emergencies, diplomatic relations, scientific, economic, environmental and political events, news of entertainment and sports around the world; and secondly, all these articles are well organized in the typical news format, i. e., with headline(s), lead and detailed news story. Texts from blogs are not included in the data because they are not edited and do not have to meet the standards of accuracy and fairness required for news reporting even though they also provide timely information as other news texts do. Interviews, sections such as news briefings, opinions, are also not included in the data.

As this study is based on the assumption that metonymy structures our way of thinking and metonymic expressions should be omnipresent in texts of any kind, the data were not collected based on how many metonymic expressions they contain. However, all the examples were meticulously selected according to their typicality of metonymic representation to support the analysis.

4.3 Analytical Procedures

Cognitive research is sometimes accused of relying solely on intuition and de-contextualized examples. There have been an increasing number of corpus-based studies on this issue in recent years (Stefanowitsch & Gries, 2006). Geeraerts even puts forward the concept of "empirical revolution" in his cognitive linguistic research (Geeraerts, 2006: 25). Stefanowitsch (2006) emphasizes the role of corpus-based approach to metaphor and metonymy study. However, the use and interpretation of metonymy is heavily context-dependent, which also makes it difficult to study metonymic expressions with the help of computerized tools. Thus, this study combines the methods of observing, instrospection, extrospection and deductive reasoning to analyze the data.

van Dijk (1980a) distinguishes two kinds of coherence. Local and global coherence. The former is defined for relations between sentences of a textual sequence, i. e., a discourse is coherent if there are semantic relationships between successive sentences at the local level; the latter is defined in terms of whole sets of sentences, or the discourse as a whole, concerning not only events sequences, explicit expressions and information organization, but also the topic or theme of a particular discourse. Corresponding to these two levels of coherence, the textual functions of metonymy in organizing news texts are explored at two levels: the local level, focusing on the cohesive functions of metonymy among sentences within one segment of news texts, and the global level, focusing on the organizational patterns between one segment with other segments in the same text and the text as a whole. As the objective of the study is to reveal the functions of metonymy in organizing news texts, each article is subject to qualitative analysis firstly at the local level for cohesive devices and then at the global level for text patterns. This research adopts a cognitive-functional approach and the textual functions of metonymy are the focuses of the research. The experiential and interpersonal functions of metonymy are also integrated into the discussion when necessary.

There are two major objectives for the present study: firstly, to show how metonymy functions to organize news texts in terms of text cohesion, and secondly, to reveal the metonymic patterns of news text organization. Both objectives serve the ultimate goal: to demonstrate how metonymy organizes our language and makes a piece of news text a "meaningful whole". Corresponding to these two objectives, the study proposes the analytical framework, as shown in Figure 4.1.

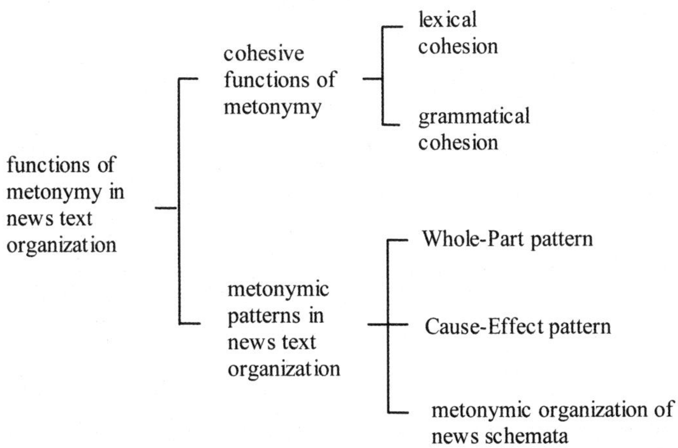

Figure 4.1 The analytical framework of the study

The cohesive functions of metonymy are discussed according to Halliday and Hasan's (1976) model of cohesion, which classifies cohesive devices into *lexical cohesion* and *grammatical cohesion*. Different from Halliday and Hasan's (1976) model, the present study emphasizes the role of metonymy in lexical cohesion and therefore, discussion on how metonymy functions to organize news text in terms of lexical cohesion is one of the focuses of the present study.

Based on the assertion of Al-Sharafi (2004) that the representational nature of metonymy is realized through contiguity and causality, this research divides the various metonymic relationships into Whole-Part metonymy and Cause-Effect metonymy, each of these two kinds subsuming various subcategories of metonymic relations. The Whole-Part metonymy subsumes WHOLE-for-PART metonymy, PART-for-WHOLE metonymy, and PART-for-PART metonymy, and the Cause-Effect metonymy subsumes CAUSE-for-EFFECT metonymy and EFFECT-for-CAUSE metonymy. Discussion is carried out to examine how each of these two kinds of metonymy functions to organize news text, or the patterns these two kinds of metonymy demonstrate in organizing news text. The analysis of metonymy's functions at the global level is focused on the functions of metonymy in organizing news schemata, answering such questions as how Summary is organized and what are the relationship between Summary and Main Events, between Main Events and Background, and between Main Events and Consequences.

Chapter 5
Cohesive Functions of Metonymy

This chapter focuses on exploring the cohesive functions of metonymy in news text organization to show how metonymy contributes to the formal continuity of discourse. The discussion starts with an explicit exploration of how metonymy contributes to lexical cohesion, and then moves on to its contribution to grammatical cohesion in an attempt to reveal how metonymy functions to realize local coherence in organizing news texts.

5.1 Functions of Metonymy in Lexical Cohesion

Lexical cohesion concerns connectivity between lexical items in the text, and is the category of cohesion that makes the most substantive contribution to texture (Hasan, 1984; Hoey, 1991). This section aims to explore the functions of metonymy in lexical cohesion in news texts in an attempt to show how metonymy provides cognitive foundations for all the types of semantic relations underlying the network of lexical cohesion. Following Halliday and Hasan's (1976) model, the discussion is carried out based on the two principal categories of lexical cohesion: reiteration and collocation.

5.1.1 Metonymic Cohesion through Reiteration

According to Halliday and Hasan (1976), *reiteration* is a form of lexical cohesion that involves the repetition of a lexical item, which may be a direct repetition, a synonym or near-synonym, a superordinate, or a general word. The following part of this subsection discusses in detail how metonymy functions in this category of cohesive devices, specifically, repetition, synonymy, antonymy, hyponymy and meronymy.

5.1.1.1 Metonymic Cohesion through Repetition

Repetition is the most direct form of lexical cohesion. Repeating a key term or phrase helps the writer focus on his/her ideas and keep the readers' attention on track. Normally, repetition of a single lexical item is not sufficient to create relatedness of sentences, and therefore in actual texts repetitions always occur in multiplicity. The following segment contains examples of direct repetition (bold type is used to highlight the repeated lexical items in the segments):

(1) **New proposals** from the Financial Services Authority on potential changes to its remuneration code which prohibit sales of shares by **bankers** are not as draconian as first feared, according to a leading pay consultant.

...

However, Terry said that the **new proposals**, published last week, would make it very difficult for **bankers** to be offered guaranteed bonuses and pointed out the FSA had "introduced the world's toughest pay rules to the UK financial services industry".

(The Guardian, May 2, 2011)

In Example (1), "new proposals" and "bankers" are repeated to remind the readers of the topic the news is about. When a repeated form has the same referent with its preceding occurrence, it can be said that the repetition of that linguistic form is the repetition of the same sign metonymy or metonymic relation of FORM-for-CONCEPT, in which the FORM that appears repeatedly in the text provides access to the same CONCEPT. Identical sign metonymy repetition can be diagramed as in Figure 5.1:

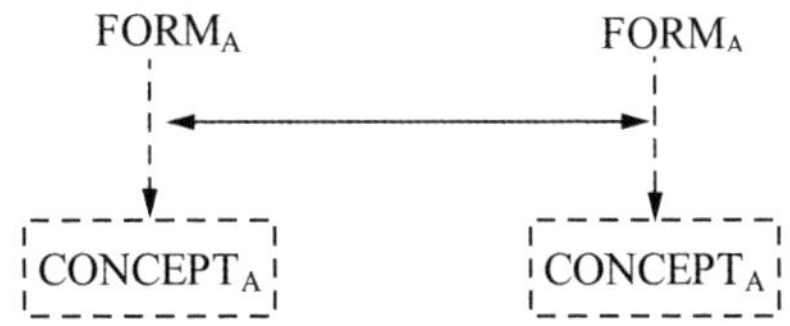

Figure 5.1 Identical Form-Concept metonymic repetition

In this figure, the dashed arrows denote metonymic relationship while the bidirectional arrows signify a cohesive tie. The figure shows that two identical sign metonymies form a cohesive tie because they have identical FORM and provide access to identical CONCEPT. It can also be said that Example (1) includes repetition of two identical FORM-for-CONCEPT metonymies.

In cases where the repeated lexical item has a different referent with its preceding occurrence, they still perform cohesive function. As Halliday and Hasan (1976: 283) suggests, a lexical item "coheres with a preceding occurrence of the same item whether or not the two have the same referent, or indeed whether or not there is any referential relationship between them", which can be illustrated by the following examples:

(2) Has the **X Factor** lost the **X Factor**?

(The Guardian, October 17, 2011)

(3) **Simon & Schuster** described it as "one of the most anticipated autobiographies of this generation," a "larger-than-life portrait of his illustrious, controversial and ever-entertaining life in and out of the public eye."

...

Simon & Schuster is expected to sell the book to foreign publishers during the upcoming Frankfurt Book Fair.

(NYT, September 22, 2011)

In Example (2), the first "X Factor" refers to the British television music competition to find new singing talents, while the second "X Factor" refers to the property that the competition is supposed to have: creativity or originality to bring novelty to its audience. Similarly, the first "Simon & Schuster" in Example (3) refers to the people who represents the publishing company and where the following quotations come from, while the second refers to the company as a whole or the marketing department of the company whose major function is to sell books. When the repeated lexical item does not have the same referent with its preceding occurrence, only part of the sign metonymy (FORM, the source entity) is repeated, as in Examples (2) and (3).

This kind of lexical cohesion in which only part of the sign metonymy (the source) is repeated may be labeled as identical source metonymic repetition. In a sense, in this kind of repetition, only the linguistic form is repeated, instead of the whole sign, which can be diagramed as in Figure 5.2:

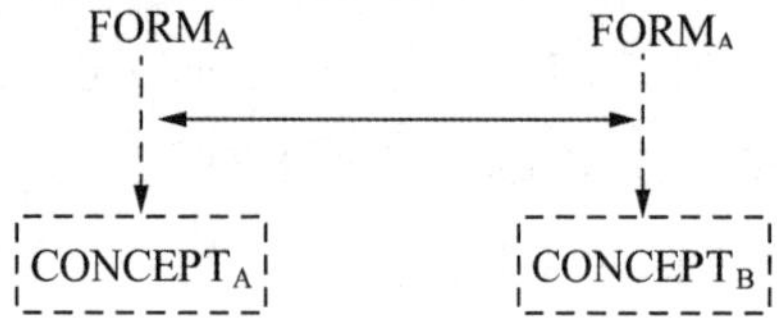

Figure 5.2 Identical FORM metonymic repetition

Figure 5. 2 shows that the two metonymic relations, $FORM_A$-for-$CONCEPT_A$ and $FORM_A$-for-$CONCEPT_B$, form a cohesive tie because they have identical source.

In the two kinds of metonymic repetition discussed above, the same lexical items are repeated, which generate cohesive powers no matter whether they have the same referent. From the perspective of metonymy, the repeated FORMs (the sources) form cohesive ties whether these forms activate or provide access to the same CONCEPT or not.

In Example (1), there is another case of repetition, the abbreviated form "FSA" which is used to substitute for its complete form "Financial Services Authority". Abbreviations (the term abbreviation is used here as a general term which subsumes acronyms and initialisms) occur regularly in news texts. Readers can easily find numerous abbreviations on the news websites or the daily news papers, such as GDP (Gross Domestic Products), NASDAQ (National Association of Securities Dealers Automated Quotations), and NATO (North Atlantic Treaty Organization). Some of these abbreviated forms are so conventionalized that it is no longer necessary to mention their complete forms, such as ATM, PIN, AIDS, UN, NATO, U. S. , U. K. , BBC, IRA, while the less conventionalized ones usually appear later than their complete forms in the same text or accompanied by their complete forms which are usually bracketed after them, as in Examples (4) and (5):

(4) In the turf war that has come to characterize the computer chip market, **Advanced Micro Devices**, appears to have stumbled in the fourth quarter. **A. M. D.** , the second-largest maker of the microprocessors, issued a warning late Thursday that its fourth-quarter revenue would miss Wall Street's forecasts because of lower unit prices, signaling that the price war between **A. M. D.** and its main rival, Intel, had taken its toll.

(NYT, January 13, 2009)

(5) The 69-year-old former leader of the governing **Democratic Party of Japan** (**DPJ**) is accused of overseeing false accounting by his staff.

...

The scandal has deeply divided the **DPJ**, which has been losing public support.

(BBC, October 6, 2011)

In news texts, the most frequently occurring abbreviated forms are the names of organizations (e. g. FBI, UN) and specialized terms (e. g. PTSD for "post trauma stress disorder", OD for "overdosed"), especially in the fields of technology and medical conditions, where the words are usually long and therefore are commonly abbreviated. The reason of using abbreviated forms seems quite obvious: long names like "Bavarian Motor Works" are easier to be remembered as "BMW" than their complete forms by the consumers of its products, not to mention its shareholders. Some acronyms become everyday words, such as "laser" (light amplification by stimulated emission of radiation), "radar" (radio detecting and ranging), and "zip" (zone improvement plan) code and no one still cares about whether they are actually abbreviated forms or not.

Abbreviation is a typical phenomenon characterized by metonymy based on a relation between linguistic forms: a part of a formal representation stands for the whole formal representation motivated by the PART-for-WHOLE metonymy. Bierwiaczonek (2007) makes a detailed research into metonymies based on linguistic forms. According to Bierwiaczonek, the ontological realm of linguistic form may be divided into the domain of sound and the domain of graphic representations, which give rise to two kinds of ICMs, the speech-sound ICM, associating sounds with concepts, and the writing ICM, in which graphic symbols represent speech sounds. Typical cases of the first kind of metonymy are homophonic alphabetism, which is represented by alternative shortened forms of spelling in which the sound representations of letters or numbers are usually used, such as 2 for to or too, 4 for for, U for you, C for see. The most common form of writing metonymy is abbreviations, in which a part, consisting of first letters of all or most of the words, stands for the whole form consisting of all letters.

The justification underlies formal metonymy is obvious. It is far easier to write and pronounce DNA, than to write or pronounce "deoxyribonucleic acid". Other abbreviated forms, such as etc., e.g., i.e., Dr., Prof., are created for the same reason, to spare both the writers and readers the trouble of having to spell out long words or phrases repeatedly without even the slightest change of meaning.

Metonymy plays an important part in word formation, especially process involving shortening and conversion, but the role of metonymy in word formation is not one of the major concerns of the present study, and what the study is interested in is the role abbreviations play to realize text cohesion. Radden and Kövecses (1999) distinguish this metonymy as a type of concept metonymy and label it as FORM_A-CONCEPT_A FOR FORM_B-CONCEPT_A metonymy. In this situation, the form of an expression changes while the concept remains the same. This metonymy applies to reductions of form as in the abbreviation in Example (1), in which the form "Financial Services Authority" changes into "FSA", but the referent as well as the concept it activates remains the same.

An abbreviated form and its complete form constitute a cohesive tie, in which different forms provide access to the same concept, as Figure 5.3 shows.

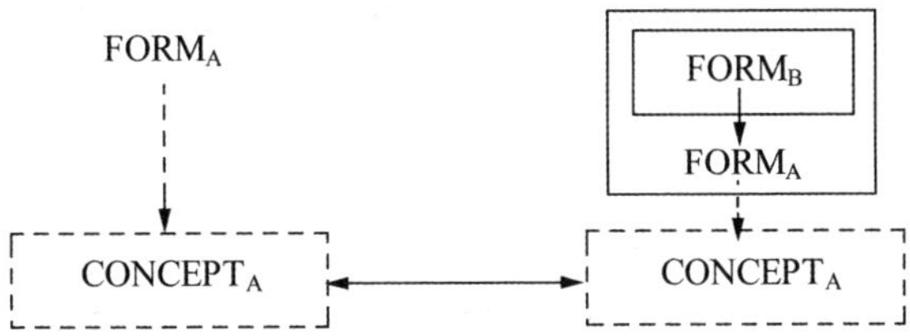

Figure 5.3 Identical CONCEPT metonymic repetition

$FORM_B$ is a part of $FORM_A$ and used to stand for $FORM_A$. Both $FORM_A$ and $FORM_B$ have the same referent, or provide access to the same concept. In this kind of metonymic cohesion, metonymy works at two levels: at the lexical level, $FORM_B$ is part of $FORM_A$, constituting a PART-for-WHOLE metonymy; at the textual level, two FORMs provide access to the same CONCEPT, creating a cohesive tie.

It can be concluded that whether it is the whole metonymic relation or only part of the relation, FORM or CONCEPT, that is repeated, a cohesive tie is formed. As suggested by Halliday and Hasan (1976), a cohesive tie is usually strengthened by the fact that the items have the same referent, when two linguistic forms have the same referent, the cohesive link between these two pairs of Form-Concept relation is strengthened, but it is not required for these two items to be cohesive, and when two linguistic forms have different referents or provide access to different concepts, they still form a cohesive tie. As a matter of fact, there is an inclination that speakers or writers are apt to choose different linguistic forms to avoid direct repetition of words, and there is usually less repetition in written texts than in spoken texts. The rest part of this subsection will discuss how metonymy functions to realize lexical cohesion through lexical items of different semantic relations.

5.1.1.2 Metonymic Cohesion through Synonymy

Lyons (1981: 50-51) claims that "synonyms are completely synonymous if, and only if: (i) all their meanings are identical; (ii) they are synonymous in all contexts; (iii) they are identical on all (relevant) dimensions of meaning". In other words, expressions are full synonymous only when they have identical meanings in all contexts and are semantically equivalent in all aspects of their meanings, and therefore full synonyms in natural discourse of any kinds are very rare. It should be emphasized here that Lyons focused on context-free lexical synonymy. This study focuses on context-bound textual synonymy, which focuses on the aspect of meaning in context. Thus, the term synonym in the present study refers to not only the context-free synonyms, but also the context-bound synonyms even if they are not semantically synonyms.

Metonymy is a phenomenon in which one entity is used to refer to another, while in synonymy, different lexical items, phrases, or even clauses are brought together to have the same referent. This can account for why metonymy and synonymy are related. Consider Examples (6) and (7) of lexical cohesion by synonymy:

(6) These developments are a growing victory for the rule of law, since international human rights law absolutely prohibits **corporal punishment** of children. In this instance, the rule of law is consistent with most social science research showing that the punishment has no real positive educational or moral effects on children. The studies instead show that **physical chastisement** is correlated with multiple adverse effects on children, some of which are serious and may persist into adulthood.

(NYT, April 7, 2011)

(7) In birds, the **dads** often shoulder some or all of the responsibility for their **young.** Many **fathers** incubate eggs, feed **babies**, and guard nests. This behavior is rare in other animals.

(NYT, December 18, 2009)

"Corporal punishment" and "physical chastisement" in Example (6) are synonymous and they have the same referent and the CONCEPTs they activate are the same. The writers use different FORMs to refer to the same CONCEPT and the identical target in the reiterated metonymic relations enables these two forms to form a cohesive link. In Example (7), "dads" and "fathers" have the same referent, and so do "young" and "babies". Strictly speaking, "young" and "babies" are not semantically synonymous but they trigger the same concept of "infant birds" in the specific context described in Example (7), as Figure 5.4 shows.

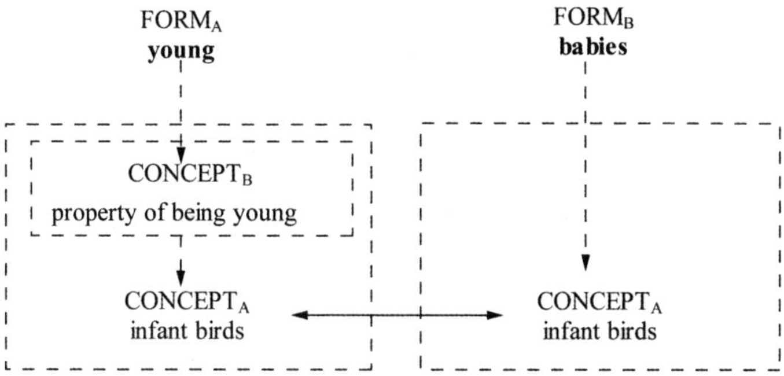

Figure 5.4 Metonymic cohesion in the "young" example

"Young" is a property of infant birds, used in this context to refer to the infant birds, which is motivated by the PROPERTY OF AN ENTITY-for-THE ENTITY metonymy. The two forms, "young" and "babies" are not synonymous, but they provide access to the same concept and constitute a cohesive tie.

The case is also true when the synonymous items are not nouns, as in Examples (8) and (9):

(8) The Obama administration **supported** the lawsuit in the Mazda case, and **sided with** the vaccine maker in that case.

(WP, February 24, 2011)

(9) But opposition figures and experts **expressed** skepticism, noting that al-Qaeda has never conducted operations in Syria before. Some also **voiced** suspicions that Assad's own officials could have staged the attacks to discredit the opposition and buttress state claims that "terrorists" are behind the uprising.

(WP, December 23, 2011)

In Example (8), "sided with" is an expression involving multiple metonymic mappings. Firstly, it maps from the form "side with" onto the concept of "to show support by taking a side with", which further maps onto the concept of "to support". Figure 5.5 shows the metonymic cohesion between "sided with" and "supported":

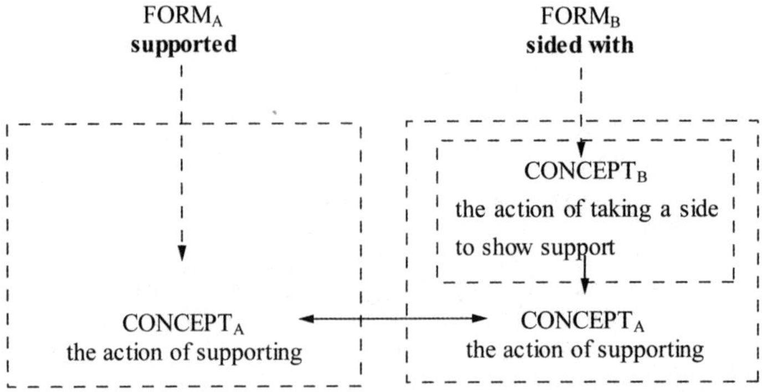

Figure 5.5　Metonymic cohesion in the "sided with" example

Concept metonymy, i. e., metonymic transfer occurs between two concepts, will be discussed in details in the following chapters and what is of interests here is the cohesive power generated by different forms that provide access to the same concept, no matter whether these forms are semantically synonymous or not. Similarly, "voiced" in Example (9) provides access to the same concept with "expressed", which is also motivated by metonymy even though they do not literally share the same meaning.

Different from direct repetition, synonymy is not a repetition of the same metonymic relations of FORM-for-CONCEPT; instead, different FORMs are adopted to trigger the same CONCEPT. To avoid direct repetition of a certain lexical item and make the text more appealing is one of the reasons why writers choose different forms to trigger the same concept. The metonymic relation between synonyms in creating cohesive ties may be sketched in Figure 5.6.

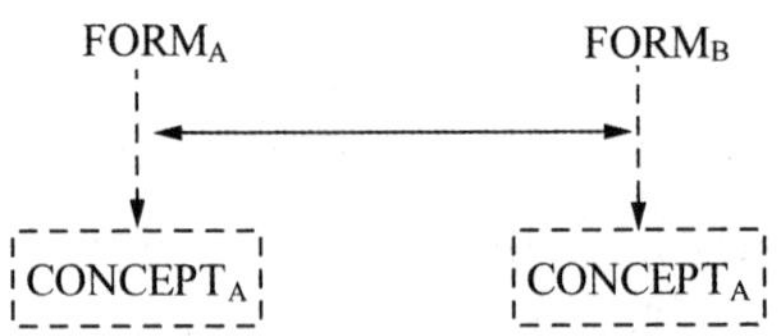

Figure 5.6　Metonymic cohesion through synonymy

Figure 5.6 shows that $FORM_A$ and $FORM_B$ provide access to the same concept. Synonyms can generate cohesive forces because the concepts they provide access to are identical. This case is opposite to the "X-factor" example in which the repeated item provides access to a different concept even if it has the same linguistic form with its former occurrence.

To sum up, two synonymous items form a cohesive tie because they activate or provide access to the same concept. They belong to the kind of lexical cohesion in which only a part of the FORM-CONCEPT relation is repeated, which may be labeled as identical CONCEPT metonymic cohesion. Even when the two items are not semantically synonymous with each other, as long as they provide access to the same concept they form a cohesive tie.

5.1.1.3 Metonymic Cohesion through Antonymy

Antonymy is one of the major sense relations structuring the lexicons of natural languages. *Antonyms*, lexical items opposite in meaning, also function as cohesive links in texts. In Halliday and Hasan's (1976) model of cohesion, a cohesive force can be extended to pairs of opposites of various kinds: complementaries, such as "boy" and "girl", "stand up" and "sit down"; antonymous such as "like" and "hate", "wet" and "dry", "crowded" and "deserted"; and converses, such as "order" and "obey". The term antonym in the present study refers to pairs of opposites based on conceptual association rather than lexical association.

In actual language use, a positive concept can be used to stand for its opposite, which is well demonstrated in expressions of irony, as in the examples given by Voßhagen (1999: 290-297): "X is a fine friend" and "big idea". Voßhagen also provides another type of metonymy involving opposition, namely THE POSITIVE END OF A SCALE-for-THE WHOLE SCALE, which is best demonstrated by such expressions as "How big/much is it?" "Big" or "much" do not necessarily mean big or much, but are used to mean the size or the quantity.

In colloquial English, words such as "terrific", "awesome", "wicked" are used to denote something excellent or wonderful, which are the opposite of their standard meanings. The fact is that it would be very strange to say something and mean the opposite in a largely descriptive, non-ironic context, such as news texts which are required to be accurate and precise in conveying messages. However, it is both possible to utter a positive term in order to convey a negative concept and to utter a negative term in order to convey a positive concept. In natural language, there exist phenomena when negatives are used to express a positive meaning, such as "not bad", and vice versa, such as "could be better" (Zhang Hui & Lu Weizhong, 2010). The construction of "could not have done" has become so conventionalized that almost no one still pays attention to its negative meaning, as in Examples (10), (11) and (12):

(10) But the timing **could not have been better.**

(NYT, April 14, 2011)

(11) The rest of Wednesday's session in Federal District Court in Manhattan **could not have stood in sharper contrast**.

(NYT, April 13, 2011)

(12) Calhoun knew Oriakhi **was not alone** in his feeling.

(NYT, March 18, 2011)

In Example (10), the literal meaning of "could not have been better" indicates a failure to be better, but the utterance meaning indicates that the timing is perfectly good. In Example (11), the reporter conveys his/her opinion that the contrast was very sharp through a negative form. "Was not alone" in (12) provides access to the concept that other people have the same feeling with Oriakhi.

Voßhagen (1999) is one of the first studies to systematically analyze the metonymic potential of antonymic relations. In his works he claims that metonymy is conceptually grounded and that linguistic metonymies have to be regarded as manifestations of general conceptual metonymies and argues that: (i) opposites belong to one conceptual domain; and (ii) the relation between opposites is one of close mental contiguity (Voßhagen, 1999: 291). This mental contiguity between opposites within one conceptual domain enables antonymic pairs to co-occur frequently in texts, which makes a text connected. Among the classes of lexical items related by opposition, adjectives constitute an important part, as in Example (13):

(13) The Chinese continue to resist mandatory ceilings on their emissions. They argue that the **developed countries** have churned out greenhouse gases for decades and should bear a greater burden in reducing them. **Developing nations**, they add, should not be restrained in using economic development to raise their standards of living, even if greater emissions result.

(NYT, December 18, 2009)

"Developed countries" and "developing nations" in Example (13) are opposite with each other with regard to their degree of development and are complementary with each other in a more general ICM. Mentioning the two opposite poles can activate the general ICM which these two poles belong to as the background. According to Voßhagen (1999), the opposite concepts represented by two expressions are contiguous with each other within one conceptual domain and this contiguous relationship makes it possible for pairs of opposite expressions to form cohesive links.

The present study agrees with Voßhagen's (1999) argument that it is not the antonym that provides access to its opposite, but is the concept it triggers that provides access to another concept. Figure 5.7 shows the metonymic representation of antonymy:

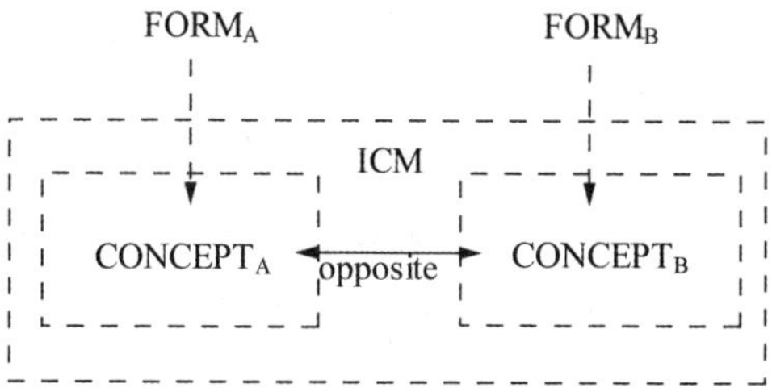

Figure 5.7 Antonymous CONCEPTs metonymic cohesion

Figure 5.7 shows that two forms, FORM$_A$ and FORM$_B$, provide access to two opposite concepts, CONCEPT$_A$ and CONCEPT$_B$. As two opposite concepts are contiguous with each other within the same ICM, this conceptual contiguity enables each of these two opposite concepts to provide access to the other and the more inclusive ICM which both of them belong to at the same time. Therefore, a cohesive link is formed between FORM$_A$-CONCEPT$_A$ and FORM$_B$-CONCEPT$_B$.

Even when the lexical items are not semantically antonymous with each other, as long as the concepts they activate are opposite with each other, these two items form a cohesive tie, as in Examples (14) and (15):

(14) All of the **Republican** districts headed for a special election went for President Obama in 2008. All the **Democratic** districts targeted went for Walker in 2010.

(WP, May 5, 2011)

(15) **Wal-Mart** Wins. **Workers** Lose.

(NYT, June 20, 2011)

"Republican" and "Democratic" in Example (14) are not semantically antonymous, but they activate the concepts of two opposite groups in presidential election.

In Example (15), there is no direct opposition between "Wal-Mart" and "workers", and as a matter of fact, workers can be considered as a part of the larger concept of Wal-Mart. However, in this specific context, "Wal-Mart" stands for the employer while "workers" stands for the current and former females employees of Wal-Mart who proceed against their employer, Wal-Mart, for crimination. There is meaning reduction in both the cases where words with broader connotation are used to refer to more specific concepts. There is no intrinsic opposition between the concept of "Wal-Mart" and the concept of "workers"; however, there is opposition between employer and employee. Thus, "Wal-Mart" and "workers" are linked because the concepts they trigger stand in an opposite relation, as Figure 5.8 shows.

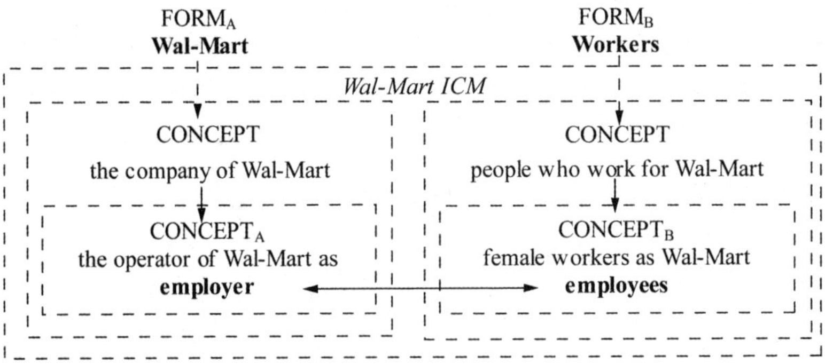

Figure 5.8 Metonymic cohesion in Example (15)

In Example (15), there is another metaphorically used pair of opposite words, "win" and "lose", in which the law suit is metaphorically compared to a war, which also denotes the opposite relationship between the two referents.

The relation of opposition can also be found among verbs, as in Example (16):

(16) Police **rounded up** at least 1,200 protesters in New Delhi and more than 3,000 in Mumbai, but many were later **released**, wire services reported.

(WP, August 16, 2011)

"Round up" is motivated by the PREVIOUS EVENT-for-RESULT metonymy, and the target meaning is "arrest", which is the opposite of "release". These two opposite actions in the same ICM form a cohesive tie, as Figure 5.9 shows.

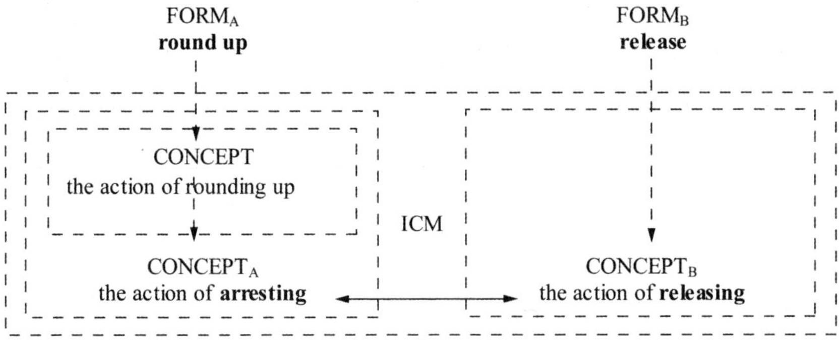

Figure 5.9 Metonymic cohesion in the "round up" example

To sum up, opposite concepts are closely associated within an ICM, and one of them can be used as a reference point affording mental access to the other as well as the more inclusive ICM which both of these opposite concepts are parts of. The analysis shows that two linguistic forms form a cohesive tie when the concepts they trigger are opposite to each other within the same ICM, regardless of whether these two linguistic forms are semantically antonymous or not.

5.1.1.4 Metonymic Cohesion through Hyponymy

Hyponymy is the relationship between a specific word and a general word when the former is included within the latter. A *hyponym* is a subordinate, specific term whose referent is included in the referent of a *superordinate*, which is a general term that includes various different words representing narrower categories. This relationship plays a significant part in verbal interaction, and is also an important source of cohesion. However, it does not have a status of familiarity among people that equal its importance in text organization compared with synonymy and antonymy.

Hyponymy has proven to be one of the most effective ways of understanding how words relate to each other. Understanding hyponymy helps people define words used in everyday life. Metonymy allows us to perceive a subcategory through mentioning its superordinate. When one of the subcategories is mentioned, we can conceive of its superordinate even if it is not explicitly present in the text. Moreover, the theory of metonymy as a textual tool does not necessarily require that the superordinate be mentioned in the text. When the superordinate is mentioned in the text, the hyponym and superordinate form a cohesive tie, as in Examples (17) and (18):

(17) **The hooded pitta** is a new **species** for the trip, and one that we would find only on the mainland. It is **a ground bird** that rummages through leaf litter on the forest floor looking for food.

(NYT, October 4, 2011)

(18) The simple muscular exertions involved in producing the familiar ha, ha, ha, he said, trigger an increase in **endorphins**, **the brain chemicals** known for their feel-good effect.

(NYT, September 13, 2011)

The topic of Example (17) is about "the hooded pitta", which is a kind of "species" as well as a kind of "ground bird". Through mentioning its superordinate, "ground bird" and "species", features of this new species are profiled. Though the readers may not be familiar with the hooded pitta, and don't know what thing it is or what kind of species it is, they would have a general idea of ground birds and species of animals. Mentioning its superordinate can make a hyponym better understood. Similarly, in Example (18), "endorphins" is a hyponym of "brain chemicals". The concept that "endorphins" denotes is a subcategory of the concept that "brain chemicals" denote. With the help of its superordinate, people who have no idea of what "endorphins" are can have some idea of what kind of things they are and what functions they have.

The cohesive link between a hyponym and a superordinate is metonymic in that when the superordinate is mentioned, the hyponym is still in focus. Readers projects features of the superordinate onto the hyponym. The easy-to-perceive aspect of a superordinate provides a mental path for the interpretation of its subcategories and therefore contributes to text coherence.

The nature of metonymy as a conceptual device can be clearly manifested in the structure of categories. Lakoff (1987: 79-90) argues that a member of a category may stand for the whole category. For instance, the category "nurse" is usually perceived in terms of "female nurse". In languages, such as English, superordinates are used frequently to refer to their hyponyms, as in the following Examples (19) and (20):

(19) Under **kidney** transplant proposal, younger patient would get the best organs.

(WP, February 24, 2011)

(20) A federal regulation that allows **automakers** to choose what kind of seat belts to install in minivans does not protect the **companies** from being sued if they pick one that is less safe, the Supreme Court ruled Wednesday.

(WP, February 24, 2011)

"Organs" in Example (19) is a superordinate of "kidney" but in this specific situation, it has the same referent with "kidney"; and "companies" in Example (20) has the same referent with "automakers". Figure 5.10 shows the metonymic relations in hyponym-superordinate cohesion in Example (20).

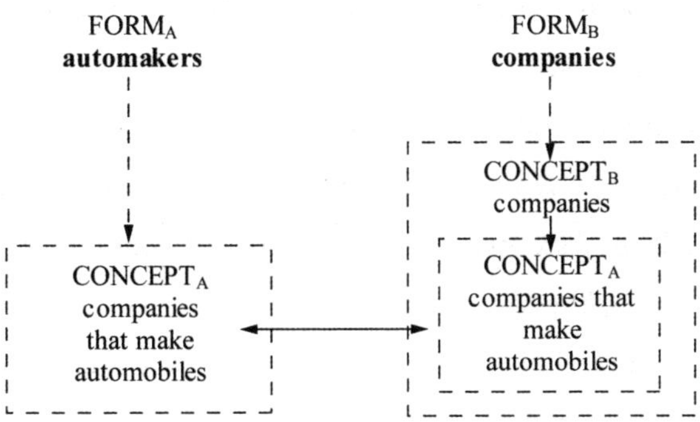

Figure 5.10 Metonymic cohesion in Example (20)

Figure 5. 10 shows that $FORM_B$ triggers two metonymic processes: the FORM-for-CONCEPT and CONCEPT-for-CONCEPT metonymy. In the first process, $FORM_B$ triggers $CONCEPT_B$; in the second process, $CONCEPT_B$ triggers $CONCEPT_A$, i. e., both $FORM_A$ and $FORM_B$ provide access to the same concept, constituting a cohesive tie. It is obvious from the figure that there is a meaning reduction from the source concept (companies) to the target concept (companies that make automobiles), which is a part of the concept triggered by $FORM_B$ (companies). We can see that lexical items like "automakers" and "companies", as well as "kidney" and "organs" are connected because they are related by the CONCEPT-for-CONCEPT metonymic relation between hyponym and superordinate.

The hyponym-superordinate metonymic cohesion exemplified by Examples (19) and (20) can be simplified somewhat and sketched as in Figure 5.11.

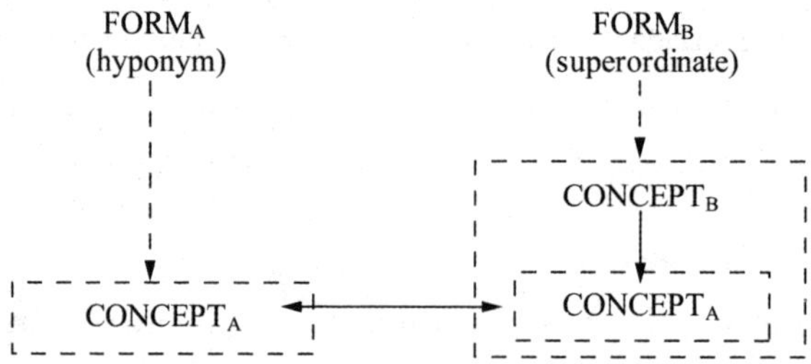

Figure 5.11 SUPERORDINATE-for-HYPONYM cohesion

From Figure 5. 11 we can see that two different forms, $FORM_A$ and $FORM_B$, stand in a hyponymic relationship. The concept activated by the hyponym is included in the concept activated by its superordinate. The meaning reduction of the superordinate enables it to provide access to its hyponym and therefore both the hyponym and superordinate provide access to the same concept. It can also be categorized into the kind of cohesion in which different forms provide access to the same concept.

Another thing that should be noted here is that, the metonymic relation between a superordinate and a hyponym is bidirectional, i. e., a superordinate can be used to stand for a hyponym and vice versa, a hyponym can also be used to stand for its superordinate.

To sum up, the concepts triggered by a hyponym and its superordinate stand in a Part-Whole relation, in which the concept triggered by the hyponym is part of the concept triggered by the superordinate. Cohesion realized through hyponymy has two representations. Firstly, a hyponym and a superordinate form a cohesive tie because the concepts they provide access to stand in a relation of inclusion. When the superordinate is mentioned, the hyponym is still in focus because features of the superordinate are projected onto the hyponym. The easy-to-perceive aspect of a superordinate provides a mental path for the interpretation of its subcategories and therefore contributes to text coherence. Secondly, as the concepts triggered by a hyponym and a superordinate stand in a Whole-Part relation which enables one of them to stand for another through meaning extension of reduction, thus, in a piece of text, both the hyponym and superordinate may provide access to the same concept and constitute a cohesive tie.

5.1.1.5 Metonymic Cohesion through Meronymy

Meronymy is a semantic relation very similar to hyponymy, for both of them denote relations of inclusion. They are different from each other because hyponymy denotes a kind-of relation while meronymy denotes a part-of relation (Seto, 1999). In other words, hyponymy is the relation between a more comprehensive category and a less comprehensive one while meronymy is the relation between an entity and its parts. Hyponymy is usually illustrated by the formula "A is a kind of B", e. g., "a dog is a kind of animal," or simply "a dog is an animal", while meronymy is usually illustrated by the formula "A is a part of B" or "A has B", e. g., "A page is part of a book", or "a book has pages" (Saeed, 1997). A "page" is a meronym of a "book" and a "book" is a holonym of a "page".

Just from the spelling we may see that there must be some connection between meronymy and metonymy. Meronymy and metonymy are linked because both of them are grounded on the Whole-Part relation. Consider Examples (21) and (22):

(21) The country has also been pouring money into biomass plants and solar **installations**—millions of **panels** now sit on German roofs and fields.

(NYT, August 29, 2011)

(22) Young people and families with children are increasingly facing **homelessness**,

according to a study, which says rising numbers of people are finding themselves **without a roof over their head.**

(The Guardian, December 5, 2012)

"Panels" in Example (21) is used anaphorically to refer to "solar installations", since the panels are the most important power generating components of solar installations. In this case, "panels" and "solar installations" refer to the same thing and activate or provide access to the same concept. In Example (22), "without a roof over their head" stands for "with no house to live in" as the roof is part of the house and "without a roof" there will be "no house". In each of these two cases, one part of an entity is used to refer to the whole entity. Figure 5.12 shows how metonymy realizes cohesive functions in Example (21).

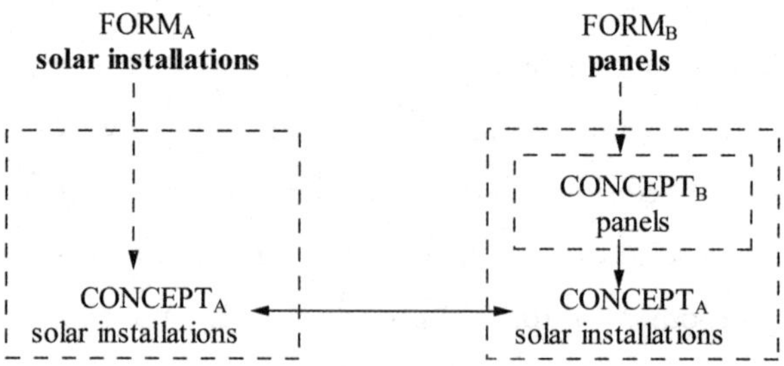

Figure 5.12 Metonymic cohesion in Example (21)

The CONCEPT-for-CONCEPT metonymic relation is responsible for connecting "panels" and "solar installations" because they are metonymically related as part and whole. Different from the SUPERORDINATE-for-HYPONYM metonymic cohesion in which there is a meaning reduction in the metonymic transfer from the concept triggered by the superordinate to the concept triggered by the hyponym, there is a meaning extension in the metonymic transfer from the concept triggered by the meronym to the concept triggered by the holonym in the MERONYM-for-HOLONYM cohesion.

A general model of MERONYM-for-HOLONYM metonymic cohesion can be diagramed as in Figure 5.13.

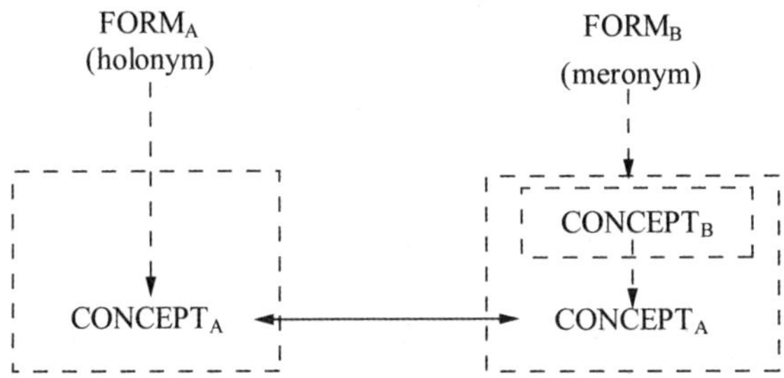

Figure 5.13 MERONYM-for-HOLONYM cohesion

From Figure 5.13 we can see that two different forms, $FORM_A$ and $FORM_B$, bear a meronymic relationship. The concept activated by a meronym is included in the concept activated by a holonym. The meaning extension of a meronym enables it to provide access to its holonym and therefore both the holonym and meronym provide access to the same concept contributing to text cohesion and coherence. It can also be categorized into the kind of identical target metonymic cohesion.

To sum up, cohesion realized through meronymy is quite similar to cohesion realized through hyponymy. The concepts triggered by a meronym and a holonym also stand in a Part-Whole relation, in which the concept triggered by the meronym is a part of the concept triggered by the holonym. Cohesion realized through meronymy also has two representations. Firstly, a meronymy and a holonym form a cohesive tie because the concepts they provide access to stand in a relation of inclusion. When one of the pair is mentioned, the other will also be triggered as background. Secondly, as the concepts triggered by a meronymy and a holonym stand in a Whole-Part relation which enables one of them to stand for another through meaning extension of reduction. Thus, in a piece of text, both the meronymy and holonym may provide access to the same concept, constituting a cohesive tie.

This section discusses the five kinds of cohesive devices within the category of reiteration of lexical cohesion in Halliday and Hasan's (1976) model. Metonymic thinking functions both in the formal world and the conceptual world, guiding the selection of linguistic vehicles which provide access to the targeted concepts. On one hand, various linguistic vehicles that provide access to the same target make a text unpredictable and interesting; on the other hand, repeated linguistic vehicles make a text formally connected even though they provide access to different targets.

5.1.2 Metonymic Cohesion through Collocation

Different from reiteration, which involves the repetition of a lexical item, either identically or in a modified form, collocation indicates a relationship of associated meaning between regularly co-occurring lexical items (Halliday & Hasan, 1976). Halliday calls collocation a "co-occurrence tendency" and states that "collocation is one of the factors on which we build our expectations of what is to come next" (Halliday, 1985: 312-313). Tanskanen (2006) suggests that compared to reiteration, collocation is more intricate because the association between the items is subtle and subjective: what is considered as a valid collocational relation will vary from one communicator to another. Some researchers hold that it is debatable whether collocation properly belongs to the notion of lexical cohesion, and even Halliday and Hasan themselves acknowledge that "collocation is the most problematic part of lexical cohesion" (Halliday & Hasan, 1976: 284). However, although subjectivity is probably unavoidable as regards some instances of collocation, there is by no means a ground for excluding collocation from an analysis of lexical relations.

Taylor (1995: 123-124) observes that the "essence of metonymy resides in the possibility of establishing connections between entities which co-occur within a given conceptual structure". It can be argued here that it is the conceptual contiguity or causality that motivates these lexical items to "keep each other company". Lexical items belong to the same ICM have a highly possible tendency to co-occur. Consider Example (23):

(23) The martial art of wushu provided the first of an onslaught of **gold medals** for China at the Asian **Games** in Guangzhou, with the host nation excelling in competitions ranging from weight lifting (two gold medals) to dance (five).

On the first morning of the event, in which 45 nations are competing, the two-time world **champion** Yuan Xiaochao won **a gold medal** in the changquan discipline. Yuan set the tone for China, which won 18 of the next 27 finals. China had 28 medals over all. Japan and South Korea each picked up four gold medals.

(NYT, November 13, 2010)

In Example (23), we may find a strong collocational bond between the lexical items, such as "games" and "competitions", "champion" and "a gold medal", "competitions" and "finals", "games" and "medals", which makes the text cohesive. It is obvious that all the lexical items belong to the same Games ICM, and each item is connected with others directly or indirectly, as Figure 5. 14 shows.

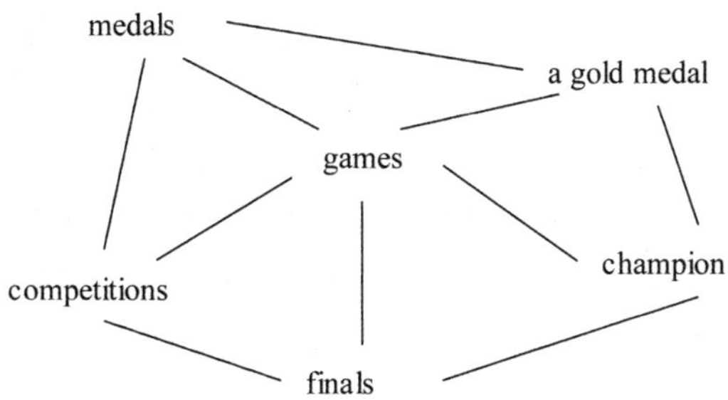

Figure 5. 14 The collocational bonds of the lexical items in the Games ICM

Once the topic of a sports competition is introduced, we can go on to talk about the champion, the finals, the medals, and so forth. These concepts are perceived as associated or contiguous with each other depending on people's world knowledge. More examples may be found in Examples (24) and (25):

(24) Police said in a statement Tuesday that they **arrested** 26-year-old Emmett Bramble after a routine search at Golden Grove prison in St. Croix. It was not clear if Bramble had an **attorney.**

(WP, July 29, 2011)

(25) The **violence** also reached Tunisia, one of the most moderate Muslim countries and the birth place of the Arab Spring. Three people **died** during **clashes** as protesters stormed the U. S. Embassy compound, climbing over walls and breaking a locked gate.

(WSJ, September 16, 2012)

(26) The **gas boom** is transforming small towns like this one (population 4,400 and growing) and revitalizing the **economy** of this once-forgotten stretch of rural

northeastern Pennsylvania. The few **hotels** here have expanded, **restaurants** are packed and **housing rentals** have more than doubled.

(NYT, October 16, 2010)

In Example (24), when someone is arrested, he/she usually has an attorney to represent him/her during the investigation and the trial. Thus, it is naturally coherent for "attorney" to appear after "arrest"; in Example (25), where there is "violence", there is always "clashes" and possibly people would "die". In Example (26), "gas boom", "transforming small towns", "revitalizing the economy", "hotels have expanded", "restaurants are packed", and "housing rentals have more than doubles" are connected by a causal relationship. Usually, when the economy is revitalized, the business of hotels and restaurants would be expanded, and more people would be attracted to the place and thus the housing rentals would rise with increasing demand. Moreover, it can also be said that hotels, restaurants and housing rentals are indicators of economy. When we talk about economy, there is a tendency that we will talk about restaurants and housing rentals next because these items are so closely associated within the same Economy ICM.

Two forms may form a cohesive tie if the concepts they provide access to belong to the same ICM even though there is no systematic semantic relationship between them. The connectedness of items in collocation can be sketched as in Figure 5.15.

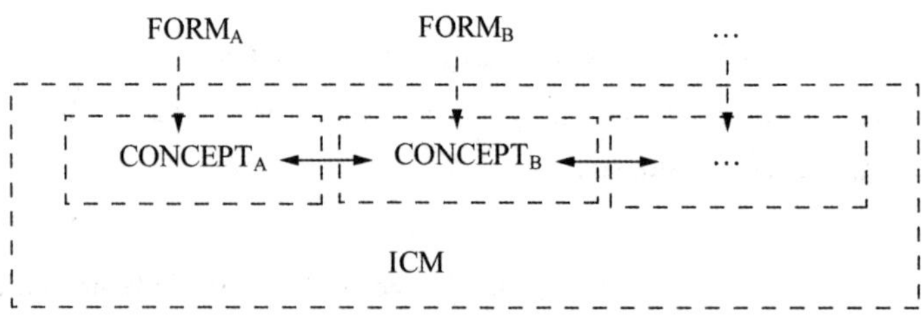

Figure 5.15 Metonymic representation of collocation

Figure 5.15 shows that the connectedness between items that co-occur is not on the linguistic level but on the conceptual level, i. e., the items are not associated by their semantic relations but by the conceptual connection within one ICM. This conceptual connection by contiguity or causality provides possibility for these items to form cohesive links if they occur in adjacent sentences.

To sum up, this section discusses the functions of metonymy in organizing news texts in terms of lexical cohesion. The discussion shows that the Form-Concept model of metonymy accounts for all types of lexical cohesion, which ensure the maximum ease of text processing as a unified whole. On the hand, the formal connectedness is realized through the conceptual connectedness: different forms, whether semantically related or not, generate cohesive force as long as they provide access to the same concept, or concepts that are contiguous with each other within the same ICM. On the other hand, different linguistic forms which provide access to the same concept make the topic of texts focused but the linguistic patterns flexible and interesting.

5.2 Functions of Metonymy in Grammatical Cohesion

Halliday and Hasan (1976) classified the grammatical links into four broad types, reference, substitution, ellipsis and conjunction. For the purpose of the present study, the analysis concerns only three of the four types, namely, reference, substitution, and ellipsis.

5.2.1 Metonymic Cohesion through Reference

The issue of reference has been investigated from various perspectives within linguistics and psychology. Halliday and Matthiessen (1999: 530) consider reference as "the way of referring to things that are already semiotically accessible: either actually, in the text, or potentially, in the context of situation". The former refers to textual reference while the latter refers to situational reference. Both situational and textual reference serve the function of showing how the message fits into its context, but situational reference links the language to the external context, and does not contribute to the texture of the text, since it does not bind two elements together into a text, whereas "textual reference signals how the message fits specifically into its textual context, or the co-text" (Thompson, 2008: 181).

Although the nature of metonymy is still under discussion, it is generally accepted that referring is the primary function of metonymy (Lakoff & Johnson, 1980; Lakoff, 1987; Gibbs, 1994a, 1994b; Nunberg, 1995; Stirling, 1996; Warren, 2002). For this reason, this subsection is devoted to exploring metonymy's functions in textual reference, while its functions in situational reference will be covered in the following chapters of this book, because referring to people, things, situations or events in the real world is indispensable in texts of any kinds, especially for news reports.

As the most important part of reference, anaphora has attracted a lot of academic attentions in particular from a variety of theoretical perspectives (e. g. Reinhart, 1983; Erku & Gundel, 1987; Clark, 1977, Clark & Haviland, 1977; Sanford & Garrod, 1981; Huang, 1994). Studies on anaphoric and cataphoric relations concentrate mainly on the question of how they are signaled by determiners, such as the definite article (the) and demonstratives. Metonymy is traditionally regarded as a phenomenon of referring, designating the relationship between a linguistic expression and a person, an object, an action or event in the world. This property of metonymy obviously may interact with other referential phenomena. The subsequent discussion is intended to reveal the various interaction patterns for metonymies and anaphora, including both *direct anaphora* and *indirect anaphora* in Quirk et al.'s (1985) terminology.

According to Quirk et al. (1985), *direct anaphora* is the kind of anaphora whose anaphor and antecedent stand in the relation of explicit co-reference. In Halliday and Hasan's (1976) model, reference items in English can be divided into personal, demonstrative and comparative. Personal reference is by means of personal pronouns, such as "he", "she", "him", "they"; demonstrative reference is reference by means of location, such as "this", "that", "these", "those" and the article "the"; comparative reference is indirect reference by means of identity or similarity, realized by such items as "same", "other", "more". A complete list is given in Halliday and Hasan (1976: 37-39). Example (27) is an example of reference in Halliday and Hasan's (1976) model.

(27) **Tillman died** last Sunday after a random attack at a house party. Investigators say

he was stomped, kicked and punched to death.

(WP, November 13, 2010)

In English, proper nouns or common nouns are usually used at the beginning of the text and pronouns are used to refer back to the proper or common nouns in the rest of discourse unless they may arouse ambiguities. In the ontological and conceptual realms, "Tillman" and "he" in the particular context of Example (27) refer to the same target, the man who named Tillman and died at a house party. The two items is cohesive because they form a tie and maintained the identical referent, or because of their coreferentiality.

According to Al-Sharafi's (2004) model of textual metonymy, interpretation of the reference item "he", the third-person-singular pronoun, depends on its antecedent "Tillman", which means the form "he" provides access to the form "Tillman" as well as the person who is named "Tillman" and the relevant concepts about "Tillman" in this particular context. There exists a metonymic interpretation of this relation no matter whether we perceive the relation between "Tillman" and "he" as forms or as concepts.

Figure 5.16 shows the metonymic relation between "he" and "Tillman" in Example (27).

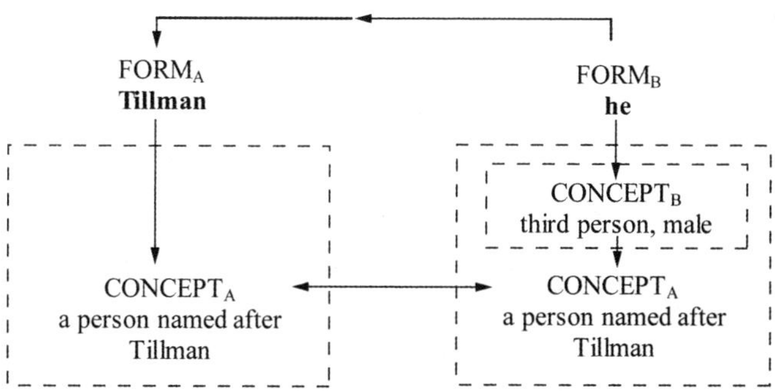

Figure 5.16 Metonymic cohesion in Example (27)

In Figure 5.16, the one-way arrow signifies that the interpretation of $FORM_B$ is dependent on its antecedent. To interpret "he" we need to look backward for its antecedent because the concept activated by "he" is just a part of a more inclusive ICM, i.e., the ICM of its antecedent. $FORM_B$(he) is used to stand for $FORM_A$ (Tillman) because both nouns and pronouns are forms of language (Al-Sharafi, 2004).

Al-Sharafi (2004) argues that the function of the referential item "he" in the organization and interpretation of the texts should be perceived as a component in the ICM of its antecedent. As in Example (27), "Tillman", a family name used to refer to a person who is male, determines that the pronoun that used to stand for it must be one denoting a male person. Thus, the concept triggered by the third person singular pronoun, "he", becomes a part of the "Tillman" ICM and is used to stand for the whole ICM of "Tillman".

The first and second person pronouns, according to Halliday and Hasan, normally are interpreted exophorically. In news texts, first person pronouns frequently occur in quoted speech, and they also contribute to cohesion, because the readers need to look in the text, either anaphorically or cataphorically, to find out who the speaker is, as in Example (28).

(28) But Representative **Mike Coffman**, Republican of Colorado, who is on the Armed Services Committee, said: "**I** don't have any fascination with looking at gunshot wounds to the face."

(NYT, May 12, 2011)

The first person pronoun, "I", and "Mike Coffman" refer to the same referent and thus form a cohesive tie. Both the forms provide access to the same target.

In Halliday and Hasan's (1976) model, the demonstratives regularly refer exophorically to something within the context of situation. Confined by the purpose of the current research, the book only focuses on demonstratives that contribute to text cohesion, as the one in Example (29).

(29) "**The objective of the meeting was to try and convince us not to participate in the demonstrations, and when we did, our punishment was the order to close our offices**," Mr. Helfi said. "**That** doesn't reflect Maliki's speech about the right of the Iraqis to protest."

(NYT, March 8, 2011)

The demonstrative pronoun, "that", anaphorically refers back to the fact stated in the preceding sentence. The concept triggered by "that" must be recovered from the concept its antecedent triggers. Consider Example (30):

(30) The **Central Intelligence Agency** is allowing members of the House and Senate Intelligence and Armed Services Committees to see **photographs of Osama bin Laden's corpse**, a C. I. A. spokeswoman said Wednesday. Lawmakers will view **the photos** in a secure room at **the agency's** headquarters in Langley, Va., and cannot take copies of **the photos** with them.

(NYT, May 12, 2011)

The two occurrences of "the photos" refer back to "photographs of Osama bin Laden's corps" and "the agency" refers back to "the Central Intelligence Agency". In Example (30), the form of anaphor is part of the form of its antecedent, in which part of the form, "the photos", is used to stand for the whole form, "photographs of Osama bin Laden's corps", and therefore both the anaphor and its antecedent provide access to exactly the same concept in this specific situation.

Based on the discussion above, a universal model for metonymic cohesion through direct anaphora can be sketched, as Figure 5.17 shows.

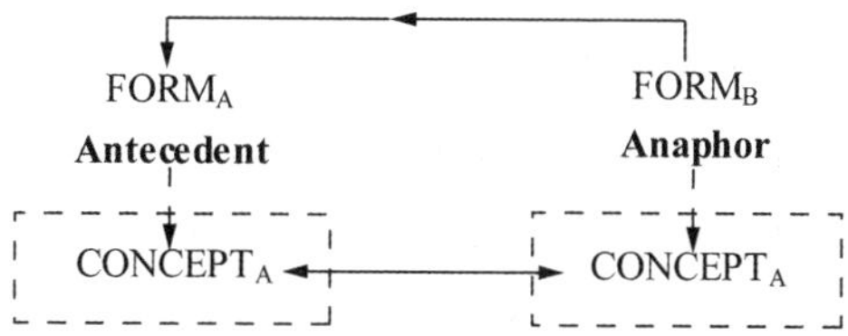

Figure 5.17 Metonymic representation of direct anaphora

Figure 5.17 shows that the metonymic relations of FORM-for-FORM can explain reference in text as a phenomenon in the world of forms, but reference relations are not confined to the formal world (Al-Sharafi, 2004). Strictly speaking, an anaphor and its antecedent are connected because they provide access to the same concept. The concept triggered by the anaphor should be perceived as an element of the concept triggered by its antecedent.

The phenomenon of *indirect anaphora* has been treated under different names, such as *bridging* (Clark, 1977; Mastui, 2000), *associated anaphora* (Hawkins, 1978; Sidner, 1979), *inferables* (Prince, 1981), *indirect anaphors* (Quirk et al.,

1985), *inferred entity* (Ariel, 1990), *cross-reference* (Huang, 1994), or *associative anaphora* (Charolles & Kleiber, 1999). According to Quirk et al. (1985), indirect anaphora is the type of anaphora where the relation between anaphor and antecedent is implicit or indirect, as in Examples (31) and (32).

(31) **Other Midwest states** are engaged in similar battles and have set aside neighborliness for easy growth as **they** search for answers to rising unemployment in their still-struggling economies.

Though **they** may say their development efforts are designed to help them compete with the two coasts for companies, they often end up fighting over companies already in the region.

(NYT, April 08, 2011)

(32) Tracey Guest, a spokeswoman for **Simon & Schuster**, said there was no announced first printing yet, but **they** "expect the first printing and initial e-book sales to be completely commensurate with the worldwide attention and interest that Schwarzenegger commands".

(NYT, September 22, 2011)

In Example (31), the two occurrences of "they" anaphorically refer back to "other midwest states", but the antecedent refers to nonhuman things and cannot "search for answers" or "may say" something. Therefore, this antecedent must be interpreted metonymically, in which the concept of "states" triggers the concept of "people in those states".

In Example (32), there is no direct antecedent for the third person plural pronoun "they"; however, the sentence can still be perceived coherent by the readers. In this sentence, there is a referential metonymy of COMPANY-for-MEMBERS OF THAT COMPANY in which "Simon & Schuster" refers to "the members, especially the operators of the company of Simon & Schuster". Thus, "they" refers back to the targeted referent, "the operators". The metonymic cohesion in Example (32) can be sketched as in Figure 5.18.

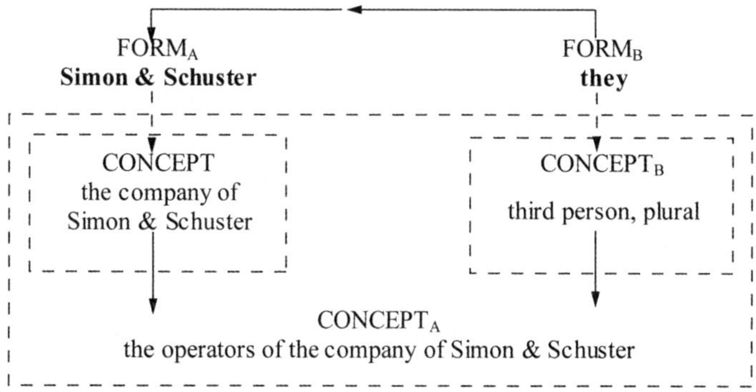

Figure 5.18 Metonymic cohesion in Example (32)

Figure 5.18 shows that the antecedent, "Simon & Schuster", triggers the concept of the company which further triggers the concept of the operators of the company; the anaphor, "they", triggers the concept of third person, plural, which is a property of the target concept of the antecedent, the operators of the company of Simon & Schuster.

(33) "The United States military has a zero-tolerance policy for **sexual assault**, and we will hold **the perpetrators** appropriately accountable," he said.

(CNN, January 19, 2012)

(34) The crime reporters say that one reason for the "Yard's failure is that, when the Yard tried to stop **the corruption**, serving officers tipped **them** off so **they** could evade detection".

(The Guardian, June 8, 2011)

"The perpetrators" refer to "the perpetrators of sexual assault in the U. S. military" in this particular situation described by Example (33), because the crime of sexual assault has already been mentioned; and our world knowledge tells us that that a crime is done by a perpetrator or perpetrators. Similarly, in Example (34), "them" and "they" refer back to an implicit antecedent "(people involved) in the corruption". In this case, "the perpetrators" can also be regarded as an elliptical variant of "the perpetrators of the sexual assault".

Based on the discussion, a universal model for indirect metonymic representation or anaphora can be sketched as in Figure 5.19.

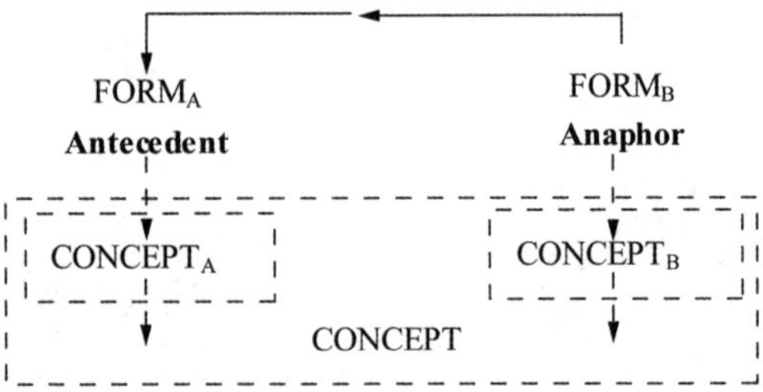

Figure 5.19 Metonymic representation of indirect anaphora

Figure 5.19 shows that the concept triggered by the anaphor can be perceived as a component of the ICM of the antecedents. Both antecedent and anaphor provide access to the same concept. However, anaphoric pronoun agrees in gender and number either with the metonymic target or with the metonymic source, depending on which one is more conceptually salient to the speaker or writer.

To sum up, FORM-for-FORM and CONCEPT-for-CONCEPT metonymies are responsible for cohesion realized through reference. At the formal level, both the anaphor and antecedent are forms of language no matter they are pronouns, demonstratives or common nouns. At the conceptual level, these two forms provide access to the same concept, contributing to text cohesion.

5.2.2 Metonymic Cohesion through Substitution

As Cornish (1986: 1) points out, people tend to use the "semantically attenuated expression in place of the full, lexical expression initially used" in order to avoid redundancy or repetition in communication. Substituting one element for another in a text can provide a text with formal connectedness, which corresponds to the fact that metonymy is basically a process of substitution in nature; thus it can be said that as a cohesive device, substitution is fundamentally metonymic.

Halliday and Hasan (1976) distinguish the items that can occur as substitutes in English into three types: nominal substitution, which is often realized by pronouns "one" and "ones", and a nominal phrase "the same"; verbal substitution, realized by the verb "do" and its variations, and clausal substitution, realized by the pronoun "so" and the adverb "not".

Substitute items that can be used to stand for nominal phrases vary in different works. For instance, Quirk at al. (1985) holds that words such as some, none, any, few, fewer, many, more, most, less, several, enough, etc. can all act as substitutes for noun phrases. Analysis on nominal substitutes in the present study is limited to the use of "one/ones", which can be illustrated by Examples (35) and (36).

(35) They may avert a future **debt crisis**, but won't solve this **one.**

(NYT, October 2, 2011)

(36) "I think this is part of a longer term trend," said Chu Shulong, a political scientist at Tsinghua University in Beijing. "Over the last five or six years, this **administration** has become much more sensitive about social stability than the previous one. Some measures might be temporary, but most of them will be long term."

(WSJ, April 11, 2011)

"One" substitutes for "debt crisis" in Example (35) and substitutes for "administration" in Example (36). At the formal level, one form is used to stand for another, but at the conceptual level, substitutes do not necessarily have the same referent with their antecedents. The substitute, "one" is "grammatically and semantically equivalent" to its antecedent, but it does not refer to the same referent as its antecedent does (Quirk, et al., 1985: 803). In Example (35), the form "one" stands for the form "debt crisis", but "a future debt crisis" could be any debt crisis, while the debt crisis activated by "one" refers to a specific debt crisis. It can be said that "a future debt crisis" denote a category while "this one" denotes a specific crisis and there is a kind-of relationship between the referents activated by substitute and its antecedent.

In Example (36), "one" substitutes for "administration", but these two forms do not refer to the same referent. To put it simply, the antecedent, "administration", refers to the current administration of the Chinese government, while the substitute, "one", refers to the former administration. Therefore, substitution is a formal relation of FORM-for-FORM as well as a conceptual relation of CONCEPT-for-CONCEPT, but whether the substitute and its antecedent provide access to the same concept depends on specific context. In a word, substitutes and their antecedents do not have to have a relationship of coreference.

Verbal substitution is usually realized by "do", sometimes "do so" or "do the same", as in Examples (37) and (38).

(37) Greek public debt **continues to mount**, and **so does** the pressure on the government to find more revenue and make more cuts.

(NYT, October 2, 2011)

(38) French Foreign Minister Laurent Fabius told high-level representatives here that Maj. Gen. Manaf Tlas, a longtime member of Assad's inner circle, had **fled Damascus.** In a news conference later Friday, Clinton seized the moment to encourage others close to Assad **to do the same.**

(WP, July 6, 2012)

Interpretation of the "so + do + subject" construction in Example (37) depends on its antecedent. In this specific context of Example (37), "so does the pressure on the government" means "the pressure on the government continues to mount". One form, "so does", is used to stand for another form, "continues to mount", and both forms provide access to the same concept. Similarly, in Example (38), "to do the same" is used to stand for "to flee Damascus". The substitute and antecedent have different forms but they provide access to the same concept.

In English, "so" and "not" can be used to replace clauses representing a state, belief, an assumption or an emotion, as illustrated in Examples (39) and (40).

(39) "It was an individual act, which could have various reasons or motives, but it does not mean at all that the security situation is bad in the province," said the governor of Faryab Province, Abdul Haq Shafaq. He said the American trainers had good relations with the border police battalion. "It's early to say if **the shooting had links with the Holy Koran burning** or **not.**"

(NYT, April 4, 2011)

(40) Like Mr. Comey, Mr. Fitzgerald now has the public identity of a Republican political appointee. Moreover, **his demonstrated willingness to challenge the Bush White House could give its current occupants pause**, though they would never say so in public.

(NYT, May 1, 2011)

In Example (39), "not" substitutes for "the shooting did not have links with the Holy Koran burning" and in Example (40), "so" substitutes for "his demonstrated willingness to challenge the Bush White House could give its current occupants pause". Substituting clauses with words as short as "so" or "not" makes a text as brief as possible.

Substitution shares the same attribute with anaphora, because a substitute usually refers back to elements mentioned earlier in the same text. Therefore, it implies a repetition at the formal level which can literally take the place of their antecedent, or it can be said that one form is used to signify another.

Based on the discussion, metonymic representation of substitution includes three subtypes of substitutes, which can be diagramed in Figure 5.20.

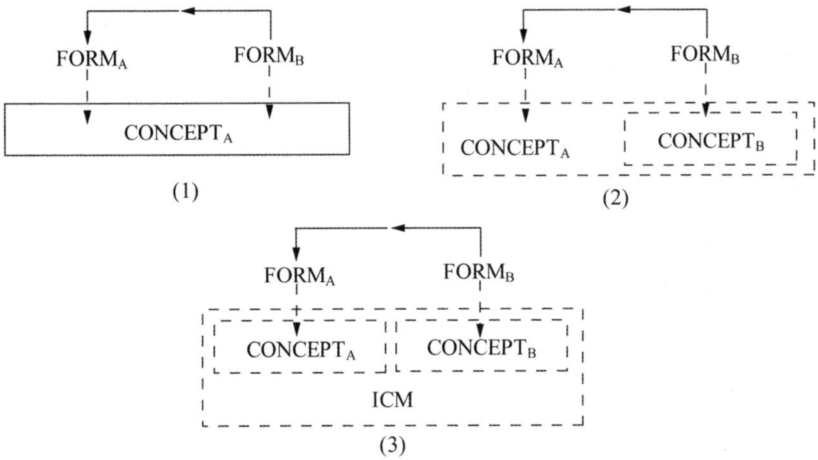

Figure 5.20 Metonymic representation of three types of substitutes

In each of these three figures, $FORM_A$ signifies the antecedent and $FORM_B$ signifies the substitute. Figure (1) shows that the antecedent and substitute provide access to the same concept. Figure (2) shows that the concept triggered by the substitute is included in the concept triggered by its antecedent. Figure (3) shows that the concept triggered by the substitute and the concept triggered by the antecedent are contiguous with each other within the same ICM.

To summarize, cohesion realized through substitution lies in the fact that the concept that the substitute triggers and the concept that the antecedent triggers stand in a metonymic relationship. Substitution can be regarded as using a semantically attenuated form to replace a repeated occurrence of the antecedent. The cohesive force of substitutes and antecedents is generated from the relationship between the concepts they provide access to, which can be an identical relationship, a contiguous relationship or a relationship of inclusion.

5.2.3 Metonymic Cohesion through Ellipsis

Ellipsis refers to the cohesive device in which full repetition of a clause or clause element is avoided. Ellipsis expresses "something unsaid" but there is no implication that what is unsaid is not understood; on the contrary, "unsaid" implies "but understood nevertheless" (Halliday & Hasan, 1976: 142). Like substitution, ellipsis is classified into three main types: *nominal ellipsis*, *verbal ellipsis*, and *clausal ellipsis*.

Nominal ellipsis refers to the type of cohesion that takes place within the nominal group, as in Examples (41), (42) and (43).

(41) Japan's **Meltdown** and the Global Economy's

(NYT, March 18, 2011)

(42) To test the relationship of laughter of this sort to pain resistance, he did a series of **six experiments.** In **five**, participants watched excerpts of comedy videos, neutral videos or videos meant to promote good feeling, but not laughter.

(NYT, September 13, 2011)

(43) "We left school with a mountain of **debt**," Mr. Obama said in 2008. "Michelle I know had at least $60,000. I had at least $60,000. So when we got together we had a lot of loans to pay."

(NYT, April 11, 2011)

Example (41) is a news headline which consists of two NPs; the second is an elliptical form, standing for "global economy's meltdown". The slot can be retrieved from the preceding NP, even though they do not necessarily have the same referent: the first "meltdown" refers to the meltdown of Japan's nuclear operator, while the omitted one metaphorically refers to a situation which is as severe as the melting down of a nuclear reactor core.

In Example (42), "five" is an elliptical form, standing for "experiment number five". To understand elliptical forms, the readers should go back of the text to fill in the slot. According to Barcelona (2005), in the construction of "NP + [number] + CARDINAL", the cardinal regularly indicates serial order rather than quantity, as "five" in "[experiment] five" should be "the fifth experiment". Barcelona calls this kind of metonymy CARDINAL NUMBER-for-ORDINAL NUMBER metonymy, in which the cardinal part of the construction is the part that is salient and informative enough to stand for the whole construction. In Example (43), "$60,000" stands for "$60,000 of debt"; "of debt" is left unsaid but still understood nevertheless.

When a part of the NP is omitted, it can be said that the whole NP is substituted by only part of the NP, motivated by the PART OF A FORM-for-THE WHOLE FORM metonymy (Bierwiaczonek, 2007).

In verbal ellipsis, part of the verbal phrase is omitted, as in Example (44).

(44) **A Palestinian attacker wounded seven Israelis, one critically**, near a Tel Aviv nightclub early Monday, hitting a police checkpoint with a stolen taxi and then stabbing others, police said.

(NYT, August 29, 2011)

In Example (44), "one" is the elliptical form of "one Israeli", motivated by the PART OF A FORM-for-THE WHOLE FORM metonymy. Apart from this nominal ellipsis, there is another structural slot between "one" and "critically", which has to be recovered from the preceding utterance that "a Palestinian attacker wounded seven Israelis", and therefore this slot should be filled by "was wounded". Thus, the form, "one critically", provides access to the concept of "one Israeli was wounded critically". Using part of a form to stand for the whole form can avoid redundancy and keep the readers focused on the new information.

It is hard to find cases of clausal ellipsis in the data collected for the present study. The low frequency of clausal ellipsis is consistent with Halliday and Hasan's (1976) assertion that the two types of cohesive ties, substitution and ellipsis, occur more frequently in informal, conversational texts than they do in formal and highly descriptive text. There are lots of elliptical forms in news headlines. However, in Halliday and Hasan's (1976) model, *ellipsis* is "something left unsaid", but not everything "left unsaid" is an example of ellipsis. In other words, not all elliptical forms contribute to text cohesion. There are two requirements for "something left unsaid" to be ellipsis: being cohesive and related to textual relations. Quirk et al. (1985) clarify the issue of ellipsis somewhat and argue that an elliptical form contributes to text cohesion only when its full form is recoverable from the linguistic context. Although elliptical forms motivated by the PART OF A FORM-for-THE WHOLE FORM metonymy prevail in news texts, not all of them contributes to text cohesion, and therefore, further discussion on the role of metonymy in shortening linguistic forms will not be covered in this chapter.

To summarize, the Form-Concept model of metonymy proposed by the present study deals with only two of the three ontological realms in which metonymy may occur: the world of forms and the world of concepts, and does not deal with real referents in the world, because words, sentences and whole discourses are not interpreted relative to the world, but to the way we believe the world to be. Thus, as long as language is concerned, there is always a FORM and a CONCEPT involved. From the discussion of this chapter, it can be concluded that two linguistic items (or two FORMs) are cohesive as long as they satisfy one of the following conditions:

(1) they have identical FORM;

(2) they provide access to the same CONCEPT;

(3) they provide access to CONCEPTs which are related by inclusion; or

(4) they provide access to CONCEPTs which are contiguous within the same ICM.

Repetition is the kind of lexical cohesion in which the same Form-Concept relation or only part of the relation, the Form, is repeated. The discussion shows that whether it is the whole Form-Concept relation or only the FORM that is repeated, a cohesive tie is formed. When the repeated linguistic forms trigger the same concept with its previous occurrence, the cohesive link between these two pairs of Form-Concept relation is strengthened, but it is not required for these two forms to be cohesive. When the repeated form has a different referent, or provides access to a different concept with its previous occurrence, they still form a cohesive tie.

Synonymous items provide access to the same concept. Even when they are not semantically synonymous with each other, as long as they provide access to the same concept, they form a cohesive tie. Antonymous items provide access to CONCEPTs that are opposite to each other within one ICM. Concepts related by opposition are conceptually contiguous and one of them can be used as a reference point affording mental access to the other as well as the higher-level ICM which both of these opposite concepts are parts of. Even if two linguistic forms are not semantically antonymous, as long as they provide access to CONCEPTs that are opposite with each other within one ICM, they generate cohesive powers.

The concepts triggered by a hyponym and its superordinate stand in a Part-Whole relation, in which the concept triggered by the hyponym is part of the concept triggered by the superordinate. Cohesion realized through hyponymy has two representations. Firstly, a hyponym and a superordinate form a cohesive tie, because the concepts they provide access to stand in a relation of inclusion. Secondly, as the concepts triggered by a hyponym and a superordinate stand in a Whole-Part relation which enables one of them to stand for another through meaning extension of reduction, thus, in certain context, both the hyponym and superordinate may provide access to the same concept, contributing to text cohesion.

Cohesion realized through meronymy is quite similar to cohesion realized through hyponymy. The concepts triggered by a meronym and a holonym also stand in a Part-Whole relation, in which the concept triggered by the meronym is a part of the concept triggered by the holonym. Cohesion realized through meronymy also has two representations: the concepts triggered by the meronymy and holonym stand in a relation of inclusion; or the meronymy and holonym provide access to the same concept.

Items that have the tendency to co-occur have cohesive power, because the CONCEPTs they provide access to are contiguous with each other within one more inclusive ICM. The items that co-occur in collocation are connected by relations at the conceptual level instead of the linguistic level, i. e. , the items are not associated by their semantic relations but by conceptual connection within one ICM.

The relations between pronouns, substitutes, or even structural slots and their antecedents are also metonymic. These semantically attenuated forms are used to stand for the whole form which can be recovered from the preceding clauses. The FORM-for-FORM and CONCEPT-for-CONCEPT metonymies are responsible for cohesion realized through grammatical cohesive devices. At the formal level, one form is used to stand for another form, because no matter what category they belong to, pronouns, demonstratives or common nouns, they are all forms of language. At the conceptual level, these different forms provide access to the same concepts, two concepts that are related by inclusion or conceptual contiguity within the same ICM.

Chapter 6
Whole-Part Metonymy in News Text Organization

This chapter aims to reveal the patterns Whole-Part metonymy demonstrates in organizing news texts. It starts with an elaboration on the contiguity principle underlying the Whole-Part metonymy followed by an analysis on the experiential functions of Whole-Part metonymy, and then moves on to the Whole-Part pattern of news text organization.

6.1 The Contiguity Principle underlying Whole-Part Metonymy

The notion of *contiguity* is the key component in defining and interpreting metonymy recognized by both the rhetoricians and cognitive linguists (Lakoff, 1987; Croft, 1993; Panther & Thornburg, 1998; Radden & Kövecses, 1999). It plays a central role in metonymic thinking and is the defining feature that distinguishes metonymy from metaphor (Norrick, 1981; Feyaerts, 2000; Dirven, 2002).

Different from the traditional approach which located contiguity based on objective or natural contiguity in the world of reality, cognitive linguistics explores contiguity at the conceptual level (Radden & Kövecses, 1999) and describes it as a relationship based on experiential closeness. According to Koch (1999: 146), contiguity is "the relation that exists between elements of a frame or between the frame as a whole and its elements", which can be demonstrated in the most frequently quoted example in the literature of metonymy: "the ham sandwich is waiting for his check". In this sentence, two entities, the item the customer ordered and the customer, are experientially associated, or conceptually contiguous with one another, so that one entity (the item the customer ordered) can be used to stand for the other (the customer).

Metonymy is defined by Seto (1999: 91) as "a referential transfer phenomenon based on the spatio-temporal contiguity as conceived by the speaker between an entity and another in the (real) world". Cognitive approach sees reality as a domain that does not "exist independently of human understanding, knowledge and belief" (Feyaerts, 1999: 317), which agrees with the cognitive assumptions that meaning is created, not found, by human beings. As Bredin (1984: 57) says, "metaphor creates relation between its objects, while metonymy presupposes that relation", i. e., conceptual contiguity exists before the metonymic transfer.

The concept of contiguity may refer to any possible connections established between entities within a given conceptual structure, an ICM, frame, schema, domain or scenario. In other words, contiguity can take any form, spatial, temporal or abstract, as long as there are possibilities for people to construe a communicatively associated relation between the entities involved (Seto, 1999: 91). According to Seto (1999), temporal and abstract entities are metaphorically construed. Events can be metaphorically considered as spatial entities. In this way one temporal entity can be continuous with another temporal entity as special entities are. Abstract entities, such as properties, are considered as abstract because they are not bounded by space or time, even though they are not necessarily abstract.

To summarize, contiguity exists in our conceptualization of the world and the concept of contiguity must be metaphorically construed. It should be noted that contiguity exists in our conceptualization does not mean that contiguity can only exist between concepts, or between two conceptual entities within the same conceptual domain or ICM. It can also be found between word forms

(Bierwiaczonek, 2007) and between real-world referents (Radden & Kövecses, 1999). The various contiguous relationships between two entities within the same ICM, or one part of the ICM within the whole ICM produce various kinds of metonymies, which can all be subsumed into the broad category of Whole-Part metonymy.

6.2 Experiential Functions of Whole-Part Metonymy

The Whole-Part metonymies are primarily metonymies based on contiguity between the parts and the whole or between the parts within the same whole. This subsection investigates into the experiential functions of Whole-Part metonymies to show how metonymy "structures our thoughts, attitudes, and actions" on the ground that "metonymic concepts are grounded in our experience" (Lakoff & Johnson, 1980: 39). The traditional approaches treat metonymy as a figure of speech whose prime function is reference, while cognitive approaches stress the non-referential functions of metonymy. This section will firstly examine the referential use of Whole-Part metonymy and then move on to analyze its non-referential use.

6.2.1 Referential Use of Whole-Part Metonymy

Referring to people, things or events in the real world are indispensable in verbal communication, because they help the addresser and the addressee to locate the entities they are talking about. When a speaker or writer uses a definite referring expression, he/she must presuppose that the listener or reader could have a mental representation of the entity being referred to (Prince, 1978; Kronrod & Engel, 2001). The referential function of metonymy is motivated by the experiential associations among entities, which means the mental path from the source entity to the target entity can only be successfully established in the mind of the addressees who can perceive the empirical association between these two entities.

When the source entity is a part of the whole, the target entity may be the whole or other part within the same whole. And the whole may also be used as a source entity providing access to its part. Thus, the category of Whole-Part metonymy may be further divided into three subcategories: PART-for-WHOLE, WHOLE-for-PART, and PART-for-PART metonymies. The rest part of this subsection will examine the referential functions of these three types of Whole-Part metonymy in news text organization.

6.2.1.1 PART-for-WHOLE Metonymy

The most obvious cases of PART-for-WHOLE metonymy have been called synecdoche by traditional rhetoricians, where one part stands for the whole. Jakobson (1956) argues that the formal frame of any visual image, painting, drawing, photograph, film or television frame, are synecdochic in nature, because what is being presented is only a piece of reality. He further argues that any attempt to represent reality can be seen as involving synecdoche, as in Examples (45), (46) and (47).

(45) A look back at the past few **summers** reveals how tough the economic (and political) sledding has been for Obama.

(WP, July 6, 2012)

(46) Young people and families with children are increasingly facing homelessness, according to a study, which says rising numbers of people are finding themselves without **a roof** over their head.

(The Guardian, December 5, 2012)

(47) Former governor and Democratic National Committee Chairman Tim Kainewill hire **a well known face in Virginia politics** to oversee his U. S. Senate campaign next year.

(WP, July 7, 2011)

Summer is just one of the four seasons of a year, or a part of a year. "The past few summers" is used in Example (45) to refer to "the past few years", because the text was produced in summer and "summer" is conceptually more salient than "year" from the perspective of both the reporter and the readers. "A roof", a part of a house, is used to stand for "house" in Example (46); thus, "without a roof over their head" coheres with "homelessness" which occurred earlier. "A well known face in Virginia politics" in Example (47) refers to "a well known person in Virginia politics", because the face is the most prominent part of a person when we try to recognize this person. These three cases of metonymy include meaning extension where the most salient part of an entity stands for the whole entity.

An element of a conceptual frame is conceptually contiguous with the whole. Thus, we may refer to an entity by naming one of its parts, such as a season can be used to stand for a year, a roof for a house, a face for a person, and so forth. It should be noted here again that the relationship between a part and a whole must be construed metaphorically, i. e., a part may also be a subcategory or a property of an entity. By mentioning a subcategory under a higher category, or a property of an entity, the whole category or entity would be activated. In English, the construction of "definite article + adjective" can be used to stand for a group of people who share the same attribute designated by the adjective, as in Examples (48) and (49).

(48) This week, we hosted a renowned expert in HIV/AIDS care currently practicing at a hospital known for serving **the poor and vulnerable** in New York.

(CNN, December 2, 2011)

(49) For four years, the Virginia General Assembly has scrimped, scrounged and borrowed to pay for schools, highways, police and public programs that care for **the mentally ill, the disabled and the poor.**

(WP, March 13, 2011)

In Examples (48) and (49), "the poor and vulnerable" and "the mentally ill, the disabled and the poor", refer to the groups of people who are poor and vulnerable, mentally ill, disabled or poor. According to Bierwiaczonek (2007), this process includes generic personal nouns in combinations with adjectives designating a particular physical or social condition. For instance, "the blind", "the deaf", "the rich", "the poor", "the needy", "the jobless" stand for people who are blind, deaf, rich, poor, needy, or jobless. In a word, one property of an entity can provide access to the entity because this property can highlight certain attribute of this entity.

Adjectives in English are usually used as nouns to refer to entities that share a certain attribute, as in Examples (50), (51) and (52).

(50) Military spouses and adult **dependents** will be able to file confidential sex assault reports and get victim support services, he said.

(CNN, January 19, 2012)

(51) But publishing detailed descriptions of how to synthesize a pathogen with the capability of triggering **a pandemic** is worse.

(NYT, March 13, 2012)

(52) A small plane headed from New Jersey to suburban Atlanta crashed onto **an interstate** shortly after takeoff Tuesday, killing five people, authorities said.

(CNN, December 22, 2011)

In Example (50), "dependents" refers to people who rely on other people especially for financial support; "a pandemic" in Example (51) refers to a pandemic disease caused by pathogen; "an interstate" in Example (52) refers to the highway connecting two or more states in the United States.

Ruiz de Mendoza (2001) investigates into the impact of metonymy on grammar and labels the metonymy as A DEFINING PROPERTY-for-AN ENTITY, as in "blacks" for "black people", "nobles" for "noble people", and "classics" for "classic works". Defining properties are designated by adjectives and entities by nouns, and this metonymy recategorizes adjectives into nouns.

Barcelona (2005) argues that the conversion of adjective lexemes into nouns is motivated by a process of ellipsis in the realm of form, where the head in the NP is omitted. He labels this metonymic process as the "SALIENT PART OF FORM (MODIFIER)-for-WHOLE FORM (MODIFIER-HEAD CONSTRUCTION)" metonymy (Barcelona, 2005: 323). The omitted head can be inferred from the text, either anaphorically or cataphorically.

According to Quirk et al. (1985), nouns are commonly used attributively, for instance, "the bus station" and "the large station", but nouns do not satisfy other criteria that adjectives do. For instance, we can say "the station seems large", but we cannot say "the station seems bus" (Quirk et al., 1985). Examples (53), (54) and (55) include some examples of nouns used attributively.

(53) She concurred with **the Mazda decision** Wednesday but wrote separately to "emphasize the court's rejection of an overreading of **Geier** that has developed

since that opinion was issued."

(WP, February 24, 2011)

(54) Since the **March** 11 **disaster**, which has caused energy shortages in Japan and will necessitate billions of dollars worth of government spending on reconstruction, the yen had hovered until this week in the low 80s against the dollar.

(WP, July 29, 2011)

(55) **The Cairo agreement** comes three and a half months after a broader reconciliation pact was signed by the leaders of the two factions in Doha, Qatar, and a year after they first reached a unity accord.

(NYT, May 21, 2012)

"The Mazda decision" in Example (53) refers to "the court decision against the company of Mazda", while "Geier" is an elliptical form for "the courts decision against the company of Geier". A participant involved in an event is used as a trigger for the whole Event ICM, exemplifying a prototypical category of PART-for-WHOLE metonymy. "March 11 disaster" in Example (54) refers to "the disaster happened on March 11" and "the Cairo agreement" in Example (55) stands for the "agreement signed in Cairo". In each of the cases above, one aspect of an event, the date, the agent, or the location, is highlighted to help both the reporter and the readers in locating the targeted referent. This construction motivated by metonymy is prototypical in designating referents: one salient part of an entity can be selected as a trigger to provide access to the whole entity.

In news reports, when the reporters are not at liberty to reveal the names of the people concerned in the report or there is no need to do so, they commonly refer to these people by their vocation, position, or the role they assume in a news event, such as Examples (56) and (57).

(56) "We're not there yet; we don't have the votes yet. But today is the day," Boehner had told members at a morning meeting, according to a GOP **source** who was not authorized to publicly discuss the private conversation.

(NYT, July 28, 2011)

(57) **The crime reporters** say that one reason for the "Yard's failure is that, when the Yard tried to stop the corruption, serving officers tipped them off so they could

evade detection".

(The Guardian, June 8, 2011)

A GOP "source" in Example (56) refers to the person who assumes the role as an information source. Crime reporter is a profession, and "crime reporters" in Example (57) are used to refer to a group of people whose profession is to report events concerning crimes. Panther and Thornburg (2001, 2002) discuss in detail how metonymy functions in the English *-er* nominals and argue that the verbal base in an *-er* nominal evokes the whole scenario of an action or an event, as in Examples (58) and (59).

(58) The Chinese film industry and Hollywood are squaring up to each other, Ellen E. Jones reported last week, with China seeking a chunk of Hollywood's business, and Hollywood seeking to part Chinese **cinema-goers** from their cash.

(The Guardian, June 16, 2011)

(59) Royals **watchers** crowd Carpinteria polo club

(NYT, July 9, 2011)

The verbal base "watch" and "go" evoke the whole scenario of people watching polo, and going to cinema to see movies.

Adjectives related to nationality may also profile a nominal character, even though they occupy a premodifying position in a NP, as in Examples (60) and (61).

(60) Electronic cigarette incites bomb scare on **British highway**

(WP, July 6, 2012)

(61) **Syrian unrest** raises fears about chemical arsenal

(NYT, August 29, 2011)

Despite the fact that these nationality words occupy a premodifying position, their attributive character is backgrounded and their nominal character is profiled. Such expressions may be changed into phrases of the "noun + postmodifer" construction; for instance, "British highway" in Example (60) can be changed into "highway in Britain" and "Syrian unrest" in Examples (61) into "unrest in Syria".

One feature of the PART-for-WHOLE metonymy is that the most salient part in an ICM functions as a shortcut to provide access to the whole ICM.

Consider Examples (62) and (63):

(62) "I'm not going to drop the F-bomb like Melissa did," the British actor said in his **thank-you.** "I've done that plenty."

(WP, February 28, 2011)

(63) But any "**no**" from any regulator—for being a pound overweight, or having a bumper an inch too short, or failing to have adequate airbags, or a thousand other issues—means at best delays and at worst a failed project.

(WP, March 12, 2011)

"Thank you" is an expression used to show gratitude. In the context specified by the news text where Example (62) is extracted from, it refers to the speech given by the winner of an award to express his gratitude to those who have helped him in winning the award at an awarding ceremony. Similarly, "no", an expression used by people when they refuse others, is used here to refer to a refusal in Examples (63).

6.2.1.2 WHOLE-for-PART Metonymy

The instances of the referential use of metonymic expressions above are all motivated by PART-for-WHOLE metonymy. Cases of metonymy in which the whole stands for only a part of it are also very common in news texts, as in Examples (64) and (65).

(64) The final insults came when with five laps left in the race the rookie driver Vitaly Petrov, in a **Renault**, passed Schumacher before on the final lap Felipe Massa, Schumacher's former teammate at Ferrari, passed him and pushed him into 10th position, where he finished the race.

(NYT, April 18, 2010)

(65) The most active stock in the sector was **Exxon Mobil**, which was up more than 1 percent during the day, at $70.63.

(NYT, November 9, 2010)

"Renault" in Example (63) refers not to the company that produces cars but to a car produced by that company; in Example (64), "Exxon Mobil" refers to the stock of the company of Exxon Mobil. In the context concerning car racing or stock exchange as described by Examples (63) and (64), it would be the most efficient way to use the company to identify the car it produced or the stocks of that company, saving efforts for both the writers and readers in locating the referents.

It has been repeatedly mentioned in this book that the Whole-Part relation should be metaphorically construed, and therefore, the relationship between a general category and a specific subcategory is also deemed as a kind of Whole-Part relation. Thus when a general concept is used to refer to a specific concept, a metonymic mapping occurs. In news texts, expressions with general connotations are often used to denote something specific, as in Examples (65), (66) and (67).

(65) Depending on age, **erectile function**, the extent of cancer and the type of treatment, a man's chances of returning to a somewhat normal sex life can range from less than 10 percent to 70 percent or more.

(NYT, September 24, 2011)

(66) While not naming Mr. Romney, the line was clearly a reference to him changing his position on abortion rights. Mr. Romney was **pro-choice** before becoming the governor of Massachusetts but later changed his position to **pro-life.**

(NYT, October 7, 2011)

(67) Brief descriptions of the incidents include "**inappropriate level of support** given to students," and "three teachers in three classrooms **provided aid to students**".

(WP, May 18, 2011)

"Erectile function" stands for "sexual impotence", "pro-choice" stands for "pro-abortion", "pro-life" stands for "anti-abortion", and "inappropriate level of support given to students" and "three teachers in three classrooms provided aid to students" stand for the specific description of "cheating with the help of teachers". These cases are all motivated by WHOLE-for-PART metonymy, where general categories are used to stand for specific categories.

Sometimes, referring to entities indirectly may cause the readers a price of spare effort in locating the right referent from, but yield a gain at the same time for achieving particular pragmatic effects—to say something euphemistically. How much spare effort would be caused depends on the conceptual distance of these two concepts in the readers' mind, i. e., how closely these two concepts are related. When the two concepts are closely related, the readers would have little difficulty or spend little extra effort in locating the target; when the two concepts are loosely related, more efforts would be cost.

As a way shaping people's ideology, news texts are full of euphemistic expressions, especially when sensitive topics are concerned, such as abortion, taxes, war, sex, gays and lesbians, etc. News texts, in paper or in digital forms, are an important source of new euphemisms, though journalists are trained to avoid euphemisms for the sake of clarity, precision and honesty.

Socially, the motives for using euphemisms are complex: they may be used to avoid offending the feelings or sensibilities of the listeners, e. g., "underachiever" instead of "poor students", "seniors" instead of "old people", "gender" instead of "sex", "domestic violent" instead of "wife-beating", "physically challenged" or "differently abled" instead of "handicapped", "remains" instead of "corpse", etc. (Lu Weizhong & Kong Shujuan, 2006; Zhang Hui & Lu Weizhong, 2010; Gradečak-Erdeljić & Milić, 2011). Moreover, selecting a vehicle for a referent definitely shows how the language users perceive the referent, such as the rebels consider themselves freedom fighters, while others may look upon them as terrorists.

Usually, a whole is used to provide access to a part when the whole is more conceptually salient than the part. For instance, when we say "to clean a table", we actually mean "to clean the surface of a table". However, as far as euphemism is concerned, the case turns to its opposite. An expression with a more general connotation is used to blur a specific concept, i. e., the whole actually blurs the part.

6.2.1.3 PART-for-PART Metonymy

In addition to the WHOLE-for-PART and PART-for-WHOLE metonymy, a third subtype of the Whole-Part metonymy is the PART-for-PART metonymy. Contiguity, which is grounded in our cognitive ability, links two related entities within the same ICM together, so that one can be used to stand for the other in appropriate contexts. Consider Example (68):

(68) **Fukushima** changed everything.

(NYT, August 29, 2011)

"Fukushima" refers to the nuclear disaster happened in Fukushima. In this case, the location of an event is used to refer to the event happened in that place. The conceptual relationship that holds between an event and the location where it happens is a very common metonymy-producing relationship. Radden and Kövecses (1999) label this kind of metonymy as LOCATION-for-EVENT metonymy. Truszczyńska (2003) also stresses the role of experience in the forming of metonymical patterns and argues that people conceive of the relation between place and event in terms of some spatial contiguity.

Place names can be used to switch between more than one metonymic target depending on specific contexts because the relation between source entity and target entity is contingent (Panther, 2005). Consider Examples (69) and (70):

(69) Clinton told the conference that Russia and China, who declined invitations to attend, "are holding up progress—blockading it—[and] that is no longer tolerable." The chief U.S. diplomat said **Moscow** and **Beijing** were not "paying any price at all—nothing at all—for standing up on behalf of the Assad regime."

(WP, July 6, 2012)

(70) Rogge warned however that **London** faces a tough task to match **Beijing**, which has had spectacular ceremonies, more than a million volunteers, and unprecedented control over areas such as transport, labor, resources and security.

(The Guardian, August 24, 2008)

"Beijing" in Example (69) appears to be a typical instance of the CAPITAL CITY-for-GOVERNMENT metonymy, in which the capital city stands for the government of the country. "Beijing" in Example (70) is used to refer to the Olympics Games held in Beijing in 2008, which is another instance of LOCATION-FOR-EVENT metonymy. Usually the texts provide enough information for the readers to find the right target entity; if not so, the readers should activate their world knowledge. As in the case of Example (68), the nuclear disaster in "Fukushima" drew attention from the world because its outcome would influence the whole world. Thus, by mentioning the location of the event, the whole event would be activated in the readers' mind.

One tricky property of PART-for-PART metonymies lies in the fact that sometimes, the relation between one part and another part may be indirect, i. e. , multiple conceptual shifts may be involved, as in Example (71).

(71) "**The ballot boxes** will decide who will win at the end of the day," Mr. Zomor said during an interview in his large family compound in this hamlet on Cairo's western edge.

(NYT, April 2, 2011)

"The ballot boxes" triggers the concept of "the marked ballots deposited in those boxes" which continue to trigger the concept of "the people who deposit the ballots in the boxes in a voting". Chained metonymies involve process with more than one conceptual shift (Hilpert, 2006b). In metonymic expressions like the one in Example (71), a series of metonymic mappings account for the complex meaning transfer from "the ballot boxes" to "voters". The associations between "ballot boxes" and "ballots", and between "ballots" and "voters" are well-motivated with a strong experiential basis, while the association between "ballot boxes" and "voters" is indirect, which must be construed from the chained metonymic transfer. There is a prerequisite for a successful mapping in Example (71): only a person can lead the extension of the attribute onto non-human results, as neither the ballot boxes nor the ballots can decide anything; only people can make a decision.

Cases in which human traits are given to non-living objects prevail in actual language use, which are usually treated as personification in the field of rhetoric, as in Examples (72), (73) and (74).

(72) And **a local television station reported** that the town of Marysville was leveled and multiple fatalities were expected.

(NYT, March 2, 2012)

(73) Military **report finds** Pakistani government not involved in killing of U. S. officer

(CNN, October 31, 2011)

(74) "We firmly believe federal bureaucrats should not be unilaterally setting national climate change policy," **the statement said.**

(WP, February 3, 2011)

"A local television station" cannot actually report anything and neither can "military report" literally find anything; it is the reporters working for the station who reported the news and the unmentioned military investigators who wrote what they found in that report. Similarly, it is the congressmen who said in that statement, because the statement cannot virtually say anything. And it can be argued that these cases are metonymic in nature on the ground that the source and target are conceptually contiguous with each other.

Panther (2005) argues that metonymy is a process of meaning elaboration, where the target is a more elaborated expression of the source. For instance, the target meaning of "the statement said" in Example (72) should be "a congressman said in the statement". Metonymy not only makes an utterance economical but also accounts for the clash between an inanimate subject and a verb which requires an animate subject, such as "find", "report", and "say". Lakoff and Johnson (1980) treat this phenomenon as personification motivated by metaphors, in which human qualities are imputed to non-human things. However, Examples (72), (73) and (74) seem to be better accounted for by metonymy, in which non-living objects are used instead of the person or persons who are responsible for or have connection with that objects to show more objectivity and authority.

To summarize, the referential use of Whole-Part metonymy has the following major functions: firstly, it provides an efficient and economic way to direct the readers to the intended target(s), and also facilitates the reference of things that the readers are already familiar with through shortening the distances; secondly, selecting the proper vehicle can highlight or obscure certain part(s) of an ICM in accordance with the language producers' specific purposes; this also evidences the assumption suggested by cognitive linguists that metonymies are not arbitrary single expressions but reflect general principles: people conventionally use the salient and well-understood aspects of an entity to stand for the entity as a whole or some other aspect of it (Deignan, 2005; Gibbs, 1994a, 1994b; Lakoff, 1987; Lakoff & Johnson, 1980, 1999); and thirdly, switching metonymic vehicles can avoid direct repetition and maintain topic-contiguity between multiple metonymic targets which are conceptually contiguous.

6.2.2 Non-referential Use of Whole-Part Metonymy

The cognitive approach emphasizes the non-referential functions of metonymy, specifically, the predicative function and the illocutionary function of metonymy. Predicational metonymies prevail in description of states, actions and processes, while illocutionary metonymies are omnipresent in conversational communications, and therefore, discussion of this subsection is focused on the predicative use of metonymies. This subsection focuses on three of the most common predicational metonymies, namely, AGENT/INSTRUMENT-for-ACTION, MANNER-for-ACTION, and CONCRETE ACTION-for-ABSTRACT ACTION metonymies.

6.2.2.1 AGENT/INSTRUMENT-for-ACTION Metonymy

Kövecses and Radden (1998) examine a number of metonymic configurations based on the formulation of a number of ICMs, such as the Action ICM, and propose that an Action ICM is composed of different parts, each part can be used to stand metonymically for the action; for instance to "shampoo one's hair" is motivated by the metonymy of INSTRUMENT-for-ACTION. Ruiz de Mendoza and Perez (2001) also investigate into the role of metonymy in affecting grammar and argue that the agent or instrument in an Action ICM is usually used as a vehicle for providing mental path to the whole Action ICM. Consider Examples (75) and (76):

(75) Signals apparently also malfunctioned, causing another train to **rear-end** the stationary train.

(NYT, July 23, 2011)

(76) Ironically, he was taken to Tihar Jail, which **houses** a former government minister and other senior officials and businessmen accused in recent corruption scandals.

(WP, August 16, 2011)

The word "rear-end" in Example (75) is used as a verb to stand in a representational metonymic relation of PART-for-WHOLE for the whole action of "one train runs into another from behind". In Example (76), "houses" means "to provide living facilities for". The most salient and important element in the action comes to stand for the whole action, exemplifying the non-referential use of PART-for-WHOLE metonymy.

6.2.2.2 MANNER-for-ACTION Metonymy

Talmy (1985, 2000) assumes that motion events involve a *figure* moving along a *path* with respect to a series of *grounds*, including the *source* and *goal* of the motion, as well as a *manner* or *cause*; thus when an Action ICM includes event(s) of motion, the manner, the cause or even the destination of the motion may also have a metonymic relation with the motion. In Seto's (1999: 107) model of metonymy, the notion of subevent is extended in the case of reporting verbs in such a way that "the sound, manners, gestures, etc, that accompany events can all be good candidates for the metonymy of this type". Consider Examples (77), (78) and (79):

(77) Within hours after the military call for the protests to disband, thousands of Mubarak supporters were **bused** into the square in what appeared to be an orchestrated campaign.

(WP, February 2, 2011)

(78) That ordinary Syrians have **braved** bullets and tanks to take to the streets for 18 consecutive weeks seeking the ouster of President Bashar al-Assad is an indicator of their movement's resilience.

(WP, July 29, 2011)

(79) Mr. Lin **hurried** down a ramp, past trash bags and through a door into the basement...

(NYT, March 2, 2012)

In Example (77), "bus" is used as a verb to refer to the action of taking a bus, in which the manner of transporting stands for the action of traveling by the vehicle. In Example (78), "brave" is used here metonymically to refer to the action of undergoing or facing something courageously and in Example (79), "hurried" refers to moving rapidly. In each of these three instances, an attribute of a behavior or the manner of an action is metonymically used to refer to the action or motion.

Verbing is a way of conversion, in which adjectives, adverbials or nouns are converted into verbs, such as "to rear-end", "to house", "to brave", "to be bused" and "to hurry" (Dirven, 1999; Koch, 1999; Warren, 1999; Panther &

Thornburg, 2002). Conversion is a productive way of word formation in English motivated by metonymy (Dirven, 1999). A word of one lexical category is converted to a word of another lexical category, which can be motivated by both the contiguity principle and the causality principle.

The above examples belong to a prototypical category of the Whole-Part metonymy which is described by Langacker (1993: 31) as "active-zone/profile discrepancies", in which an entity's active zone is defined as comprising "those portion of the entity that participate most directly and crucially in that relationship", or to make it simply, by mentioning one profiled part or aspect of a concept, the whole target concept will be activated in the mind of addressees through metonymic inference. For instance, the instrument involved in an action or the manner of an action becomes the active zone and is profiled, while the action itself becomes a background (Langacker, 1993).

6.2.2.3 CONCRETE ACTION-for-ABSTRACT ACTION Metonymy

Kövecses (2002) distinguishes various ICMs that give rise to lots of metonymic relations, one of which is the Complex Event ICM. In the Complex Event ICM, the successive events, the initial, central, and final subevents may be conventionally used to stand for the entire complex event. In Event ICMs, the various metonymic relations may be guided both by the contiguity principle and the causality principle, or in other words, metonymic relations may occur between a PART and the WHOLE, between different PARTs of the same WHOLE, or between a CAUSE and an EFFECT in the same Event ICM. One of the guiding principles in choosing which part of the Event ICM to be the vehicle is the principle of CONCRETE over ABSTRACT, i. e., concrete actions in Complex Events ICMs are usually used as vehicles to provide mental paths to abstract actions. Consider Examples (80), (81) and (82):

(80) Republican and Democratic leaders **returned to the bargaining table** and struck a deal on a $1 trillion spending bill to keep the government operating after Friday.

(WSJ, December 16, 2011)

(81) Approximately 100 men stood in front of the city's largest hotel **shouting slogans** against the U. S. and the anti-Islamic video.

(WSJ, September 15, 2012)

(82) He lives the high life in Monaco and London, **rubbing shoulders with celebrity friends such as Jean-Claude Van Damme and Fifty Cent.**

(BBC, October 5, 2011)

In Example (80), "returned to the bargaining table" is a subevent of resuming the bargaining, and in Example (81), "shouting slogans" is a subevent of protesting. In Example (82), "rubbing shoulders with celebrity friends" means to socialize with or have a close relationship with celebrities. In each of these cases, a concrete event is used to stand for an abstract event.

These three cases evidence the argument by cognitive linguists that people tend to use the "well-understood or easy-to-perceive aspect of something and use it to stand either for the thing as a whole or for some other aspect or part of it" (Lakoff, 1987: 77). This is based on the nature of human cognition that the concrete events are usually perceptually and conceptually more salient than the abstract events. For example, the event of reading and marking a student's term paper is described as "marking a paper" in British English and as "grading a paper" in American English; here, a final subevent is used to stand metonymically for a whole event. Many events are hard to describe and only expressible by way of their subevents. Expressions, such as "score a goal", metonymically profile the subevent of the player's action, its succeeding result, the score.

6.3 Whole-Part Pattern of News Text Organization

Jakobson (1956) proposes that the nature of discourse is defined as either metaphoric or metonymic and further argues that it is metonymy rather than metaphor that structures the sequence of events. This section discusses how Whole-Part metonymy structures description of entities and then moves on to its functions in narration of events.

6.3.1 Whole-Part Pattern in Description

The examples extracted in the last section are typical metonymic expressions which are familiar to both linguists and non-scholarly language users. However, people use metonymy unconsciously in organizing our everyday language into texts. As a matter of fact, it is not compulsory for metonymy to be figurative, even though it has been traditionally treated as a figure of speech.

Referring to the subjects of a news story is indispensable, regardless of the subjects being persons, institutions, countries or things. Usually, the full name of a person is sufficient to locate the person who is named after that name, such as "George W. Bush" and "Barack Obama". If the person is well-known enough, just a family name is sufficient in directing the readers to the right target. For instance, "Obama", unless otherwise specified, refers to the president of the United State of America, Barack Obama. There is only one condition for the referential use of FAMILY NAME-for-FULL NAME metonymy in referring to people: no confusion can be aroused. For instance, "Clinton" may refer to the former U. S. president, Bill Clinton or the current Secretary of State, Hillary Clinton.

However, names unfamiliar to the readers are usually avoided to appear alone in news texts; otherwise, the readers may fail to have a mental representation of the person being referred to, i. e., the readers may fail to get access to the targeted ICM or fail to perceive the relevance between the subject and the main topic of the report as the writer intended. Consider Examples (83), (84) and (85):

(83) **State Senator Jamie Eldridge, a Democrat whose district includes Devens**, said he was initially excited for Evergreen to come to his district, but even before the announced loss of 800 jobs, he had come to oppose such large corporate assistance.

(NYT, January 14, 2011)

(84) **Robert R. Provine, a neuroscientist at the University of Maryland, Baltimore County, and the author of "Laughter: A Scientific Investigation"**, said he thought the study was "a significant contribution" to a field of study that dates back 2,000 years or so.

(NYT, September 13, 2011)

(85) **Zyad Elelaiwy**, 32, **a lawyer who is one of the online organizers and a member of the umbrella opposition group founded by Mohamed ElBaradei, the Nobel**

laureate, acknowledged a generational divide in the movement.

(NYT, February 7, 2011)

In Example (83), the name "Jamie Eldridge" alone is enough for referring to a specific person but only for readers who know the person. For readers who have no idea of who Jamie Eldridge is, a detailed description of the person is obligatory. The reporter provides the subject's social position, "state senator", political background, "Democrat" as well as one of his jurisdictional responsibilities, "whose district includes Devens", to show the importance of the person's opinion. Thus, even readers who do not have any idea about the person who is named as "Jamie Eldridge" can also perceive the relevance between the subject and the main topic and be directed to the intended target ICM by "State Senator" and "a Democrat whose district includes Devens".

In Example (84), the selected information of "neuroscientist at the University of Maryland" and "author of 'Laughter: A Scientific Investigation'" helps the readers have a general idea of who the person, "Robert R. Provine", is and at the same time indicates the authenticity of the opinion that the reporter has quoted. Similarly, in Example (85), "Zyad Elelaiwy" is described as "a lawyer who is one of the online organizers and a member of the umbrella opposition group founded by Mohamed ElBaradei" and "Mohamed ElBaradei" is described as "the Nobel laureate". Occupation and the major event the subject has been involved are provided to help the readers relate this particular person with something they are familiar with. For instance, "Zyad Elelaiwy" is related to "a lawyer" and "Mohamed ElBaradei" is related to the "Nobel laureate".

Aspects, such as the occupation, position of a person, major action or event he/she has been involved or the role he/she has assumed, are usually selected as linguistic vehicles to provide access to the ICM of a person. Sometimes, a person's age can also be important, because from one's age, the readers may speculate about his/her background in general, such as his/her social experience, health condition, etc. Which aspect or aspects should be selected depends on what information the reporter wants to highlight, as in Example (86):

(86)

Headline	**Sarah Palin** says she will not run for president in 2012
Lead	**Former Alaska Governor Sarah Palin** has declared she will not run for the White House next year.
News Story	**Mrs Palin** said in a statement that the decision came after much thought, and that she and her husband, Todd, "devote ourselves to God, family and country". **The** 47**-year-old's** announcement ends months of uncertainty over her plan. ... **The mother-of-five** has signed a number of lucrative television deals, published two best-selling books and set up a successful fundraising machine.

(BBC, October 6, 2011)

The reporter chooses the full name of the subject "Sarah Palin" in the headline. In the lead, the subject's previous political position "former Alaska Governor" is added to her full name in referring to the same person. As for political figures, their positions enjoy more conceptual salience than their full names. In the news story, the reporter uses three different expressions, "Mrs. Palin", "the 47-year-old" and "the mother-of-five" to designate the subject. Each of these three addresses highlights one part of the ICM of Sarah Palin, emphasizing different aspects of the subject.

From the perspective of metonymy, different FORMs are used to provide access to the same person of Sarah Palin, contributing to text cohesion. In each of these expressions, both the concepts of the source entity and the target entity are activated, which is another evidence for the argument that metonymy is an "efficient means of saying two things for the price of one, i. e. two concepts are activated while only one is explicitly mentioned" (Brdar & Brdar-Szabó, 2009: 240). For instance, both "the 47-year-old" and "the mother-of-five" refer to the same person, Sarah Palin, but the former also triggers the concept that she is 47 years old, and the latter provides access to the concept that she is a mother of five children.

Ruiz de Mendoza (2001) observes that, the referential use of metonymy is an economical way of achieving a communicative effect similar to the one that is obtained by means of an elaborate definite description; the greater the number of adjectives and modifying noun phrases we add to them, the greater the precision with which the referent is denoted, as in the example: "the tall man" vs. "the tall, strong man wearing a brown hat and carrying an umbrella". Ariel (1988, 1990, 1991) puts forth the accessibility theory and argues that the more informative an expression describes about the entity, the easier the addressee will be directed to the ICM of that entity.

However, no text can ever include all relevant information pertaining to any experience. Besides, too much information brought together would make the description clumsy. Therefore, a textual reference must be selective in the information it presents. It is evident that every piece of information is selected for a purpose: to direct the readers to the intended target. The principle guiding the selection of information is similar to the principle that guides the selection of metonymic vehicles: the degree of conceptual prominence (Panther, 2005). Consider Examples (87) and (88):

(87) A growing number of celebrities are also opposed, including Chris Tarrant and **James and Oliver Phelps, who played the Weasley twins in *Harry Potter***, while the Rambers Association, the Campaign for the Protection of Rural England, the Woodland Trust, the RSPB, and the Wildlife Trusts have expressed reservations.

(The Observer, September 18, 2011)

(88) **Former Penn State football coach Jerry Sandusky's wife, Dottie**, told CNN that she is angry about accusations of child sexual abuse occurring in her home, calling them "absolutely untrue".

(CNN, December 9, 2011)

In Example (87), "the Rambers Association", "the Campaign for the Protection of Rural England", "the Woodland Trust", "the RSPB" and "the Wildlife Trusts" are all used to refer to the people who represent them, motivated by the INSTITUTION-for-PEOPLE RESPONSIBLE metonymy. The referential use of

Whole-Part metonymy has been discussed in last section, and what is of interest here is how the information in bold type is organized. From the text, it can be inferred that "Chris Tarrant" and "James and Oliver Phelps" are all celebrities. Chris Tarrant is the host of one of the best known television game shows *Who Wants to Be a Millionaire*. Most of the people in U. K. reading this piece of news would have no trouble in getting access to the person through just the name of him. However, James and Oliver Phelps are actors and for most people, the roles that actors have played may enjoy more salience than the name of the actors themselves. To put it simply, the name of "James and Oliver Phelps" may not be familiar to the readers, but the roles they have played, "the Weasley twins in Harry Potter", are better known for people who have viewed the *Harry Potter* movies. Similarly, in Example (88), "Dottie", the subject, is of interest to the readers because of her relationship with her husband, the "former Penn State football coach Jerry Sandusky".

To summarize, this way of referring to unfamiliar individuals is metonymic in nature because one or more salient properties, i. e., parts of an ICM, are chosen to refer to or co-refer to the individual as a whole in order to highlight the connectedness and importance of this individual to the news story. When more information about an entity is provided, a more vivid mental representation of the target entity will be triggered. Moreover, when more salient parts of an ICM are presented, the ICM will be easier to be accessed.

In the examples discussed above in this section, the whole ICM of a person is accessed through a part or several parts of it. Description of entities, such as a person or an event, is also organized in a Whole-Part pattern, in which the whole is activated by a part or parts of it. Consider Example (89):

(89) Redgrave was **a complex man—bisexual**, **alcoholic**, **demon-driven**—and his story, which concerns the disappearance of a famous Austrian actor, Joseph Charles, explores in nightmarish fashion the age-old question of the true identity of actors: Do they, in fact, have one?

(WSJ, September 16, 2012)

Example (89) firstly describes Redgrave as "a complex man", followed by three adjectives: "bisexual", "alcoholic", and "demon-driven", specifying the way how complex Redgrave is. It can be said that there is a kind of relationship between the concepts of "bisexual", "alcoholic", "demon-driven" and "complex". The relationship between a general category and its subcategories can be metaphorically viewed as a relationship between a whole and its parts, with the general category as the whole and its subcategories as its parts. Figure 6.1 shows how these concepts in Example (89) are organized.

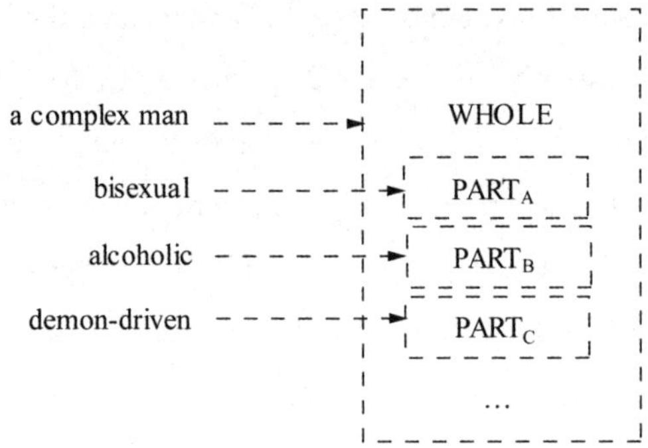

Figure 6.1 Whole-Part organization in Example (89)

The column on the left represents the linguistic vehicles or the textual forms while the boxes with broken lines on the right represent concepts these forms provide access to. "A complex man" triggers a general concept, which consists of several subcategories, and "bisexual", "alcoholic" and "demon-driven" trigger concepts which belong to those subcategories, which can be seen as parts of the same whole. Similar relationship can be found in Examples (90) and (91).

(90) The American soldier at the centre of the WikiLeaks revelations was so **mentally fragile** before his deployment to Iraq that **he wet himself**, **threw chairs around**, **shouted at his commanding officers and was regularly brought in for psychiatric evaluations**, according to an investigative film produced by the Guardian.

(The Guardian, May 27, 2011)

In Example (90), "he wet himself, threw chairs around, shouted at his commanding officers and was regularly brought in for psychiatric evaluations", are particular descriptions of the state of being "mentally fragile", because it is unusual for physically and mentally healthy people to wet themselves, throw chairs around, or shout at their commanding officers. These particular descriptions are all selected to show how mentally fragile the people in question is. They are the selected parts to help the readers get access to the whole.

> (91) [1] While state executives and government officials are regularly arrested on corruption charges, only a handful have received the death penalty in recent years. [2] Four years ago, the head of China's Food and Drug Administration was executed for corruption and failing to protect consumers.
>
> [3] In 2009, the former chairman of Sinopec, the Chinese oil giant, was also sentenced to death with a two-year reprieve for accepting millions of dollars in bribes. [4] And this week, two former vice mayors in China were executed for accepting millions of dollars worth of bribes.
>
> (NYT, July 22, 2011)

The numbers in Example (91) and Examples (92) and (93) are added for convenience in analysis. Sentence [1] in Example (91) activates an ICM in which a small number of corrupted officials were sentenced death penalty and sentences [2]-[4] activate particular ICMs of specific officials who were executed for corruption which are all included in the broader ICM activated by sentence [1]. The executives and officials that are arrested for bribery are by no means confined to the following three cases. They are just selected examples to support the argument of sentence [1].

Organization of Example (91) is metonymic also because even the cases were replaced by other cases on the condition that they are of the similar significance, or as long as they have the same prototypical effect and arranged in the same chronological sequence, the communicative effects will still be the same. This is because the functions of the three examples are to provide access to the generalization that "many executives and officials are arrested by corruption". As long as the selected parts all direct the readers to the same whole, the text will cohere.

The particular concepts in Example (91) is arranged in the chronological order of the events, and Example (92) represents another Whole-Part pattern:

(92)[1]They know the life of a rural physician is not easy. [2]Patients tend to be older, poorer and often uninsured. [3]The job generally pays less than lucrative specialties. [4] And many rural doctors have so little support that they are essentially on call permanently.

(NYT, July 22, 2011)

In Example (92), sentence [1] is a general statement signifying a general ICM, and sentences [2]-[4] are specific situations signifying specific ICMs. The chosen three situations are examples of the general statement, arranged according to their prominence. The most significant situation is arranged first and the least significant one is arranged last. If the sequence is changed, the communicative effect would be changed accordingly. Figure 6. 2 shows the Whole-Part organization of Example (92).

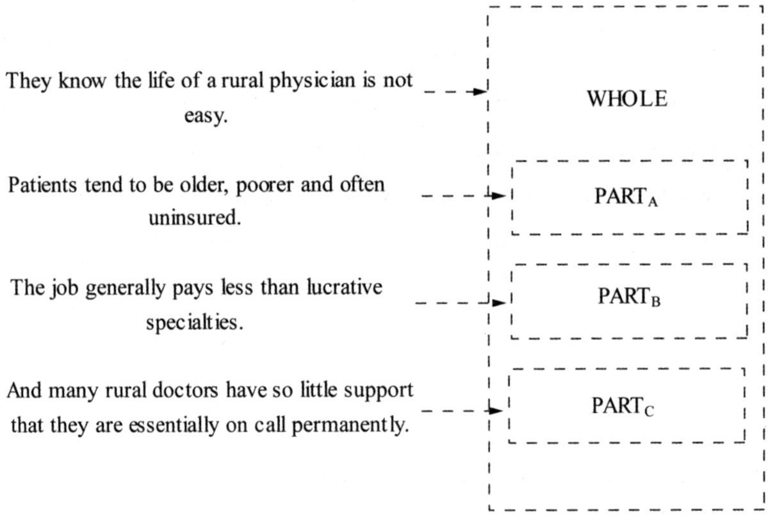

Figure 6.2 Whole-Part organization in Example (92)

Figure 6.2 shows that sentence [1] provides access to a general ICM; each of sentences [2]-[4] provides access to a specific ICM, constituting a part of the general ICM. The general ICM is the whole and the specific ICMs are parts of the whole.

The sentences in Example (92) are connected because the concepts they provide access to are connected by Whole-Part relations. When the specific ICMs are triggered, the general ICM is also activated as the background. For instance, when the concept that patients tend to be older, poorer and often uninsured is triggered, the concept that the life of rural physician is not easy is also activated as the background.

Hoey (1983a) distinguishes an important pattern of discourse organization, the General-Particular pattern, which can be further divided into Generalization-Example pattern and Preview-Detail pattern. Examples (89)-(92) discussed above are organized in the Generalization-Example pattern and Example (93) is organized in Preview-Detail pattern.

> (93) [1] Boehner's bill would raise the debt limit in two stages—one that could cover borrowing through the end of the year and another to cover 2012. [2] The first increase is paired with $915 billion in spending cuts over 10 years. [3] The second would be contingent on passage of a larger deficit-reduction package crafted by a new congressional committee.
>
> (NYT, July 28, 2011)

In Example (93), sentence [1] provides access to the concept that Boehner's bill would raise the debt limit in two stages and sentences [2]-[3] provide details of these two stages, each of them providing detail of one stage. Different from the pattern displayed by Examples (89)-(98), in which the Whole-Part relation arises between a general concept and a specific concept, the Whole-Part pattern displayed by Example (93) includes a Whole-Part relation between a whole and its parts.

To summarize, both the Generalization-Example relation and the Preview-Detail relation in Hoey's (1983a) terms can be reduced to a Whole-Part pattern in which the Particular/Detail member is a part of the General/Preview member. This pattern of organization is metonymic in that each particular ICM functions as a trigger to provide access to the general ICM. Normally, when the readers are reading the examples or details, their attention is still directed to the general proposition expressed in the general sentence, in other words, the whole is still in focus.

6.3.2 Whole-Part Pattern in Narration

Jakobson (2003) proposes that metonymy, because of its character as a figure defined by contiguity, facilitates forward movement of the narrative when seen in a macro-context. Steen (2005) summarizes three functions that metonymy plays in narrative: firstly, metonymy, as a figure of speech, plays a rhetorical role; secondly, metonymy is pervasive in the language of narrators as well as the characters and thus plays a linguistic role; and thirdly, metonymy, as a mode of narration, plays a structural role in narrative.

Narratives are metonymic in nature because the formal text is just a part of the cognitive text that represents the social reality. It is impossible and unnecessary to cover every detail of what has happened or what is happening in a news report, just as Al-Sharafi (2004: 105) claims that "by means of cognitive reasoning we interpret something from the text without it being explicitly stated in the formal text". Moreover, it is economical to be able to refer to a whole domain by using just a part of it, as in Example (94).

(94) Secretary of State Hillary Clinton **arrived** in Afghanistan on an unannounced visit Wednesday, just one day after **landing** in Libya.

(CNN, October 19, 2011)

Arriving or landing in a place is part of traveling, which, again is supposed to be part of visiting a country when the people has a state-level position. Or we can say that "arriving" or "landing" is a subevent for the whole event of "visiting a country for political purposes". It should be noted here that Afghanistan, Libya, or other such names of countries or capitals are not used to refer to the locality as a whole. What is intended is not the whole domain but just a part or parts of it; specifically it is just the sphere of political life, more precisely its foreign affairs aspects. That is to say, utterances such as: "Hillary Clinton arrived in Afghanistan", or "Hillary Clinton landed in Libya" should be treated metonymically, because Hillary Clinton, as a politician, is not traveling privately for pleasure but for political purposes representing the country.

The notions of the whole event and subevent are a metaphorical extension of the spatial meanings of whole and part; and the term event is taken in the broad sense which includes processes, activities, and states of affairs (situations). In this way, description of certain aspects, details, background provides a holistic scenario of the event. In these situations, subevents or accompanying aspects of an event are highlighted but their overall event is still in focus. In Example (94), "arrived in" or "landing" may be replaced by the word describing the whole event, "visited" or "visiting" respectively.

Chatman (1978) notes that when reading two adjacent sentences describing two actions, the readers will naturally infer that there are other actions occurring in the intervals, as in Example (95).

(95) He **wheeled** his bike from the restaurant's tiny two-table dining area, checked the charge on its lithium-ion battery, good for about four hours, and made sure there was a spare one powering up in the cramped basement... Mr. Lin **strapped** on a red-and-gray helmet, **zipped** his black puffy jacket to the neck and prepared for a long day.

(NYT, March 2, 2012)

"Wheel" and "strap" are verbalized nouns, referring to the action of riding a bike and fastening with a strap; "zip" was initially used to describe the sound caused by the action of zipping a zipper and is used here to refer to the act of fastening by a zipper. The three action verbs in Example (95) do not describe virtually consecutive actions but they activate the whole scenarios in the minds of the readers who may automatically fill in the gaps and make the scenarios consecutive, adding actions such as ascending on a bike, pedaling, descending from the bike, looking for the battery, and so forth.

In our everyday language use, a connection is made between all kinds of concepts and other concepts that are related in one more encompassing knowledge structure. And in narrative structure, aspects of the plot can stand for the whole series of events, or aspects of a situation can stand for the complete evoked situation. Thus the chronological and causal sequencing of distinct events in a plot has been analyzed as so many metonymic moves by the narrator, with the situations constituting contiguous parts evoking a larger whole that is left unexpressed. Consider Example (96):

(96) The sun is up, first rays streaming through the canopy, and the two hunters pause to inspect tracks—big, dusty imprints with five toes—on the forest floor.

They move on, boots crunching twigs as they climb a ridge.

(The Guardian, December 2, 2012)

The passage starts with a description of the scene in which two hunters are hunting bears and then moves on to a narration of a series of actions of the two hunters. "The sun is up, first rays streaming through the canopy" provide information about the time, early morning, and weather condition, sunny. The reporter chooses just a few action verbs, "pause", "inspect tracks", "move on", and "crunching twigs" to evoke the whole scenario of hunting.

To sum up, in narratives, not all possible details of these actions should be punctiliously and tediously elaborated (Steen, 2005). Some should be left to the comprehension and inference of the readers. The events or subevents provided by the reporter bear the greatest cognitive salience, representing the whole event or a series of events. The successful recovery of the missing details depends on the background knowledge of the readers. Cognitive approaches to text coherence hold that coherence is achieved through an interaction between shared knowledge which is metonymically constructed and organized in memory, and inferencing principles that are metonymically motivated.

To summarize, this chapter analyses how Whole-Part metonymy functions at different levels of text organization, starting from discussion of the experiential functions of Whole-Part metonymy, including both the referential use and non-referential use.

The referential use of Whole-Part metonymy has the following major functions: firstly, it provides an efficient and economic way to direct the readers to the intended target(s); secondly, selecting the proper vehicle can highlight or obscure certain part(s) of an ICM in accordance with the language producers' specific purposes; and thirdly, switching metonymic vehicles can avoid direct repetition and maintain topic-contiguity between multiple metonymic targets which are conceptually contiguous. Verbalized nouns are a phenomenon better perceived as an outcome of metonymy affecting the language structure. The most salient and important element in the action comes to stand for the whole action, exemplifying the non-referential use of PART-for-WHOLE metonymy. Another guiding principle in choosing which part of the Event ICM to be the vehicle is the principle of CONCRETE over ABSTRACT, i. e., concrete actions in Complex Events ICMs are usually used as vehicles to provide mental paths to abstract actions within the same Event ICM.

No text can ever include all the relevant information pertaining to an event. When organizing a news text, the reporter has to select the most prominent aspects of the event and put them in the text to represent the whole news event. These selected aspects of information function as linguistic vehicles to provide access to the whole scenario of the event, forming a PART-for-WHOLE relation between the formal text and the conceptualized world of reality.

Chapter 7
Cause-Effect Metonymy in News Text Organization

This chapter aims to reveal the patterns that Cause-Effect metonymy demonstrates in organizing news texts. It starts with an elaboration on the causality principle underlying Cause-Effect metonymies, followed by an analysis on the experiential functions of Cause-Effect metonymies, and then moves on to the Cause-Effect patterns of news text organization.

7.1 The Causality Principle underlying Cause-Effect Metonymy

Causality concerns the ways in which one situation or event affects the conditions for some other ones. It is the relationship between a cause and an effect. According to Beaugrande and Dressler (1981), events and states are stored in human memory in ordered sequences by time proximity and causality and text coherence can be realized by causal relations. The earlier event or situation causes, enables, or provides the reason for the later one and the later event or situation may be the result or purpose for the earlier one.

There are also a lot of debates concerning the notion of causality. Traditional approaches treated causality as a causal contiguity, i. e., two physical events which are spatially and temporally contiguous usually stand in a relation of causality. Two sequential events are connected by causality because of their temporally contiguous relationship. Moreover, unified events can be broken up into causal chains constituted by more elementary events, in which an event is the effect of the previous one and the cause of the following one (Fauconnier & Turner, 2002). The earlier event may be seen as the cause or precondition of the later event and the later may be seen as the result of the earlier event. And this contiguous relationship enables either one of them to be used to stand metonymically for the whole scenario or the other. Therefore, a given event may contextually lead us to anticipate a later event as its result or to assume an earlier event as its cause.

Influenced by this contiguity approach of causality, some scholars group the metonymic relation between a cause and an effect as one of causal contiguity, and hold that the relationship between a cause and an effect is one that is also based on contiguity. However, some other researchers argue that the notion of contiguity alone is not comprehensive enough to group all the relations that underlie metonymy into one general term and the causality principle is as fundamental as the contiguity principle in producing metonymic relations (Al-Sharafi, 2004).

The way of treating causality as spatial contiguity can be misleading because there are numerous physical events within the realm of our everyday experience that consistently violate spatial contiguity; moreover, there is still causality between two entities even if they are not connected by spatial contiguity. For instance, concepts in the mind which stand in causal relations are not located in space.

Causal relations may arise between a state and its previous or consecutive event, between an activity or a process and its purpose or aim, its cause or preconditions, or its products or results, which may produce various metonymic relations. All of these metonymic relations can be subsumed into two broad categories of CAUSE-for-EFFECT and EFFECT-for-CAUSE metonymies, each of which subsumes various subcategories.

7.2 Experiential Functions of Cause-Effect Metonymy

Radden and Kövecses (1999) distinguish several kinds of ICMs which give rise to various metonymy producing relationships and one of them is Causation ICM, which may give rise to reversible metonymies of EFFECT-for-CAUSE metonymy and CAUSE-for-EFFECT metonymy, and each of these two categories includes many subcategories. This section starts with discussion of the referential use, and then moves on to the non-referential use of Cause-Effect metonymy.

7.2.1 Referential Use of Cause-Effect Metonymy

Causal links occur regularly in modifier-head construction, i. e., noun-noun compounds, adjective-noun combinations, genitive constructions and in noun derivatives, as in Examples (97) and (98).

(97) In **difficult talks** yesterday with the Treasury chief secretary, Danny Alexander, Clark pointed out he had last year won Treasury agreement that if the government's so-called rehabilitation revolution did not deliver a lower jail population, then the Treasury would bear the costs from the reserve.

(The Guardian, June 8, 2011)

(98) With time running short and budget negotiations this week having reached **an angry impasse**, Congressional leaders are growing increasingly pessimistic about reaching a bipartisan deal that would avert a government shutdown in early April.

(NYT, March 26, 2011)

"Talks" in Example (97) is metonymically used to refer to a conference motivated by the PART-for-WHOLE metonymy. There is a second metonymic extension in it: it is not the talks that are difficult but the agreement that is difficult to reach because of the divergence in opinions. Thus, "difficult talks" triggers the ICM of great divergence in opinions. The philosophical studies on causality always argue that effect and cause are sometimes inseparable, and people tend to unite cause and effect in our understanding of the world (Fauconnier & Turner, 2002). This nature of causality makes it possible to transfer the modifier of an effect to its cause or vice versa.

Similarly, in Example (98), an impasse cannot be angry; it is the people who are angry and what makes them angry is the impasse, or it is the impasse that causes the anger. This construction is motivated by the EFFECT-for-CAUSE metonymy. Radden and Kövecses (1999: 38) provide a similar construction which is motivated by the CAUSE-for-EFFECT metonymy, "healthy complexion". The good state of health brings about the effect of healthy complexion.

Similar construction may also be found in VPs, as in Example (99).

(99) The past may be a foreign country, as L. P. Hartley **famously observed**, but at least one of its landscapes—the political scene on election eve, a century ago—looks familiar to this time traveler.

(NYT, November 02, 2010)

What is famous is not the action of observing, but is what was observed or the result caused by the action. This construction is motivated by the CAUSE-for-EFFECT metonymy, in which the modifier of the effect is transferred to the cause.

All of the examples above involve the metonymic relationship between an effect and the cause of that effect. Sometimes a similar construction may have different interpretations, as in Example (100).

(100) Mr. Lin strapped on a red-and-gray helmet, zipped his black puffy jacket to the neck and prepared for **a long day**.

(NYT, March 2, 2012)

The expression "a long day" is used to refer to "a day with long time of work". The meaning of "day" is reduced to refer to the working hours of a day, which is apparently just a part of the day. There is another possible reading of this phrase: hard work makes people feel as if the day were prolonged. Thus, "a long day" refers to hard work which causes the effect that the day seems to be prolonged. Therefore, the boundary between a Whole-Part relation and a Cause-Effect relation is not clear and sometimes the two relations may intertwine with each other.

Compared to specific actions, which would cause various effects and consequences, the ultimate effects or consequences caused by those actions can directly attract the news readers' attention. Therefore, effects are used more often as metonymic vehicles than causes. Consider Examples (101), (102) and (103):

(101) Business group are hoping for **big changes**.

(WSJ, May 7, 2011)

(102) Donors demand **a bigger voice** in catholic schools

(NYT, February 7, 2011)

(103) In a statement, the congressmen said the legislation's intent is to show that the Clean Air Act was not meant to address climate change, stop the EPA "from imposing a backdoor cap-and-trade tax" on industries identified as polluters, and **protect American jobs**.

(WP, February 3, 2011)

In the context of Example (101), "big changes" are resulted from effective economic policies which are supposed to bring about changes, and therefore, what the business group really wants is that the government would make some effective policies to change the current situation in a remarkable way.

"A bigger voice" in Example (102) refers to more powers in expressing one's opinions, which is motivated by the EFFECT-for-CAUSE metonymy based on the logic that more power will bring more influential opinions which are metonymically represented by bigger voices.

"Protect American jobs" in Example (103) means to "protect American people from losing their job", because losing jobs would cause loss to people, thus making people in a venerable condition and it is the government's responsibility to avoid this situation.

To summarize, effects and causes are sometimes inseparable, and people tend to unite them in our understanding of the world around us. This nature of causality makes it possible to transfer the modifier of an effect to its cause or vice versa. This closeness of causality also makes the boundary between a Whole-Part relation and a Cause-Effect relation not clear and sometimes the two relations may intertwine with each other. Compared to specific actions, which would cause various effects and consequences, the ultimate effects or consequences caused by those actions can directly attract the news readers' attention. Therefore, effects are used more often as metonymic vehicles than causes.

7.2.2 Non-referential Use of Cause-Effect Metonymy

The examples discussed above concern the referential use of Cause-Effect metonymies. As causes and effects are largely involved with actions or motions, metonymic expressions based on Cause-Effect relations prevail in predication and speech act. This subsection is devoted to the non-referential use of Cause-Effect metonymies.

An expression of a result may be used in English to stand for the action that is presupposed by the result, which is labeled by Panther and Thornburg (2000) as RESULT-for-ACTION metonymy, which is a subcategory of the higher-level EFFECT-for-CAUSE metonymy. Ruiz de Mendoza and Hernadez (2001) also find that a resultant state has a metonymic connection with actions, and it can occur in action constructions without causing semantic anomaly. Consider Examples (104), (105), (106) and (107):

(104) The company has **cleared** the biggest hurdle: building a safe flying, driving and converting vehicle.

(WP, March 12, 2011)

(105) In the economic downturn three years ago, Adam Diaz **idled** the trucks at his bluestone quarry and **silenced** the saws at his lumber mill.

(NYT, October 16, 2010)

(106) The United States and other world powers are increasingly **distancing** themselves from Assad, while a growing number of think tanks and experts are becoming convinced that his regime will not survive.

(WP, July 29, 2011)

(107) The military is dramatically **upping** its investment in drones over the next nine years, according to Pentagon plans.

(CNN, June 10, 2011)

In Example (104), "clear" is used as a transitive verb to trigger the Action ICM which contains an agent, a patient, an action, a manner and a result, and "clear" is the resultant state.

In Example (105), the resultant state "idle" triggers the ICM in which an action has been taken so as to achieve the state of being idle, i. e., "Adam Diaz" stopped production so as to make the trucks idle. Similarly, "silence" is a noun describing the condition of being silent, but it is used in Example (105) as a verb to indicate that the subject did something so that the saws are kept silent, which means the saws are no long in use. In each of these two cases, a resultant condition or state is used to provide access to the action that has caused this resultant condition, or we can say an explicit effect is used as a linguistic vehicle to provide access to an implicit cause.

"Distance" in Example (106) is also a noun used as a verb to indicate that the subjects took some actions so as to estrange with Assad. "Up" denotes the concept of being in a higher level or position, and is used in Example (106) to indicate that the military is raising its investment in drones so that the level of investment will be up.

Chapter 5 has discussed that the agent or instrument involved in an action or the manner of an action can be eligible candidates for a metonymic vehicle to provide access to the action, such as "to rear-end", "to house", "to be bused". One part of the Action ICM is used to trigger the whole ICM. The examples above, such as "to clear", "to up", "to distance", "to silence", "to up", are verbs converted from adjectives, adverbials or nouns motivated by the Cause-Effect metonymy, in which the resultant state is used to provide access to the action. In one word, a resultant state, or an effect, can be used as a trigger to provide access to the action that has caused it, or the cause of it. In this way, words that denote states or conditions can be used as linguistic vehicle to trigger the action, no matter what lexical categories they belong to. Nouns, adjectives or adverbs can all be used as verbs motivated by the RESULT-for-ACTION metonymy. Actions are usually taken for a specific purpose or to achieve a targeted result. From the result, readers can infer that the agent take some action or do something to make the result happen.

According to Panther and Thornburg (2000), a result usually is a state, such as "clear", "up", "idle", "silence" and "distance" in the examples discussed above, but it can also be a resultant event or resultant action, as in Example (108).

(108) The air strike **flattened** the home of the Dalou family in the Sheikh Radwan district of Gaza City, causing the biggest death toll in a single incident since the offensive began last Wednesday.

(The Guardian, November 19, 2012)

Panther and Thornburg (2000) also investigate into the possible acceptability of the non-actional predicates and constructions in prototypical action constructions in English and propose that the non-actional constructions that are grammatical in the text frame inherit their actional properties from the underlying RESULT-for-ACTION metonymy, as in Example (109).

(109) Lucian Cook of Savills, Mayfair, agreed. "I think the big question is: does it have an effect on the sentiments of overseas buyers in the central London market?" he said. "Frankly that remains to be seen. But... you've got to **be careful** with the central London market because it tends to lead the wider UK housing market recovery."

(The Guardian, March 21, 2012)

"Be careful" is a non-actional predicate used here to denote an implicit actional predicate of "to do something with care so as to become careful". According to Panther and Thornburg (2000), the action sense of the predicate adjective is motivated by a metonymic process. The result expressed by the predicate adjective or nominal is brought about by an unmentioned prior action. The verb phrase "be careful" is literally stative, but the target sense indicates that the hearer would do something with care so as to be careful. This kind of target sense coercion is also motivated by the RESULT-for-ACTION metonymy.

Radden and Kövecses (1999) hold that perception can be motivated by Cause-Effect metonymies, as in Examples (110) and (111).

(110) **We can't say for sure** when the first body went into the ground at the Thompson family cemetery. It might have been a veteran of the War of 1812 named Ethan Allen (not that Ethan Allen).

(WP, March 13, 2011)

(111) Hugo Chavez opponents **see an opportunity**

(WP, July 29, 2011)

In Example (110), "can't say for sure" is a resultant action of "don't know for sure", a result standing for the cause of it. Similarly, in Example (111), opportunity is something abstract and no one can actually "see" an opportunity. Here, "see" is used to stand for "perceive", because "seeing" is an important, and possibly the most important, way of perception.

The Cause-Effect relationship between an emotion and certain physiological or behavioral responses is included in the overall ICM of emotions, as in Examples (112) and (113).

(112) On the way to work recently I **was nearly brought to** tears by the sight of the front garden of a large Victorian house ruined by a slathering of rough asphalt, devoid of life, where once there had been an overgrown but beautiful front garden.

(The Guardian, June 8, 2011)

(113) Earlier on Thursday, Mr. Hchiro **had raised eyebrows** by calling the evacuated communities around the plants "dead towns", a statement seen as insensitive to the approximately 80,000 people who had been driven from their homes by the nuclear accident.

(NYT, September 11, 2011)

Tears are a manifestation of sadness (or joy in other situations). Physical behaviors such as shedding tears or nearly to shed tears are usually used to stand for the emotion of sadness, the cause which could incur such physical behaviors. In Example (112), "I was nearly brought to tears by the sight" indicates the writer was sad when she saw the scene.

Physical behaviors are usually used to stand for emotions because physical behaviors are easier to perceive than emotions or perceptions. For the same reason, people raise their eyebrows when they are surprised in a negative way or suspicious about something. In Example (113), Mr. Hchiro "had raised eyebrows" means what he had said aroused an emotion which usually causes people to raise their eyebrows.

A potential event, such as the ability, possibility, permission, obligation to undertake an action, is metonymically linked to its actual occurrence in reality (Panther and Thornburg, 1999), as in Examples (114) and (115).

(114) In the last several days, the airline did not fly to or from Kolkata, the large eastern city formerly known as Calcutta. The airline's chief executive, Sanjay Aggarwal, said **Kingfisher had to** cancel flights to India's northeastern states because it did not have enough pilots.

(NYT, February 21, 2012)

(115) The fact that militants **were able to pull off such a wave of violence** is especially disturbing considering that U. S. forces are scheduled to leave Iraq at the end of this year, leaving the country's security in the hands of still-struggling Iraqi security forces.

(WP, August 16, 2011)

Example (114) illustrates a propositional metonymy in Panther and Thornburg's (1998) terminology, in which both the referring expression "Kingfisher" and the predicating expression "had to cancel flights to India's northeastern states" involve metonymic shifts. "Kingfisher" is motivated by the COMPANY-for-PEOPLE RESPONSIBLE metonymy to refer to the executive officers of the Kingfisher company; "had to cancel flights to India's northeastern states" motivated by the OBLIGATION FOR ACT-for-ACTUAL ACT metonymy refers to the actual action of canceling the flights to India's northeastern states.

Example (115) exemplifies the ABILITY TO ACT-for-ACTION metonymy, in which the ability "to pull off such a wave of violence" is used to refer to the actual action of pulling off the violence. Both of these two cases are based on the Cause-Effect relation on the ground that obligation and ability to do something is the motivation and precondition for the actual action. They are not the direct causes but they ensure the possibility of doing that action.

So far, the study has already discussed the referential use and non-referential use of both the Whole-Part metonymy and Cause-Effect metonymy. As a cognitive tool that governs our way of thinking, metonymy prevails in our everyday use of language, referential use and non-referential use of metonymy usually occur in combination and Cause-Effect relationships are often compressed into Whole-Part relationships in the blend. Consider Examples (116) and (117):

(116) U. S. credit card firms want to **get more plastic into Chinese wallets**

(WP, July 30, 2011)

(117) The country has also been pouring money into biomass plants and solar installations—millions of **panels now sit on German roofs and fields**.

(NYT, August 29, 2011)

There are two instances of referential use of metonymy in Example (116): "plastic" refers to "credit card", which is motivated by the MATERIAL-for-PRODUCT metonymy; and "Chinese wallets" involves multiply metonymic shifts and refers to Chinese clients, as customers always take something out from their wallets when they are paying for something. Apart from these two instances of referential use of metonymy, it also includes a case of non-referential use of metonymy. The predicate, "want to get more plastic into Chinese wallets", stands for "want to attract more Chinese people to use their credit card", which is motivated by the CONCRETE ACTION-for-ABSTRACT ACTION metonymy.

Example (117) also involves both referential use and non-referential use of metonymy. Firstly, "panels" stands for "solar installations", which is motivated by the PART-for-WHOLE metonymy. Secondly, "panels now sit on German roofs and fields" refers to the state that solar installations are equipped and used by millions of households and factory facilities in Germany, which is motivated by the PRECONDITION-for-RESULTANT STATE metonymy. The state of panels being installed in households and workplaces is a precondition for the state that the solar equipments are utilized by many households and manufacturing institutions.

Examples (118) and (119) include expressions motivated by both the Whole-Part metonymy and Cause-Effect metonymy.

(118) Israel: U. N. Asked to **Prevent Activists From Sailing to Gaza** Next Month

(NYT, April 2, 2011)

(119) A senior State Department official **who will be in Beijing with Mrs. Clinton** said the main goal of the trip was **to calm what has been an inflamed summer** across the region. "It is absolutely essential that **cooler heads prevail in every capital**," the official said.

(NYT, September 3, 2012)

"Prevent activists from sailing to Gaza" in Example (118) is another representation of how complicated metonymic shifts can be even in one single expression. Firstly, "sail" is used as a verb motivated by the PART-for-WHOLE metonymy in which one part of the ship (sail) can be used to stand for the whole ship, then further motivated by the metonymy of INSTRUMENT-for-ACTION, in which the ship is used to stand for the action of transporting by ship. Moreover, "sailing to Gaza" is also metonymically motivated by the PRECONDITION-for-RESULTANT ACTION metonymy, in which going to Gaza is a precondition for the resultant action of carrying out activist practice in Gaza and what U. N. is asked to prevent is the resultant action: the activist practice. The metonymic extension is governed by both the contiguity principle and the causality principle.

Example (119) is a passage extracted from a typical news report concerning the issue of "who" said "what" with a quoted speech as a support. The attributive clause in the first sentence, "who will be in Beijing with Mrs. Clinton" is the most relevant attribute of the official involved, and is provided by the reporter to highlight the authenticity of the information. "Be in Beijing with Mrs. Clinton" is motivated by the PRECONDITION-for-ACTION metonymy, to indicate that the official will be visiting China with Mrs. Clinton for political purposes, or to meet with leaders of China in Beijing. The expression, "to calm what has been an inflamed summer", includes two cases of EFFECT-for-CAUSE metonymic expressions: the first one is "to calm", in which the resultant state is used to stand for the action of mitigating the tense diplomatic relations among countries in southeast Asia; and the second one is "an inflamed summer", which involves semantic coercion with the target meaning of "a summer with agitated atmosphere", i. e., the agitated atmosphere makes the summer inflamed. There are two PART-for-WHOLE metonymies in the expression of "cooler heads prevail in every capital". "Cooler heads" refers to people who can make composed decisions. "Cooler heads prevail in every capital" means that the people whose opinions would affect decision making of the government should make composed decisions.

To summarize, effects and causes are sometimes inseparable, and people tend to unite them in our understanding of the world around us. This nature of causality makes it possible to transfer the modifier of an effect to its cause or vice versa. This closeness of causality also makes it hard to draw a clear line of demarcation between Whole-Part relations and Cause-Effect relations and sometimes the two kinds of relations may intertwine with each other. Compared to specific actions, which would cause various effects and consequences, the ultimate effects or consequences caused by those actions can directly attract the news readers' attention. Therefore, effects are used more often as metonymic vehicles than causes. As a cognitive tool that governs our way of thinking, metonymy prevails in our everyday use of language; referential use and non-referential use of metonymy usually occur in combination and Cause-Effect relationships are often compressed into Whole-Part relationships in the blend.

7.3 Cause-Effect Pattern of News Text Organization

Studies have shown that, causal relations between events described in a text can be foregrounded by the use of causal connectives, such as "because", "therefore", and "consequently" (Bybee & Pickering, 1998; Zwaan & Radvansky, 1998). Such terms show explicitly how an event leads to another particular outcome or state. However, causal connectives are not obligatory in expressing causality. Non-causal connectives may also indicate causality and even if there is no linguistic cue it is still possible to establish a causal relation between two sentences or utterances.

7.3.1 Cause-Effect Pattern with Causal Connectives

Typical causal cues are connectives from the syntactic category of conjunctions, including both coordinating and subordinating conjunctions, such as "because", "for", "so", etc. Apart from conjunctions, sentential adverbs, such as "consequently", "therefore", etc. can also indicate causality. Within the category of sentential adverbs, nominalized propositions preceded by prepositions, such as "due to" and "as a result of", also have a connective character for indicating causality. According to Halliday and Hasan (1976), connectives provide information concerning how particular associations should be built between linguistic units. They serve as cues for maintaining particular concepts in various states of activation in the course of the comprehension and are therefore critical for coherence. Connectives facilitate memory for textual information, particularly in cases involving causal relations. Consider Examples (120) and (121):

(120) Islamabad is angry at Kabul **because** the NATO aircraft that carried out the strikes that killed its soldiers were based in Afghanistan.

(WP, November 30, 2011)

(121) Re-establishing a workable relationship between Pakistan, Afghanistan and the U. S. is important **because** Islamabad is critical to the process of peace negotiations with the Taliban. Pakistan has historical ties with the group and is seen as the actor with the greatest leverage to push the Taliban to the negotiating table.

(WP, November 30, 2011)

Example (120) exemplifies the Effect-Cause pattern of organization with the causal cue "because" connecting a state as the effect, "Islamabad is angry at Kabul", with the event that causes the effect as the cause, "the NATO aircraft that carried out the strikes that killed its soldiers were based in Afghanistan". This segment is coherent which also depends on the world knowledge of the readers that Kabul is the capital city of Afghanistan and is used here to refer to the government of Afghanistan.

The connective cue "because" in Example (121) connects a state and another state, with the former as the effect and the latter as the cause. The state of Pakistan being critical to the process of peace negotiations is the cause for the state that it is important to re-establish a workable relationship between Pakistan, Afghanistan and the U. S.

Causal connectives, as linguistic forms, trigger the concept of causal connection, denoting causally related facts in the actual world.

7.3.2 Cause-Effect Pattern with Non-Causal Connectives

One of the problems with connectives is that they may incur ambiguity: the same connective may express different types of connection, and one type of connection may be expressed by various connectives. Quirk et al. (1985) notice that the sequential meaning of "after" may induce an implication of causality. The subordinators, "after", indicate the situation in the main clause occurs after that in the subordinate clause, as in Examples (122) and (123).

(122) Rescue teams searched Saturday for thousands of missing people along hundreds of miles of Japan's northeastern coast a day **after a powerful earthquake and massive tsunami wiped entire towns off the map.**

(WP, March 12, 2011)

(123) 12 Americans rescued by helicopter **after bad weather stranded them on Senegalese island**

(NYT, August 29, 2011)

The *after*-clause in Example (122) triggers the concept that it is the "powerful earthquake and massive tsunami" that brings about the rescue teams' searching for the missing people. Similarly, in Example (123), the fact that bad weather stranded 12 people on Senegalese island creates the precondition that these 12 people were rescued by helicopter.

Events happened in sequence usually denote causality between these two events, and connectives with the meaning denoting sequence can be used to indicate causality. According to the causality principle, an earlier action or situation is usually the cause of a later one, i. e., the event happened earlier is considered as a cause and the event happened later as an effect. The same is true for phrases introduced by prepositions denoting sequence, such as "after" and "in the wake of" in Examples (124) and (125).

(124) Tillman died last Sunday **after a random attack at a house party.**

(WP, November 13, 2010)

(125) **In the wake of Osama bin Laden's killing** a significant tax story did not get much notice.

(WP, May 5, 2011)

In Example (124), the phrase led by "after" indicates the time as well as the cause for the event in the proposition. An interpretation associated with the temporal expression, the *after*-phrase, is that Tillman died as a result of a random attack at a house party. In other words, there is an inference of causality: the attack caused the death of Tillman. The sentence can be interpreted as "a random attack at a house party caused Tillman's death".

The phrase "in the wake of" signifies the timing of this "tax story" and at the same time indicates the cause of this situation, i. e., why a significant tax story, which is supposed to attract public concern, did not get much notice. In

Example (125), to understand the causality between Osama bin Laden's killing and the fact that a tax story did not get much notice, the readers need to activate their world knowledge of why the death of bin Laden is more attention-catching than a significant tax story.

Causality involves a regular association between a cause and an effect with the cause contiguous with its immediate effects and preceding them, since it is a law of nature that effects follow causes. This contiguity between causes and effects makes it possible for connectives indicating co-present events, such as "when", to indicate causality, as in Example (126).

(126) A group that calls itself the Chaos Computer Club prompted a public outcry here recently **when it discovered that German state investigators were using spying software capable of turning a computer's webcam and microphone into a sophisticated surveillance device.**

(NYT, October 16, 2010)

The *when*-clause states the timing of the main event as well as indicates the cause for the event, i. e., what caused the group, Chaos Computer Club, to prompt a public outcry. The temporal proximity between a cause and an effect provides foundations for a co-present event to stand for a consecutive event. Metonymy is a conceptual operation in which one entity stands for another but both are activated or at least partially activated. As in Example (126), two concepts are activated, with the timing of the action explicitly mentioned and the cause inferred from the same *when*-clause.

Modifying phrases or clauses can also indicate causes, as in Examples (127) and (128).

(127) Family critics staff at hospital **where patient was left to die in a corridor**

(The Guardian, June 8, 2011)

(128) Army officer **who sparked controversy with remarks on Islam** pulls out of West Point address

(WP, January 31, 2011)

The attributive clause in Example (127) helps the readers locate the objects involved in the main event that the news text is reporting and offers a cause for the event, which is another illustration of "saying two things for the price of one"

(Brdar, 2007: 17). On one hand, the sentence conveys the information that there exists a hospital where a patient was left to die in a corridor; on the other hand, the staff at this hospital was criticized because they left the patient to die in a corridor.

The attributive clause "who sparked controversy with remarks on Islam" in Example (128) denotes the cause behind the resultant action of the army officer's pulling out of West Point address, i. e., the officer pulled out because of his controversial remarks on Islam. Compare with the attributive clause in Example (129).

(129) Those details were under vigorous discussion last week at College Park, said Jessica Sunshine, a U-Md. astronomy professor **who is deputy principal investigator for the comet mission.**

(WP, November 15, 2010)

There is no casual relation between being "deputy principal investigator for the comet mission" and the fact of those details being under vigorous discussion even though this attributive clause highlights the relevance of the person involved as the information source.

To summarize, we do not have to use conjunctions that signify causality to introduce a cause or an effect, such as "since", "as a result", "because of + NP", "because", "therefore", "due to + NP", "consequently", "for this reason", "so", etc. Causal relations can also be presented through other relational clauses introduced by relational pronouns, such as "who", "where", or relational adverbials, such as "when", "after", etc. Non-clausal connectives can also be used metonymically to denote one explicit semantic relation and indicate one implicit causal relation, both of which are activated at the same time.

7.3.3 Cause-Effect Pattern without Connectives

Connectives facilitate the understanding of a text but they are not compulsory for two clauses or sentences to stand in a causal relation. Even when there is no connective between two clauses or sentences, the causality principle still enables the readers to perceive the causal relation between them, as in Example (130).

(130) In December, a federal appellate court turned down **a request from utilities, oil refiners and the state of Texas to delay the regulation for green house gas**

emissions by the EPA. The companies said that **the EPA regulations would be too costly.**

(WP, February 3, 2011)

In Example (130), the first sentence triggers the concept of the main event that a federal appellate court turned down a request. The head of the NP in bold type is a nominalized action verb, "request", with the agent and patient of the action explicitly presented in the postmodifier. Thus, this NP triggers the concept of "utilities, oil refiners and the state of Texas requested EPA to delay the regulation for green house gas emission". In the second sentence of Example (130), "the EPA regulations" anaphorically refers back to "the regulation for green house gas emissions by the EPA". Thus, the second sentence triggers the concept of another event that "the EPA made some regulations for green house gas emissions and these regulations would be too costly". The two events stand in a causal relation, with the first event as an effect and the second as a cause. The causal relation between the concepts triggered by the two sentences can be sketched in Figure 7.1.

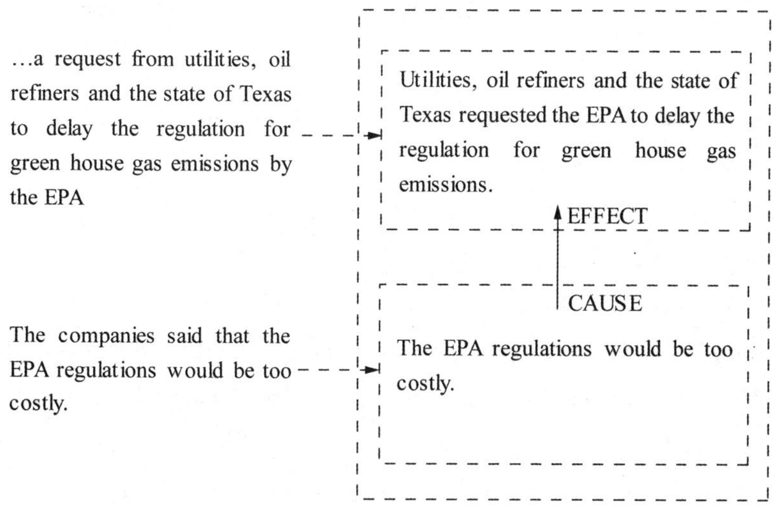

Figure 7.1 Cause-Effect organization in Example (130)

In Figure 7.1, the solid arrow signifies the causal relation from a cause to an effect, and the broken arrows signify the metonymic mapping from a linguistic vehicle to a target concept. This figure shows that the two sentences are connected as a unified whole by the causal relation between the concepts they provide access to. The concept activated by the first sentence functions as an effect, and the concept activated by the second sentence functions as a cause. The coherence of the text also depends on the metonymic reasoning of the readers: both the cause and the effect should belong to the same higher-level ICM.

More texts of the Cause-Effect pattern can be found in Examples (131) and (132).

(131) The NASA Deep Impact spacecraft carried a Maryland science mission to within 435 miles of the comet Hartley 2 and began **sending details of what it found. Those details were under vigorous discussion** last week at College Park, said Jessica Sunshine, a U-Md. astronomy professor who is deputy principal investigator for the comet mission.

(WP, November 15, 2010)

(132) Pentagon officials, who have been scouring the sergeant's military and health records for clues, have said little about what they think motivated the killings. But one senior government official said Thursday that Sergeant Bales had been **drinking alcohol** before the killings and that he might have had **marital problems.**

(NYT, March 16, 2012)

In Example (131), the action of "sending details of what it found" created the condition and made it possible for "those details were under vigorous discussion"; this relation is a weaker type of causality.

"Marital problems" in Example (132) may cause depression, which is a prototypical reason for "drinking alcohol". And the depression extrapolated from marital problems and drinking alcohol may be one of the motivations for the killing. It should be noted here that, martial problems is considered as the cause, but it does not mean that there is necessity between the cause and the effect of killing, because marital problems do not always cause killing. However, this causal relation between effect and cause makes the text connected and one can discover no such continuity in a "senseless" text.

The readers' background knowledge is instrumental to establishing causal representations without the help of linguistic cues. Apart from the textual knowledge, the readers also need to activate their background knowledge to understand the causal connection.

In the world of reality, an effect always follows a cause, but it does not mean that in language, a cause should be organized before an effect. The sentence that triggers the cause can come before or after the sentence that triggers the effect. Which one comes first depends on the nature of the event or what the reporter wants to highlight. Examples (133) and (134) exemplify the Cause-Effect pattern with the cause coming before the effect.

(133) In the second blast, **a farm tractor struck a mine** in Garmser district, **killing one civilian and wounding four others who were riding the vehicle**, Sherzai said.

(WP, July 29, 2011)

(134) Several Republicans say they will oppose the three-week spending bill House GOP leaders are offering Tuesday to avert a government shutdown, **raising the pressure on both parties to reach a long-term spending deal.**

(WSJ, March 13, 2011)

The sentence in Example (133) evokes a Complex Event ICM, which consists of several subevents, starting with "a farm tractor struck a mine", which caused a blast and killed one people and wounded four people. The event that "a farm tractor struck a mine" is the cause and "killing one civilian and wounding four others who were riding the vehicle" are the effects.

Similarly, the main clause in Example (134) triggers the Event ICM in which several Republicans claim that they will oppose a bill, while the participle phrases evokes the effect that their claim raises the pressure on both parties to reach a new deal. The main clause states an event which functions as a cause and the participle phrase states another event that immediately followed the event stated in the main clause and at the same time provides an effect caused by the cause.

In both of these two cases, the present participle phrases state events that immediately followed the events stated in the main clauses and at the same time providing effects caused by the previous events. In other words, participle phrases are saying two things at the price of only one label (Radden & Kövecses, 1999).

In news text, effects are usually organized before causes. Actually, there is a tendency for the reporters to show what has happened and then to revel what caused that. The readers can have an idea of what has happened first and then to find out the cause behind it later if they are still interested. As the worthiness of social or political events is partially determined by the seriousness of their consequences, sometimes the effect is provided before the cause. As a matter of fact, the readers may care more about the consequences of a news event than the news event itself. Consider Examples (135) and (136):

(135) Gay rights group hailed the administration's move, **saying it will bolster their argument that laws that apply a different standard to people based on sexual orientation are unconstitutional.**

(WP, February 24, 2011)

(136) Japan, **bereft of oil and** gas reserves, has developed an extensive nuclear power industry.

(WP, March 12, 2011)

Both participial phrases function as a complement to their subject and at the same time as the cause for the event in the major clause. In Example (135), "it" refers anaphorically to "the administration's move", which will have a consequence for bolstering their argument that is the reason why they hailed this move. In Example (136), being "bereft of oil and gas reserves" is the prime motive for Japan to develop nuclear power industry.

It should be noted that, the cause(s) and the effect(s) that follow an effect or cause are synecdocheic in nature because an effect may have more than one cause and vice versa and usually only the most salient one or ones are selected to be presented in the text.

Cause and effect are so closely interdependent that whenever there is a cause, there would be an effect, or a series of effects. However, this does not necessarily mean that both cause and effect should be present in the same text. The interdependency between cause and effect enables people to use one of them to imply the other, because knowledge structures are fundamentally metonymic in nature, and once a structure or ICM is triggered by a linguistic form in the text, people's ability of metonymic reasoning would help them to establish relations between parts of the text and the whole texts or other parts of the same text, or between causes and effects. Consider Examples (137) and (138):

(137) Last month, agents raided a doctor's office and revoked his license.

(NYT, April 20, 2011)

(138) In a telephone interview in August, Mr. El-Hillow said that he was desperate to avoid layoffs at the Devens factory. But he said Chinese state-owned banks and municipal governments were offering unbeatable assistance to Chinese solar panel companies.

(NYT, January 14, 2011)

In Example (137), the sentence states two events: the agents raided a doctor's office and they revoked his license. The first event is the cause of the second, but there is a causal gap between these two events. The doctor's license was revoked not because the agents raided his office but because they found illegal drugs in his office. Figure 7.5 shows the causal relations in Example (137).

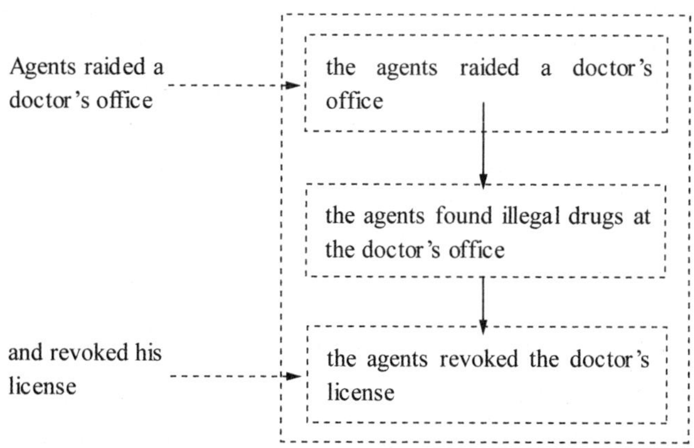

Figure 7.2 Cause-Effect organization in Example (137)

Figure 7.2 shows that the gap between the two events explicitly stated in the sentence, "agents raided a doctor's office" and they "revoked the doctor's license", can be filled by another event, "the agents found illegal drugs at the doctor's office", which resulted in the revocation of his license. In other words, there are two causal relations in this sentence: in the first one the effect is implicit while in the second one the cause is implicit.

Similar causal gap can be found in Example (138). The event of "Chinese state-owned banks and municipal governments were offering unbeatable assistance to Chinese solar panel companies" is a cause which may give rise to the potential effect of shutting down the factory in Devens in this particular context. In this way, the targeted effect of "shutting down factory in Devens" functions as an implicit cause for the "layoffs at the Devnes factory", which makes the two sentences coherent. The Cause-Effect organization between the two sentences in Example (138) can be diagramed as in Figure 7.3.

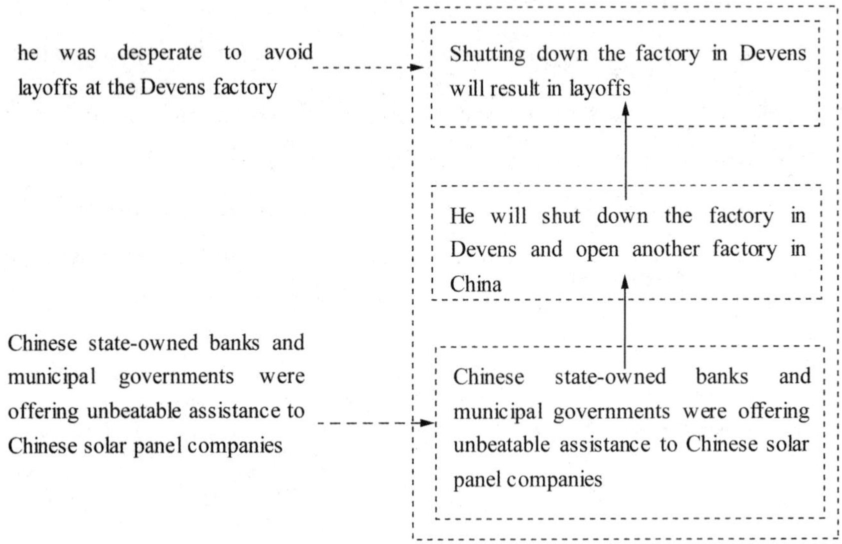

Figure 7.3 Effect-Cause organization in Example (138)

Our metonymic reasoning of causality tells us that when a country is providing favorable assistance to companies, it is attracting companies to start business in it, and quite usually, the company would shut down their current factory and open a new one in the place that offers more favorable assistance. Without establishing a causal relation between the concept of laying off and the concept of providing assistance to companies the text will not stand as a meaningful whole. In addition, the readers have to supply information that is not explicitly mentioned in the text.

Examples (137) and (138) are organized in Cause-Effect patterns with causal gaps, in which the causes are related to effects indirectly. There is an alternative explanation for this pattern: it includes two CAUSE-for-EFFECT metonymies; in the first one, the effect is implicit, and in the second one, the cause is implicit.

As is stated repeatedly that metonymy functions at several levels in one single sentence. The Cause-Effect pattern may be combined with the Whole-Part pattern in organizing texts. One cause may have more than one effect and vice versa. Determining which causes or effects to be presented in the text is a matter of selecting one part or several parts within the same whole.

To summarize, the causal connectivity in the text is the other way we can perceive metonymic roles in text interpretation alongside with the metonymic relations of structural perception of Whole-Part organization. Our metonymic reasoning of Cause-Effect relations helps us interpret a text as a meaningful whole on the ground that each state/event is either a result of another state/event or a state that initiates a further state/event (Al-Sharafi, 2004). From another perspective, this causal connection of human conceptualization makes seemingly irrelevant ICMs connected to each other.

Effects and causes are sometimes inseparable, and people tend to unite them in our understanding of the world around us. This nature of causality makes it possible to transfer the modifier of an effect to its cause or vice versa. This closeness of causality also makes it hard to draw a clear line of demarcation between Whole-Part relations and Cause-Effect relations and sometimes the two kinds of relations may intertwine with each other.

Compared to specific actions, which would cause various effects and consequences, the ultimate effects or consequences caused by those actions can directly attract the news readers' attention. Therefore, effects are used more often as metonymic vehicles than causes in news text organization. As a cognitive tool that governs our way of thinking, metonymy prevails in our everyday use of language, referential use and non-referential use of metonymy usually occur in combination and Cause-Effect relationships are often compressed into Whole-Part relationships in the blend.

Causal connectives, as linguistic forms, trigger the concept of causal connection, denoting causally related facts in the actual world, but causal relation exists in our conceptualization of events in the real world. Causal connectives do not create causality and they are just indicators to help the readers understand the causal connection between two states or events. Therefore, we do not have to use conjunctions that signify causality to introduce a cause or an effect, such as "since", "as a result", "because of + NP", "because", "therefore", "due to + NP", "consequently", "for this reason", "so", etc. Causal relations can also be presented through other relational clauses introduced by relational pronouns, such as "who", "where", or relational adverbials, such as "when", "after", etc. Non-clausal connectives can also be used metonymically to denote one explicit semantic relation and indicate one implicit causal relation, both of which are activated at the same time.

Cause and effect are so closely interdependent that whenever there is a cause, there would be an effect, or a series of effects. However, this does not necessarily mean that both cause and effect should be present in the same text. The interdependency between cause and effect enables people to use one of them to imply the other, because knowledge structures are fundamentally metonymic in nature, and once a structure or ICM is triggered by a linguistic form in the text, people's ability of metonymic reasoning would help them to establish relations between parts of the text and the whole texts or other parts of the same text, or between causes and effects. Sometimes, causes are related to effects indirectly with causal gaps, in which two CAUSE-for-EFFECT metonymies are combined; in the first one, the effect is implicit, and in the second one, the cause is implicit.

As is stated repeatedly that metonymy may function at several levels in one single sentence. The Cause-Effect pattern may be combined with the Whole-Part pattern in organizing texts. One cause may have more than one effect and vice versa. Determining which causes or effects to be presented in the text is a matter of selecting one part or several parts within the same whole.

Chapter 8
Metonymic Organization of News Schemata

This chapter attempts to show how metonymy organizes news schemata, with the aim to reveal how metonymy contributes to the global coherence of a news text. The discussion is focused on revealing how metonymy functions in organizing Headline and Lead, and the three categories that constitute the complete news Episode, Main Events, Background and Consequences.

8.1 News Schemata

van Dijk (1986) elaborates that news reports in the press are organized by a conventional news schema on the basis of his previous work on textual superstructures (van Dijk, 1980a, 1983, 1985a, 1985b, 1985c). According to van Dijk (1986: 169), a news schema is a typical example of textual superstructures, which is the conventional global form of a news text, as Figure 8.1 shows.

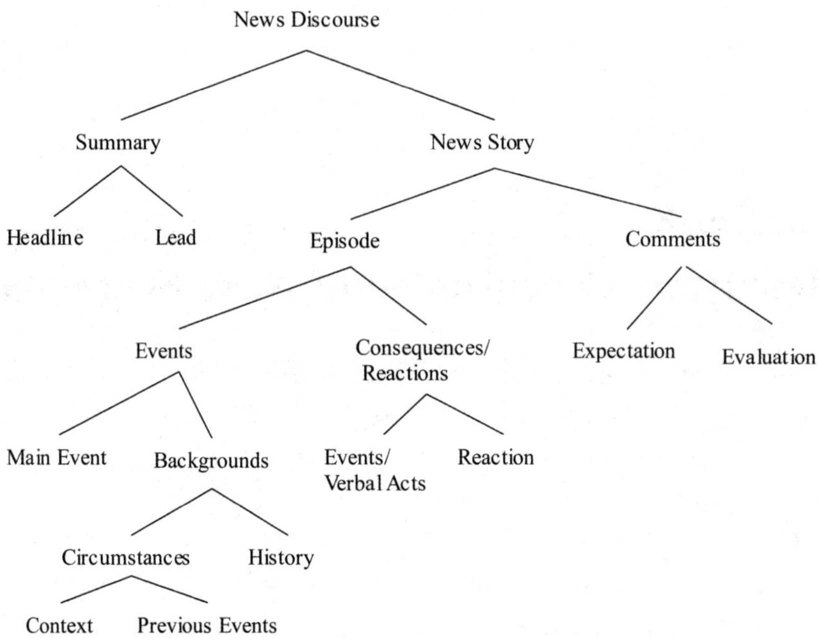

Figure 8.1 Superstructure schema of news text

In Figure 8.1, initial capitals signal that each of them is one of superstructure categories. According to van Dijk, not all these categories are obligatory in news text, but a well completed news report should at least have Summary and Main Events. Sometimes Background and Consequences are also provided. Figure 8.1 just shows a structural tendency rather than a strict rule of order (van Dijk, 1986). Summary states the main event or events through Headline and Lead. It is separated from news story because of its special functions in a news report. Episode is the core of a news story. Besides, one news article may be about several events, each with their own background and consequences.

According to Gee (1999), larger pieces of texts that have higher-level organizations with parts are much like the human body with parts: the face, trunk, hands, legs, etc. Each of these parts has their own smaller parts. Each category of the news schema can be viewed as a part of the news text and each category can have its own parts. The rest part of this chapter focuses on revealing how metonymy structures the organization of news texts at a higher level of description of discourse, or how these parts of a news schema are organized into a meaningful whole.

8.2 Metonymic Organization of Summary

According to van Dijk (1986), Summary of a news report, usually made up of a Headline or Headlines and a Lead, is of vital importance because it is the part of a news story that makes the readers decide whether to continue reading the rest part of the news report or not when they are skimming the newspaper or website. Summaries are the "verbalization of the underlying semantic macrostructure of a text" (van Dijk, 1986: 160) and they are "expedient signals to make effective guesses about the most important information of the text" (van Dijk, 1985c: 77). Therefore, Summary expresses the most important topics or themes of a text. This feature of summary echoes one of the most distinguished characteristics of metonymy: the most salient part of an entity is usually used to stand for the whole entity. This section will discuss the metonymic organization of Summary.

8.2.1 Metonymic Organization of Headline

When a reader is skimming the newspapers, his/her eyes would be easily caught by two of the most important news elements: photographs and headlines. Photographs are metonymic on the ground that they are selected as fragments of reality, and therefore they are always partial and less specific than real-world objects. Through the selected part(s), the readers or viewers can have an effective guess of the whole. If we can say that photographs tell news stories through vision, then headlines tell stories with words.

The functions of Headline are similar with those of the titles of texts of other genres such as fiction or fairy tales. Usually the title of a literary work is an easy way of referring to the book or works of other forms, such as a movie or performance adapted from the book, as in Examples (139) and (140).

(139) That's hardly an accusation that could be leveled against ***Great Expectations***. If some of Dickens's novels sprawl luxuriously across the page, this one is as trim

as a whippet.

(The Guardian, September 23, 2011)

(140) America's youth last night entrusted their adolescent hearts to ***Harry Potter***, ***Twilight***, ***Bad Teacher*** and ***The Tourist*** at the annual Teen Choice awards, held at the Gibson Amphitheater in Los Angeles.

(The Guardian, August 8, 2011)

"Great Expectations" in Example (139) is the title of one of Dickens's novels and is used here to refer to the novel metonymically; "Harry Potter", "Twilight", "Bad Teacher" and "The Tourist" in Example (140) refer to the movies entitled after them. Just the title will trigger the ICM of the whole work. Example (141) includes a more complicated case of metonymically used novel title.

(141) "It's a **Catch-22**," said Kuni Yogo, a former nuclear power planner at Japan's Science and Technology Agency. He said that the government and Tepco "try to disclose only what they think is necessary, while the media, which has an antinuclear tendency, acts hysterically, which leads the government and Tepco do not offer more information".

(NYT, March 17, 2011)

"Catch-22" was coined by Joseph Heller in his novel *Catch-22* . And the meaning of it has been extended to refer to a paradoxical situation in which an individual cannot or is incapable of avoiding a problem because of contradictory constraints or rules. Therefore, the title of the novel has been adopted as a term used to refer to similar situations as the one described in the novel. The metonymic use of "Catch-22" is different from those in Example (139) and Example (140) because the target it evokes is not the ICM of the whole novel but only a part of the content of the novel. Therefore, metonymic relationship exists not only between a title and the whole content it leads but also between the title and part of the content. Interpretation of the target concept depends on specific context. The second sentence in Example (141) describes that there is a paradox between what the media want and how they act: on one hand, they want to know more about the nuclear disaster; on the other hand, what they have done prevents the government from providing more information. Thus, the target concept of

"Catch-22" is a paradoxical situation as the one described in the novel, i. e., a part of the content of the novel instead of the novel as a whole.

Different from titles of novels or texts of other genres, such as the ones quoted above, headlines of news texts are seldom used to refer to the whole news reports or part of their contents. However, news headlines always show the readers more information than titles do, in other words, headlines communicate more than titles do.

A meticulously organized headline may draw attention of more readers. For news headlines in print, the size of the print and placement on the page can indicate the importance of a certain news story, while for news reports in digital forms, a list of headlines functions as an index so that the readers will know what the stories are about by taking just a glance at the list. The readers differ in their interests of reading because of their specific experiential, physiological or cognitive backgrounds. One way for them to choose the news texts they are interested in is to read the list of headlines.

Media language is required to be brief, especially for news headlines. Constrained by the space of the page or screen, the language of headlines has to be concise. Bell (1991) even argues that newspaper headlines make a sub-genre in the journalistic genre. Economy is one of the major pragmatic functions of metonymy; therefore, a lot of metonymic expressions are employed in news headlines. Consider Examples (142) and (143):

(142) **France** to sell Rafale fighter jet to **India**

(WP, January 31, 2011)

(143) US accuses **Tehran** over plot to kill Saudi ambassador

(The Guardian, October 12, 2011)

In Example (142), "France" and "India" are metonymically used to refer to the relevant departments from the two countries that are involved in purchasing the jet, motivated by the COUNTRY-for-CERTAIN DEPARTMENT OF THAT COUNTRY metonymy. In Example (143), "Tehran", the capital city of Iran, is used to refer to the government of that country, motivated by the prototypical metonymy of CAPITAL CITY-for-GOVERNMENT metonymy. The form

"US" is part of the form "the United States", which is used here to stand metonymically for the person who represents the government of the United States. News texts are abundant in metonymic expressions of such kind. The most obvious reason to employ metonymic expressions is to make the language as brief as possible.

In news headlines, there are lots of elliptical forms which can be found both in nominal groups and verbal groups. The PART OF A FORM-for-WHOLE FORM metonymy saves much space in headlines. The abbreviated forms are used to stand for the whole forms without the slightest change of meaning. Consider Examples (144), (145), (146) and (147):

(144) **Worst Year** for West Nile is Expected, Officials Say

(NYT, August 23, 2012)

(145) **Official** Says Bus in Crash That Killed 15 Was Speeding

(NYT, March 31, 2011)

(146) Disney **looking** into cradle for customers

(NYT, February 7, 2011)

(147) Florida Republican **at Odds** With Their Leader

(NYT, March 8, 2011)

"Worst Year" in Example (144) is an elliptical form for "the worst year" and "Official" in Example (145) stands for "an official". In each of these two cases, a part of a NP is used to stand for the whole NP. Practically, there is a tendency to avoid articles in organizing headlines and it is hard to find any "a", "an" or "the" at the start of a news headline.

"Looking into" in Example (146), stands for "is looking into", and "at Odds With" in Example (147) stands for "is at odds with". In each of these two cases, a part of a VP is used to stand for the whole VP.

Articles and different variants of the auxiliary verb "be" can be omitted in headlines because they carry no new information and even when they are missing there will not be any difficulty for the readers to be directed to the target concept.

Headlines do not have to be a sentence, in its complete or elliptical form. A clause, a phrase or phrases can function as a headline as well, as in Examples (148), (149), (150), (151) and (152).

(148) How a Doctor's Web Site Can Generate More Business

(NYT, October 27, 2011)

(149) What teachers really want to tell parents

(CNN, September 6, 2011)

(150) Where to get help with breast-feeding

(WP, March 13, 2011)

(151) No Train for the Motor City

(WSJ, December 16, 2011)

(152) Before and after McChrystal's removal, a flurry of White House activity

(WP, June 23, 2010)

In Examples (148)-(152), the clauses introduced by "how", "what" and "where" explicitly express the topics that the news reports are about. The main clauses can be omitted because they carry little information and can be easily inferred from the part left. For instance, the omitted main clause in Example (148) can be filled by "(this text is about) how a doctor's web site can generate more business".

Metonymy functions at many levels in organizing the headline in Example (151). Multiple metonymic shifts are involved in the expression of "Motor City", which is used to stand for the city of Detroit. Detroit is famous for its automotive industry. Motors are one of the most important parts of automotive products and are conventionally used as a metonym to stand for automobiles. Therefore, a city famous for its automotive industry can be referred to as "motor city". The main clause of "There is" is omitted, reducing the headline into just a NP. Moreover, "train" contrasts with "motor", creating an extra communicative effect which arouses readers' curiosity of why there is no train in a city advanced in motor vehicles.

The headline in Example (152) consists of two phrases: an adverbial phrase, "Before and after McChrystal's removal" and a NP, "a flurry of White House activity". The adverbial phrase states the timing and indicates the cause of the event. The NP is an elliptical form for "there exists a flurry of White House activity". Readers would have no problem in getting access to the information these two phrases are trying to express: the government removed McChrystal from his position, which caused a flurry of activity. "Removal" is the nominalized counterpart of the verb "remove". Nominalization motivated by metonymy can turn abstract processes into concrete states or objects and make a text to look unbiased through impersonalizing the processes (Fairclough, 1992, 2003; Billig, 2008; Basilio, 2009).

The most important function of news headlines is to show what the news texts are about. Clauses or phrases, as long as they satisfy this requirement, can all be used as news headlines.

Most news stories are about things that have already happened or things that are about to happen. But in news headlines, it is hard to find tenses other than simple present. Consider Examples (153) and (154):

(153) Gaza: Israeli Airstrike **Kills** 3 Militants

(NYT, April 2, 2011)

(154) Europe to **lead** daring Sun mission

(BBC, October 4, 2011)

In Example (153), the tense of simple present is used to stand for the tense of simple past. By making the verb "killed" into a simple present, the reporter provides us a vivid, eyewitness account: it sounds as if the event is happening now. Headline in Example (154) summarizes an event that will happen in the future, with the verb "is" omitted.

The principle of prominence is always governing the organization of breaking news headlines. Most of the headlines of hard news are highly descriptive, because this format can capture a story's essence best. The elements provided in a headline are chosen based on their importance in the Event ICM, such as the participant(s), timing, location, cause, response, consequences, etc. Any element can be viewed as a part of the whole Event ICM, and the most salient parts are chosen to be presented in the headline of a news story to provide access to the whole Event ICM. Consider Examples (155) and (156) chosen from breaking news headlines:

(155) C. I. A. Drones Kill Civilians in Pakistan

(NYT, March 18, 2011)

(156) US accuses Tehran over plot to kill Saudi ambassador

(The Guardian, October 12, 2011)

The headline in Example (155) presents the agent of an action (C. I. A. Drones), the action (Kill), the patient (Civilians) and the location (in Pakistan), which can be shown in the following formula:

(AGENT) (ACTION) (PATIENT) (LOCATION)

The headline in Example (156) presents the two participants (US and Tehran), the major action (US accuses Tehran) as well as the cause of the event (plot to kill Saudi ambassador), which can be shown in the following formula:

(AGENT) (ACTION) (PATIENT) (CAUSE)

The nature of metonymy as a conceptual operation where one entity stands for another but both are activated or at least partially activated enables metonymy to be an "efficient means of saying two things for the price of one, i. e. two concepts are activated while only one is explicitly mentioned" (Brdar & Brdar-Szabó, 2009: 240). One semantic element may be used to refer to another while both are activated, as in Examples (157) and (158).

(157) U. S. military awards contracts in Afghanistan to get money away from insurgents

(WP, August 16, 2011)

(158) China hails woman who rescued bleeding toddler left for dead

(CNN, October 19, 2011)

The headline in Example (157) presents the agent (U. S. military), the action (awards), the patient (contracts in Afghanistan to get money away from insurgents, which is metonymically used to refer to people who carried out contracts in Afghanistan to get money away from insurgents) as well as the cause of the event (people who carried out the contracts were awarded because they got or will get money away from insurgents).

Figure 8.2 shows how the information is organized in this headline.

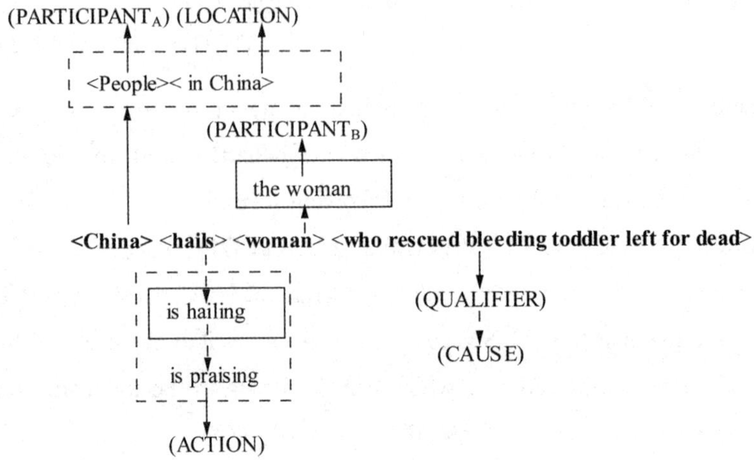

Figure 8.2　Metonymic organization of the headline in Example (158)

In Figure 8.2, dashed arrows signal metonymic links from a source to a target, while solid arrows signal specific semantic categories.

"China" in Example (158) is motivated by the COUNTRY-for-PEOPLE metonymy, in which both the source concept (the country of China) and the target concept (people in China) are activated by only one label (Radden & Kövecses, 1999; Brdar & Brdar-Szabó, 2009). The target concept motivated by the source concept is restricted by the specific context, because it is the people instead of the country who actually "hails".

"Hails" involves both metaphoric and metonymic mappings. On one hand, people hail in order to express appreciation, thus "to hail" means "to appreciate", which is a metonymic process guided by the principle that concrete actions are better understood than abstract actions; the simple present tense is used to stand for present continuous tense, mostly on the ground that the form, "hails", saves more space than the form, "is hailing". On the other hand, "hail" indicates people act in a way to show to others their attitude of appreciation, which is a metaphoric process, because people are not necessarily "hailing".

Articles in the two NPs are omitted motivated by the PART OF A FORM-for-THE WHOLE FORM metonymy: "woman" is part of the form "the woman", "bleeding toddler" is part of the form "a bleeding toddler". The *who*-clause, "who rescued bleeding toddler left for dead", functions as a qualifier of the head noun "woman" in the NP, and provides the cause for the action, i. e., people "hails" because she rescued a bleeding toddler left for dead.

Example (158) shows how metonymy functions in organizing headlines to present as much information as possible with the least words. According to van Dijk (1986), information in the headline signals the most relevant or important information of the news report, but if a headline presents only some minor details, the headline is biased. It should be noted here that news headlines of feature stories do not always summarize the main events but function as indices to trigger the readers' curiosity for further reading. Consider Examples (159) and (160) chosen from feature stories:

(159) Optimization at the Intersection of Biology and Physics

(NYT, November 2, 2010)

(160) Crab Pulsar's high-energy beam surprises astronomers

(BBC, October 6, 2011)

Reading the headline in Example (159), most readers would wonder why and how to optimize biology and physics and would like to look for further information in the news story. Similarly, curiosity would be aroused about how the high-energy beam of Crab Pulsar surprises astronomers when people read the headline in Example (160).

Questions very often appear in news headlines. On one hand, literally, the reporters may want to raise a question, but they would never expect an answer from the readers. On the other hand, the reporters may be showing their suspicion toward a so-called fact through asking questions, such as Examples (161) and (162).

(161) Can a Marketing Contest Increase Sales for This Online Retailer?

(NYT, November 16, 2011)

(162) Did U. S. forcers mistakenly kill an Afghan journalist?

(NYT, August 29, 2011)

It would also be quite natural for any reader to expect that the reporter would give the answers through the reporting, or at least provide some detailed analysis for the readers to find the answers by themselves when they are reading headlines with a question mark.

To summarize, metonymy minimizes the number of words in headlines, or even shortens the word length through abbreviation motivated by the PART OF A FORM-for-COMPLETE FORM metonymy. One tense that is used to stand for another not only brings about the metaphorical effect of reproducing the event as if it is happening now but also makes the headlines shorter. One speech act can be used metonymically to stand for another when the reporter is trying to provide an answer or oppose an opinion through asking a question. Selecting the most salient elements in an event and put them in the headline may directly show the general Event ICM to the readers and those who are attracted by the part(s) of the event showed in the headline may go to the lead and the main body of the news story for the whole event. Headlines direct readers to stories which catch their attention and help them save time as they flip through different pages. That is why headlines are usually compared to beacons.

8.2.2 Metonymic Organization of Lead

Another part in Summary that follows Headline is Lead. Lead also summarizes the major news story but carries more information than Headline does, because the space confinement on a lead is less strict than that on a headline. According to van Dijk (1986), Lead functions both as summary and introduction. There are two basic types of leads: *hard-news lead* and *feature lead*. Hard-news lead, also known as *direct lead* or *summary lead*, tells the readers or listeners the most important aspects of the news story directly, such as what happened or what was said, time and location of the event, and the source of the information. Hard-news lead is usually used in breaking news reporting. Feature lead, also known as *delayed lead* or *soft lead*, lures the readers into the story by hinting at its contents, setting a scene or evoking a mood with an incident or anecdote, which is often used with feature stories (van Dijk, 1986; Mencher, 2003; Rich, 2009).

8.2.2.1 Organization of Hard-news Leads

Usually, the leads of hard news must summarize the main event or events, providing answers to the questions readers would ask about the news story, namely the 5 Ws and one H, i. e., Who, What, When, Where, Why and How. A hard-news lead should answer several or all of these basic questions unless it looks too cumbersome to cram all these factors into one lead. van Dijk (1986) argues that leads do not express all the information and instead the selection or arrangement of information indicates what the reporter wants to highlight when reporting breaking news. As the major purpose of this chapter is to study the functions of metonymy in organizing news schemata, discussion of this subsection is focused on the metonymic relation between Lead and Headline. Examples in this subsection are all chosen from the most typical front-page hard-news reports.

(163) **Headline**: Obama creates indefinite detention system for prisoners at Guantanamo Bay

Lead: President Obama signed an executive order Monday that will create a formal system of indefinite detention for those held at the U. S. military prison Guantanamo Bay, Cuba, who continue to pose a significant threat to national security.

(WP, March 8, 2011)

(164) **Headline**: South Sudan says 80,000 displaced by Omar al-Bashir's seizure of Abyei

Lead: Up to 80,000 South Sudanese may have fled their homes after northern forces seized the contested border region of Abyei a week ago, according to a local official.

(The Guardian, May 27, 2011)

Both the headline and lead in Example (163) answer the same question about "who did what" in varying specifications, i. e., the lead elaborates on the same information provided by the headline. The expression "Obama creates indefinite detention system" in the headline is motivated by the CONTROLLER-for-CONTROLLED metonymy (Radden & Kövecses, 1999). The target concept is explicitly offered by the lead "President Obama signed an executive order

Monday that will create a formal system". In other words, the target concept activated by the headline is implicit while the concept activated by the lead is explicit.

The headline and lead in Example (164) also provide the same elements of the news event, including the source of information, the major news event, location and cause, i. e., both the headline and lead answer the same questions about "who" did "what", "where", and "why". Table 8.1 shows a comparison between the selected elements by the two parts of Summary in Example (164).

Table 8.1 A comparison between news elements provided by Headline and Lead in Example (164)

Information source	who	did what	why	where
South Sudan says	80,000	displaced	Omar al-Bashir's seizure	Abyei
according to a local official	up to 80,000 South Sudanese	may have fled their homes	after northern forces seized the contested border region of Abyei a week ago	the contested border region of Abyei

Table 8.1 shows that the lead provides elaborated information concerning the same news elements provided by the headline. For instance, concerning the information source, the headline uses the expression, "South Sudan says", motivated by the COUNTRY-for-PEOPLE RESPONSIBLE metonymy, while the lead explicitly states the people responsible, "according to a local official". These two expressions have a relationship of coreference. Concerning the "who" of the news event, "80,000" is an elliptical form of "80,000 South Sudanese"; these Sudanese were "displaced", or specifically, "have fled their homes", because of "Omar al-Bashir's seizure" of the place they lived in. The lead elaborates on the cause for this event: "northern forces (controlled by Omar al-Bashir) seized the contested border region of Abyei a week ago". The location of the event can be inferred from "Abyei" in the headline, and "the contested border region of Abyei" in the lead.

These two examples discussed above illustrate one pattern of Summary organization in which the target concept of Headline, which is usually implicit in CONCETP-for-CONCEPT metonymy, is explicitly provided by Lead. The metonymic representation of this pattern can be diagramed as in Figure 8.3.

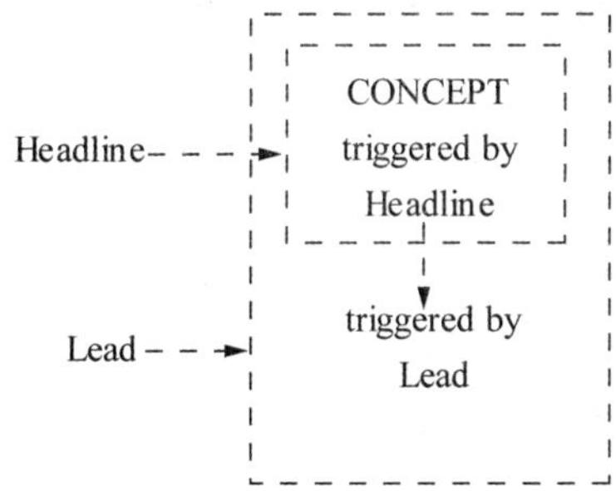

Figure 8.3 Source-Target pattern of Headline and Lead

In Figure 8.3, the concept triggered by Headline seems to be contained in the concept triggered by Lead, but Panther (2005: 358) argues that in the basic metonymic relation, "the target meaning is an elaboration of the source meaning, with the source meaning being one conceptual component of the target meaning". In other words, the containment does not necessarily mean meaning inclusion, but refers to the source meaning as a conceptual component of some more elaborated conceptual structure.

Example (165) illustrates another pattern of Summary organization.

(165) **Headline**: Growing pressure on water supplies affecting one in five global businesses

Lead: Survey reveals drought, shortages, flooding and rising prices are damaging companies in water-intensive industries.

(The Guardian, November 12, 2010)

In Example (165), "growing pressure on water supplies" in the headline activates a general concept while "drought, shortages, folding and rising prices" in the lead activate particular concepts. The general concept can be regarded as a general ICM and the particular concepts particular ICMs. Each particular ICM constitutes a part of the general ICM. When more particular ICMs within the general ICM are explicitly presented, the general ICM becomes more concrete and easier to perceive. Each of these particular ICMs affords mental access to the general ICM which they are part of, i. e. , when "drought, shortages, flooding and rising prices" are mentioned as profile, the general concept of "pressure on water supplies" is also activated as background.

The same general-particular relationship can be found between "global businesses" and "companies in water-intensive industries", as well as between "affect" and "damaging". Example (165) exemplifies another pattern of Summary organization, which can be diagramed as in Figure 8.4.

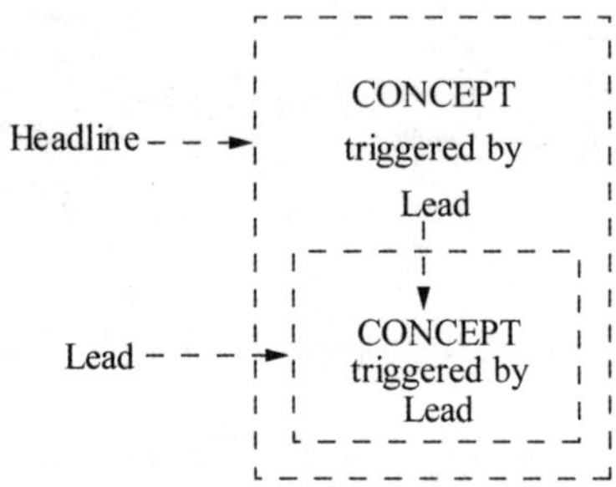

Figure 8.4 General-Particular pattern of Headline and Lead

Figure 8. 4 shows that the concept triggered by Headline is more inclusive than the concept triggered by Lead. Although the concepts triggered by Headline and Lead have different connotations, they actually refer to the same event that the news text is reporting.

From Figures 8. 3 and 8. 4, we can find a similarity between these two patterns of Summary organization, because both containment and inclusion can be regarded as a kind of Whole-Part relation. There are cases in which the concepts triggered by Headline do not contain/include or are not contained/included by the concepts triggered by Lead, as in Examples (166) and (167).

(166) **Headline**: Anders Behring Breivik declared insane by evaluation panel

Lead: Man who confessed to murders of 77 people in Norway could face psychiatric care rather than prison

(The Guardian, November 29, 2011)

(167) **Headline**: Disabled student insists Met police treated him brutally

Lead: Scotland Yard rejects complaints of assault and brutality at student fees demonstration in London

(The Guardian, May 27, 2011)

In Example (166), "Anders Behring Breivik", is the name of the confessed perpetrator of the bombing of government buildings in Oslo that resulted in 8 deaths and the mass shooting at a camp on an island of Norway where he killed 69 people. To some of the readers, the full name is enough to locate the person involved in the news event. However, to those who have no idea about the background events or who fail to recall the relationship between the people and the event that he is involved, the name only cannot evoke the intended mental representation in their minds. Therefore, the lead states the event the man was involved to help the readers get access to the targeted concept. In other words, the headline chooses the name of the agent while the lead chooses the event he was involved to locate the same person, i. e., the headline and lead choose different metonyms to provide access to the same concept. In addition, the headline describes the state of the subject being "declared insane by evaluation panel", while the lead provides one possible effect this state would cause that the subject "could face psychiatric care rather than prison".

The headline and lead in Example (167) describe two subevents within the same Event ICM from two opposite angles: the headline states one aspect of the event from the angle of the student while the lead states an opposite aspect from the angle of the police. "Met police" and "Scotland Yard" are two metonyms for the same referent, the territorial police force responsible for policing most of London. News reporting is always a matter about angles and perspectives. Reporting opinions from opposite parties involved in the same event can avoid bias.

Different from Examples (163)-(165), in which the concepts triggered by the headline and lead stand in a relationship of containment or inclusion, the concepts triggered by the headline and lead in Examples (166) and (167) are two contiguous parts within the same ICM. Figure 8. 5 shows the relationship between the concepts triggered by Headline and Lead.

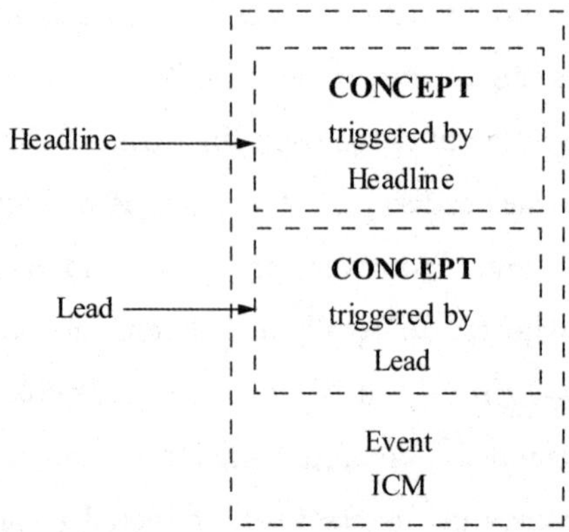

Figure 8.5　Part-Part pattern of Headline and Lead

Figure 8.5 shows that the concept triggered by Headline and the concept triggered by Lead are two parts within the same Event ICM. Headline and Lead provide information about different aspects of the same news event, or different parts of the whole Event ICM. This is in line with the hypothesis proposed by Panther and Thornburg (1998) that the more components of a scenario are presented in a text, the easier it is to identify the whole scenario.

Usually, Lead elaborates on the information provided by Headline and at the same time adds some other information of the news event, i.e., the Whole-Part relationship and Part-Part relationship between concepts triggered by Headline and Lead combine with each other in organizing Lead. Consider Examples (168) and (169):

(168) **Headline**: Afghans Avenge Florida Koran Burning, Killing 12

Lead: MAZAR-I-SHARIF, Afghanistan—Stirred up by three angry mullahs who urged them to avenge the burning of a Koran at a Florida church, thousands of protesters on Friday overran the compound of the United Nations in this northern Afghan city, killing at least 12 people, Afghan and United Nations officials said.

(NYT, April 2, 2011)

(169) **Headline**: Taliban Hit Base After Vow of Revenge

Lead: KABUL—Taliban insurgents attacked the U.S.-led coalition's main base in Afghanistan's southern Helmand province, killing two service members, after vowing revenge for the inflammatory video that has sparked violent protests across the Middle East.

(WSJ, September 15, 2012)

In Example (168), the headline tells the readers "who" (Afghans), did "what" (Avenge Florida Koran Burning) and the consequence (Killing 12). The lead tells the readers "why" (Stirred up by three angry mullahs who urged them to avenge the burning of a Koran at a Florida church), "who" (thousands of protesters), "when" (on Friday) did "what" and "how" (overran the compound of the United Nations in this northern Afghan city), and "where" (in this northern Afghan city, MAZAR-I-SHARIF), as well as the consequence (killing at least 12 people). Both the headline and lead in Example (169) answer questions about "who", did "what" and the consequence, though in different specification. The lead provides answers to more questions about "why", "when", "where" and "how".

In Example (169), questions about "who", did "what" and "when" are answered by both the headline and the lead, but other questions are also answered in the lead, including "where", "why" and "so what".

Table 8.2 shows a comparison between the news elements provided by the headline and lead in Example (169).

Table 8.2 A comparison between news elements provided by Headline and Lead in Example (169)

who	did what		where	so what	when	why
Taliban	Hit	Base			After Vow of Revenge	
Taliban insurgents	attacked	the U.S.-led coalition's main base	in Afghanistan's southern Helmand province	killing two service members	after vowing revenge	for the inflammatory video that has sparked violent protests across the Middle East

For people who are familiar with the situation in Afghan, "Taliban" in the headline is sufficient to trigger the ICM of the organization of Taliban; but for people who are not, "Taliban insurgents" in the lead is informative enough to trigger the ICM of insurgents and have a general idea of what kind of entity Taliban is. Short words are preferred to longer ones if they have synonymous meanings in Headline to save more space, and therefore the headline and lead choose different verbs in describing the same action, for "hit" is shorter than "attack".

The lead provides a detailed description about the target that was attacked. The Base ICM can be accessed without any effort (the U. S. -led coalition) and the location (southern Helmand province, Afghan). When an attack happens, people would want to know the damages the attack has caused, and therefore, the lead provides information concerning the effect caused by the attack (killing two service members). The *after*-phrases provide information about the time of the event and at the same time indicate the cause of the action in the main event.

To sum up, hard-news headlines and leads summarize the most important elements of news events. Concepts triggered by Headline and Lead usually stand in Whole-Part or Part-Part relations. When the concept triggered by Headline is contained in or inclusive of the concept triggered by the Lead, the Headline and Lead are organized in Whole-Part pattern and when the concepts triggered by Headline and Lead are different parts of the same Event ICM, the Headline and Lead are organized in Part-Part pattern. A summary with more parts of the Events ICM will direct the readers to the targeted ICM of the news event more directly.

8.2.2.2 Organization of Feature Leads

Most breaking-news stories contain hard-news lead, but it is not compulsory. Breaking-news can also have a feature lead, depending on several factors: the significance of the news, the timing, the subject matter, or even the editor's preference (Rich, 2009). If the subject is serious, such as death, disaster, a major change in the law, hard lead is preferred. Otherwise, reporters may choose a feature lead for his/her report. Consider Example (170):

(170) **Headlines**: Romney Seeks Traction in Swing States

(After Polls Show Candidate Failing to Lock Crucial States, Campaign Returns Focus to Economy)

Lead: For Mitt Romney, good news came Friday with word that President Barack Obama had added a stop to his travel schedule next week. For the first time this election season, Mr. Obama will campaign in Wisconsin, a confirmation that the traditionally Democratic state is now in play.

(WSJ, September 15, 2012)

Headline in Example (170) consists of an upper headline and a lower headline. The headlines summarize the major event of the news story that polls show Romney's temporal failure in election which makes him seek traction in swing states. Instead of elaborating on the information provided by the headlines, the lead tells another episode which could influence Romney's campaign strategy.

Other common types of feature leads are descriptive lead and narrative lead. The descriptive lead describes a person or a scene, which recounts the news event in a way of storytelling to put the readers on the scene. The description of a person or scene must be synecdochic, because it is impossible and unnecessary to cover every detail of the person or scene it tries to report, as in Example (171).

(171) **Headlines**: A Sicilian opening in the wild west

Lead: There was butter on the table, and portion packs of Nutella. But why would we eat the breakfast of a million international hotels when we could enjoy the real Sicilian experience? Locals' breakfast in the fishing village of Scopello, west of Palermo, is bread still warm from the bakery, dipped in olive oil from down the road, sprinkled with salt and eaten with pecorino cheese and, of course, a good strong caffè.

(The Guardian, May 28, 2011)

In the scene described by the lead, there must be something else except for "butter" and "portion packs of Nutella" on the table. And local people's breakfast must be far more than what has been described in the text. The reporter chooses the most prominent parts to represent the whole scene.

Many feature leads start with something about a person who is one of many people sharing the same problem. One of the general ideas for organizing feature leads is that readers can relate better to one particular person's problem than to a general statement of a common problem, as in Example (172).

> (172) **Headline**: An Addict Crosses a Line, and Is Pulled Back
>
> **Lead**: VANCOUVER, British Columbia—Gregory Reeve could hardly have picked a more Canadian way to become a heroin addict: a hockey puck in a game with friends shattered his jaw.
>
> (NYT, February 8, 2011)

Example (172) exemplifies one of many feature leads which are written following the principle from specific to general. Use a specific example at the beginning to illustrate the main point of the story. Through a part of a general ICM, the whole ICM is triggered, because a specific event is usually easier to perceive than a general one.

To summarize, feature leads do not summarize the main events like hard-news lead. They attract attention from the readers through creating scenes by synecdochic description or narration, or by stating a particular event to evoke a general phenomenon.

8.3 Metonymic Organization of News Story

van Dijk (1986) observed that news reports are not always organized to represent events in their chronological or causal order, but are arranged according to the importance or relevance to the core topic. The readers may not have enough time or patience to finish the whole story, so they always ask the most important questions first. When the readers grasp adequate information of a news story, they may stop the reading or continue with the rest of the text if they are still interested and want to know more about the story. This is especially true for news on the website, where readers have so many reading choices when they are surfing the web for news.

Breaking news is usually structured like a reverted pyramid, beginning with the most important elements of the story. As we have discussed earlier, the most important element of a new story should be presented in Summary and there are only two reasons if not so: the reporter is biased or the reporter wants to arouse the curiosity of the readers to read more to know what the story is about. Not all the categories in the news schemata are compulsory in a piece of news report. Main Events, Background and Consequences constitute the complete news Episode, which is the core of a news story (van Dijk, 1986), and therefore, this subsection focuses on the analysis of the metonymic relationship between Summary and Main Event, between Main Events and Background, as well as the relationship between Main Events and Consequences. Given the complexities of text organization and the varieties of news types and their organization, focus of this chapter is restricted to the organization of hard news reports.

8.3.1 Metonymic Relationship between Summary and Main Events

In van Dijk's (1986) model of news schemata, the body of a news report should at least include the category of Main Events, which organizes all important relevant information about the news story in the report. For breaking news report, the most important information has already been organized in Summary. The category of Main Events often elaborates on the information provided in Headline or Lead, as in Example (173).

(173)

Summary	
Headline:	Judge orders FDA to revisit decision not to ban some antibiotics in animal feed
Lead:	A federal court has ordered the Food and Drug Administration to revisit its decision not to ban the use of certain antibiotics in animal feed and criticized the agency for relying on industry to voluntarily limit the use of these drugs.
News Story	

Main Events:	This week, the federal district court in Manhattan ruled that the FDA must reconsider two citizen petitions that asked the agency to withdraw approval of some antibiotics used in food-producing animals. The agency's denial of both petitions years ago was "arbitrary and capricious," the court said. ...

(WP, June 6, 2012)

In Example (173), Headline, Lead and Main Events state about the same event that a judge from a federal district court ruled FDA to reconsider one of its decisions. Each of these three categories chooses a different metonym to refer to the same agent, namely, "judge", "a federal court", and "the federal district court in Manhattan". All these three forms provide access to the same referent, the judge representing the deferral district court in Manhattan. "Judge" in Headline is an elliptical form for "a judge", motivated by PART OF A FORM-for-COMPLETE FORM metonymy. The other two are motivated by the ORGANIZATION-for-PEOPLE RESPONSIBLE metonymy, in which the court stands for the judge who made the ruling. In this news, the purpose of the ruling is of vital importance and therefore, all the three categories describe the content of the ruling but in different degrees of specification.

Example (174) is similar with Example (173), in which the category of Main Events elaborates on the same event which has been summarized by Headline and Lead and at the same time adds some new information.

(174)

Summary	
Headline:	Bomb kills 2 at upscale Kabul hotel complex
Lead:	KABUL—A suicide bomber detonated explosives at the entrance of an upscale mall and hotel in Kabul Monday afternoon, leaving twisted metal and broken glass at a venue frequented by foreigners and wealthy Afghans.
News Story	

Main Events:	The lunchtime blast at the newly renovated Kabul City Center shopping mall and Safi Landmark hotel killed two security guards. The guards had identified the bomber as suspicious as he approached the mall, and exchanged fire with him before the blast, said Gen. Ayoub Salangi, Kabul's police chief. Two people were wounded. ...

(WP, February 14, 2011)

The subjects in Headline, Lead and the first sentence of Main Events have the same referent, but each of them highlights a different aspect of the same Action ICM. "Bomb" triggers the ICM of an explosive attack through highlighting the instrument; "a suicide bomber" highlights the actor of the action; and "the lunchtime blast" highlights the time of the action, indicating that the bomb was set off at the lunchtime. Different metonyms are chosen to provide different aspects of the same referent.

Headline and Lead choose different subevents within the same Event ICM, which stand in a Cause-Effect relation. "A suicide bomber detonated explosives" is the event that caused the blast which "killed 2". When an incident happens, the location is usually of great importance, and therefore all the three categories present information concerning the location of the incident but in different degree of specification, as Table 8.3 shows.

Table 8. 3 A comparison between metonyms of the same referent in Example (174)

Headline	... at upscale Kabul hotel complex
Lead	... at the entrance of an upscale mall and hotel in Kabul
Main Events	... at the newly renovated Kabul City Center shopping mall and Safi Landmark hotel

From Table 8. 3 we can see that each time the location of the incident is mentioned, new information is added. Apart from the information that Summary has already mentioned, the Main Events describe a previous event before the blast that "the guards had identified the bomber as suspicious as he approached the mall, and exchanged fire with him before the blast", the source of the information, "said Gen. Ayoub Salangi, Kabul's police chief" and other consequences of the event, "two people were wounded".

From the two examples discussed above, it can be concluded that Summary of hard news report is usually an attenuated version of Main Events, i. e., the information provided in Summary is usually included in Main Events or we may say that the concept activated by Summary of a news text and the information activated by the Main Events stand in a Part-Whole relation.

There are cases in news text that Main Events of the news story do not elaborate on the same information summarized in Headline and Lead, as in Example (175).

(175)

Summary	
Headline:	Clinton arrives in Afghanistan
Lead:	Kabul, Afghanistan (CNN)—Secretary of State Hillary Clinton arrived in Afghanistan on an unannounced visit Wednesday, just one day after landing in Libya.
News Story	
Main Events:	She is to meet with Afghan President Hamid Karzai on Thursday and hopes to show the United States' commitment to Afghanistan, the State Department said.
	...

(CNN, October 19, 2011)

This segment of news text is typical in news reports about a nation level leader visiting other countries. The form, "Clinton" in the headline, motivated by the LAST NAME-for-FULL NAME metonymy, is contained in the form "Secretary of State Hillary Clinton" in the lead. The form, "arrives in" in the headline, motivated by the PRESENT TENSE-for-PAST TENSE metonymy, stands for "arrived in" in the lead. Moreover, "arrived in" and "landing" in the lead are both motivated by the SUBEVENT-for-COMPLEX EVENT metonymy, standing for visiting a country for political purpose, which can be inferred from our world knowledge that when people like "Clinton" arrive or land in a foreign country, probably they are visiting that country for political purposes. "Afghanistan" is also metonymically motivated to refer to Kabul, the capital city of Afghanistan. Lead answers questions about "how" and "when", i. e., the manner of Clinton's visit (on an unannounced visit), and the time (Wednesday, just one day after landing in Libya).

Instead of elaborating on the information that has already been summarized by Headline and Lead, Main Events describes the purpose of her visiting (to meet with Afghan President Hamid Karzai on Thursday and hopes to show the United States' commitment to Afghanistan), and the source of information (the State Department said). Therefore, Main Events and Summary provide information of different aspects of the same event, affording mental access to contiguous concepts within the same Event ICM. Thus, different from the pattern exemplified by Examples (173) and (174), Example (175) shows another pattern of Summary and Main Events organization in which the concepts triggered by Summary and Main Events stand in Part-Part relations.

To summarize, the category of Main Events usually elaborates on the same information provided by Summary or describes different aspects of information with Summary, which leads to two major kinds of relation between the categories of Summary and Main Events of hard news reports: the Part-Whole relation and Part-Part relation. When Main Events and Summary state about the same aspects of information, Summary is usually an attenuated version of Main Events, i. e., the information provided in Summary is usually included in Main Events or we may say that the concept activated by Summary of a news text and the information activated by the Main Events stand in a Part-Whole relation. When Main Events state different aspects of information with Summary, the concepts triggered by Main Events and Summary stand in Part-Part relation, i. e., the concepts triggered by them are both parts within the same Event ICM.

8.3.2 Metonymic Relationship between Main Events and Background

Background is often considered an indispensable part for news texts because it helps the readers activate relevant cognitive models, i. e., personal experiences and knowledge about concrete situations that have been stored in the readers' cognitive models (van Dijk, 1986). Information given in Background is not a part of the actual news event, but provides historical or social context or conditions of these events in which the news event is better understood. In a sense, Background and Main Events trigger two different Event ICMs which are connected by causality within one higher level Event ICM. Consider Example (176):

(176)

Main Events	BP has asked United States regulators for permission to resume drilling in the Gulf of Mexico, two company officials said on Sunday, creating a delicate situation for the Obama administration as it seeks to balance safety concerns with a desire to increase domestic oil production.
Background	The petition comes less than 12 months after a rig BP had leased there exploded, causing a huge oil spill and killing 11 workers. The accident tarnished BP's image and raised questions about its safety procedure. ...

(NYT, April 4, 2011)

In Example (176), the event that BP asked for permission to resume drilling in Main Events indicates that there was a stop of oil drilling. The participle phrase "creating a delicate situation for the Obama administration as it seeks to balance safety concerns with a desire to increase domestic oil production" indicates there were safety concerns with regard to BP's resumption of drilling. The second paragraph offers background information which functions as an explanation why BP stopped drilling and why BP's resuming drilling would create a delicate situation. Figure 8.6 shows the causal relationship in Example (176).

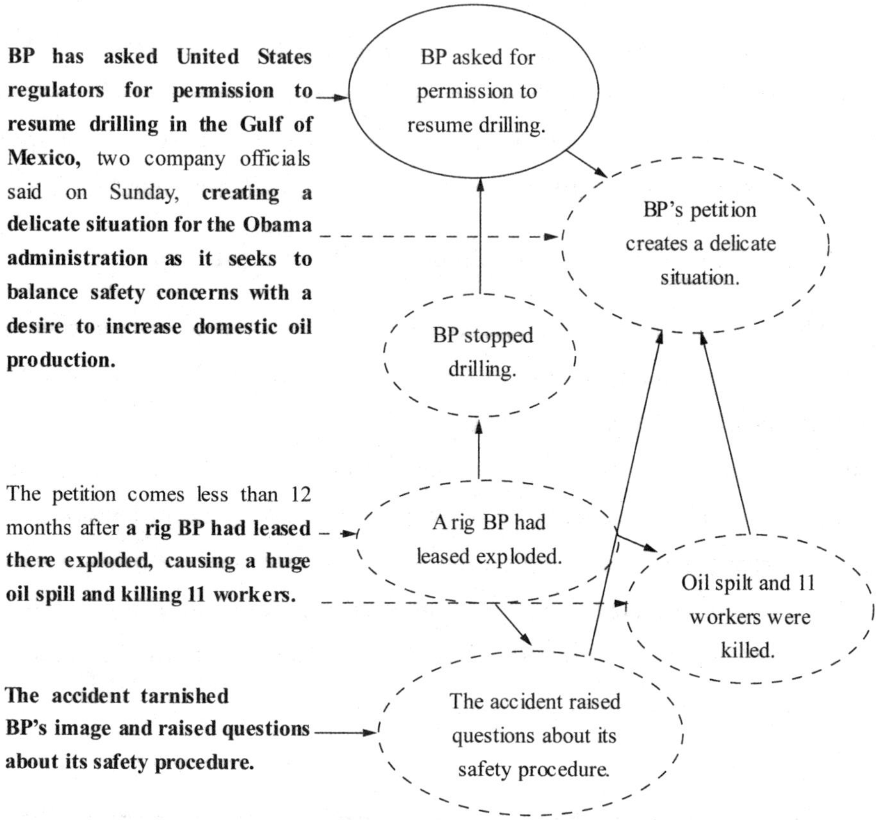

Figure 8.6 Cause-Effect organization of Main Events and Background in Example (176)

In Figure 8.6, broken arrows signify metonymic mappings from linguistic forms to target concepts and solid arrows signify the causal relations from causes to effects. From the figure we can see that, Main Events trigger concepts of two major events: BP asked for permission to resume drilling and BP's petition creates a delicate situation. These two concepts stand in a Cause-Effect relation. Background triggers concepts of three major events: a rig BP had leased exploded; oil spilt and 11 workers were killed; and the accident raised questions about its safety procedure. The former is the cause and the other two are effects. Apart from the two events which are explicitly stated by the text, there is an implicit event which is also caused by the event that a rig BP had leased exploded: BP stopped drilling. This implicit event is the cause for the event stated in Main Event: BP asks for permission to resume drilling. Figure 8.6 also shows that event stated in Background is the cause for both of the events stated in Main

Events, either directly or indirectly.

To sum up, concepts triggered by Background and Main Events stand in a Cause-Effect relation, in which Background triggers the cause and Main Events trigger the effect. Background updates our cognitive models concerning specific situations and provides information that makes a piece of news intelligible.

8.3.3 Metonymic Relationship between Main Events and Consequences

The importance of a news event is usually measured by its consequences. Journalists often include the category of Consequences in their news reports to cover the actions and events that immediately follow the main news events which may be seen as effects caused by the main events (van Dijk, 1986). Important information from Consequences may be provided before the major events in a news report the same way an effect may be provided before a cause. When the consequences of an event are the most salient part of an Event ICM, the consequences should be provided in Headline or Lead to highlight the importance of the news report, as shown in Example (177).

(177)

Summary	
Headline:	At Least 35 Killed and 210 Hurt in Crash of 2 Trains in China
Lead:	BEIJING—At least 35 people died and 210 were injured Saturday night in a train accident on a high-speed line in coastal China. It was the most serious blow yet to the country's beleaguered rail-modernization program.
News Story	
Main Events:	The accident occurred when a train traveling near Wenzhou lost power after it was struck by lightning, according to the official Xinhua news agency. Signals apparently also malfunctioned, causing another train to rear-end the stationary train. Six cars derailed; photographs and television news reports showed that at least two of the cars were thrown off a bridge 50 feet above the ground.

	The disaster prompted President Hu Jintao to declare that the rescue work was a national priority. Xinhua had graphic photos of the injured being treated in hospitals and locals lining up to donate blood.
Consequences:	China's railway minister, Sheng Guangzu, was reported to have rushed to the scene. Mr. Sheng took control of the powerful ministry earlier this year after his predecessor and several associates were fired and investigated for corruption. ...

(NYT, July 23, 2011)

The news report is about a train accident happened in China in which 35 people died and 210 people were injured. The consequences of the accident were so severe that put them in the headline would highlight the importance of the news. Main Events of the news text describe how this accident happened. The text continues with other consequences caused by the accident, such as the response of the President of China and Minister of Railway Department.

To summarize, Main Events and Consequences stand in Cause-Effect relations. Cause-Effect pattern is metonymic because when each one of the pair is mentioned, the other one is also mentally activated as background and the causal connectedness between a cause and an effect makes a text a unified whole.

To summarize, this chapter focuses on revealing how metonymy structures the organization of news texts at a higher level of description of text and shows how each category of a news schema is metonymically organized to reflect what has happened in the real world.

News schemata are constituted by different categories much like the human body by parts. Each category of the news schema can be viewed as a part of the news text and each category can have its own parts.

Summary of a news text stands in a Part-Whole relation with Main Events. Hard-news headlines and leads provide the most important elements of the news events. Concepts triggered by Headline and Lead also stand in Part-Whole relations. It can be concluded that, Summary of a news text functions as a vehicle for the readers to get access to the whole news story. It triggers the cognitive model of a news story through selecting the most prominent parts of the Event ICM, forming a PART-for-WHOLE metonymy.

The category of Main Events usually elaborates on the same information provided by Summary or describes different aspects of information with Summary, which leads to two major kinds of relation between the categories of Summary and Main Events of hard news reports: the Part-Whole relation and Part-Part relation. When Main Events and Summary state about the same aspects of information, Summary is usually an attenuated version of Main Events, i. e. , the information provided in Summary is usually included in Main Events or we may say that the concept activated by Summary of a news text and the information activated by the Main Events stand in a Part-Whole relation. When Main Events state different aspects of information with Summary, the concepts triggered by Main Events and Summary stand in Part-Part relation, i. e. , the concepts triggered by them are both parts within the same Event ICM.

Background stands in a Cause-Effect relation with Main Events. From the reporter's point of view, to make a text coherent the reporter should provide shared knowledge, which is the major function of Background. From the reader's point of view, when the background knowledge stored in the readers' mind is not adequate, textual information providing background is compulsory. Otherwise, the text would not be perceived coherent.

Consequences is a category in the news schema which provides information about the actions and events that immediately follow the main news events and that may be seen as caused by the main events and therefore there is also a Cause-Effect relation between Consequences and Main Events.

This metonymic organization of news schemata offers an explanation to the question why news reports are not always organized to represent events in chronological or causal order, but are arranged according to the importance or relevance of certain events to the core topic, and therefore, a news report is usually structured like a reverted pyramid, beginning with the most important elements of the story.

Chapter 9
Conclusion

Metonymy, as a fundamental cognitive tool, structures the way we conceptualize the world as well as the way we organize our language. This chapter summarizes the major findings, discusses implications and limitations of the present study, and provides suggestions for the future study.

9.1 Major Findings

The ultimate goal of this study is to reveal that that metonymy is far more than just a figure of speech applied only in the literary world but is an omnipresent everyday phenomenon in texts of any kind. This section summarizes the major findings of the present study corresponding to the two major research objectives: how metonymy functions to organize news text in terms of text cohesion and what patterns metonymy demonstrates in organizing news texts.

9. 1. 1 Major Findings Concerning How Metonymy Functions to Organize News Texts in Terms of Cohesion

The Form-Concept model of metonymy proposed in the present study is very convenient in providing a cognitive explanation for cohesive devices. Investigation into metonymy's functions to organize news texts in terms of cohesion finds that two lexical items (or two linguistic FORMs) are cohesive as long as they satisfy one of the following conditions:

(1) they have identical FORM;

(2) they provide access to the same CONCEPT;

(3) they provide access to CONCEPTs which are related by inclusion; or

(4) they provide access to CONCEPTs which are contiguous within the same ICM.

Repetition is the kind of lexical cohesion in which the same Form-Concept relation or only part of the relation, the form, is repeated. The discussion shows that whether it is the whole Form-Concept relation or only the FORM that is repeated, a cohesive tie is formed. When the repeated linguistic form triggers the same concept with its previous occurrence, the cohesive link between these two pairs of Form-Concept relations is strengthened, but it is not required for these two forms to be cohesive. When the repeated form has a different referent, or provides access to a different concept with its previous occurrence, they still form a cohesive tie.

Synonymous items provide access to the same concept. Even when they are not semantically synonymous with each other, as long as they provide access to the same concept, they form a cohesive tie. Antonymous items provide access to CONCEPTs that are opposite to each other within one ICM. Concepts related by opposition are conceptually contiguous and one of them can be used as a reference point affording mental access to the other as well as the higher-level ICM which both of these opposite concepts are parts of. Even if two linguistic forms are not semantically antonymous as long as they provide access to CONCEPTs that opposite each other within one ICM, they generate cohesive powers.

The concepts triggered by a hyponym and its superordinate stand in a Part-Whole relation, in which the concept triggered by the hyponym is part of the concept triggered by the superordinate. Cohesion realized through hyponymy has two representations. Firstly, a hyponym and a superordinate form a cohesive tie because the concepts they provide access to stand in a relation of inclusion. Secondly, the concepts triggered by a hyponym and a superordinate stand in a Whole-Part relation which enables one of them to stand for another through meaning extension of reduction. Thus, in certain context, both the hyponym and superordinate may provide access to the same concept, contributing to text cohesion.

Cohesion realized through meronymy is quite similar to cohesion realized through hyponymy. The concepts triggered by a meronym and a holonym also stand in a Part-Whole relation, in which the concept triggered by the meronym is a part of the concept triggered by the holonym. Cohesion realized through meronymy also has two representations: the concepts triggered by the meronymy and holonym stand in a relation of inclusion; or the meronymy and holonym provide access to the same concept.

Items that have the tendency to co-occur have cohesive powers because the CONCEPTs they provide access to are contiguous with each other within one more inclusive ICM. The items that co-occur in collocation are connected by relations at the conceptual level instead of the linguistic level, i. e. , the items are not associated by their semantic relations but by conceptual connection within one ICM.

The relations between pronouns, substitutes, or even structural slots and their antecedents are also metonymic. These semantically attenuated forms are used to stand for the whole form which can be recovered from the preceding clauses. The FORM-for-FORM and CONCEPT-for-CONCEPT metonymies are responsible for cohesion realized through grammatical cohesive devices. At the formal level, one form is used to stand for another form, because no matter what category they belong to, pronouns, demonstratives or common nouns, they are all forms of language. At the conceptual level, these different forms provide access to the same concepts, two concepts that are related by inclusion or conceptual contiguity within the same ICM.

9.1.2 Major Findings Concerning the Patterns Metonymy Demonstrates in Organizing News Texts

In the present study, metonymic relations are categorized into Whole-Part metonymy and Cause-Effect metonymy based on the two major principles underlying metonymic relations: contiguity and causality. Both Whole-Part metonymy and Cause-Effect metonymy function at different levels in organizing news texts.

Firstly, news texts are metonymic in nature because what is represented in the formal text reflects just a part of the conceptualized world of reality. No text can ever include all the relevant information pertaining to an event. When organizing a news text, the reporter has to select the most prominent aspects of the event and put them in the text to represent the whole news event. These selected aspects of information function as linguistic vehicles to provide access to the whole scenario of the event, forming a PART-for-WHOLE relation between the formal text and the conceptualized world of reality. Both the Generalization-Example relation and the Preview-Detail relation in Hoey's (1983a) terms can be reduced to a Whole-Part pattern in which the Particular/Detail member is a part of the General/Preview member. This pattern of organization is metonymic in that each particular ICM functions as a trigger to provide access to the general ICM. Normally, when the readers are reading the examples or details their attention is still directed to the general proposition expressed in the general sentence, in other words, the whole is still in focus.

Secondly, our metonymic reasoning of Cause-Effect relations underlying the text helps us interpret the text as a purposeful unit on the basis that each state is either a result of another state/event or a state that initiates a further state/event in news reporting. Causes and effects are so closely related that people tend to unite them in conceptualizing the world around us. This nature of causality makes it possible to transfer the modifier of an effect to its cause or vice versa. This closeness of causality makes it hard to draw a clear line of demarcation between Whole-Part relations and Cause-Effect relations and sometimes the two kinds of relations may intertwine with each other. Cause and effect are so closely interdependent that whenever there is a cause, there would be an effect, or a series of effects. However, this does not necessarily mean that both cause and effect should be present in the same text. Sometimes, causes are related to effects indirectly with causal gaps, in which two CAUSE-for-EFFECT metonymies are combined: in the first one, the effect is implicit, and in the second one, the cause is implicit.

Thirdly, metonymy functions at several levels even within one single sentence let alone in a text with a whole bundle of sentences. As a cognitive tool that governs our way of thinking, metonymy prevails in our everyday use of language; referential use and non-referential use of metonymy usually occur in combination and Cause-Effect relationships are often compressed into Whole-Part relationships in the blend. Metonymy is a result of the interaction of the underlying cognitive mechanism with linguistic and non-linguistic world knowledge, and it can be both figurative and non-figurative in terms of language use in organizing news texts. The Cause-Effect pattern may be combined with the Whole-Part pattern in organizing texts. One cause may have more than one effect and vice versa. Determining which causes or effects to be presented in the text is a matter of selecting one part or several parts within the same whole.

Fourthly, news schemata are also metonymically organized. This metonymic organization of news schemata offers an explanation to the question why news reports are not always organized to represent events in chronological or causal order, but are arranged according to the importance or relevance of certain events to the core topic, and therefore, a news report is usually structured like a reverted pyramid, beginning with the most important elements of the story. Summary and the main body of a news text stand in a PART-for-WHOLE relation. The more parts of the Events ICM are presented in Headline and Lead, the more possible Summary of the news text may provide successful access to Main Events. Background and Main Events stand in a Cause-Effect relation. From the reporter's point of view, to make a text coherent the reporter should provide background knowledge. From the reader's point of view, when the background knowledge stored in the readers' mind are not adequate, textual information providing background is compulsory. Otherwise, the text would not be perceived coherent. Consequences is a category in the news schema which provides information about the actions and events that immediately follow the main news events and that may be seen as caused by the main events and therefore there is also a Cause-Effect relation between Consequences and Main Events.

9.2 Implications

The present study combines both the cognitive and functional approaches to study the textual functions of metonymy in organizing news texts and the findings contribute both to studies on discourse analysis and research on metonymy.

Theoretically, this study proposes a Form-Concept model of metonymy which is very convenient in analyzing the textual functions of metonymy in terms of text cohesion. Through reducing the three ontological realms in which metonymy may occur to two, the realm of form and the realm of concept, this Form-Concept model treats metonymy as a conceptual operation in which one entity stands for another but both are activated or at least partially activated across the ontological realms of form and concept. Based on the two guiding principles of contiguity and causality, the present study categorizes the various metonymic relationships into Whole-Part metonymy and Cause-Effect metonymy and investigates into the organizational patterns each of these two categories of metonymy demonstrates in news text organization. Most importantly, this study extends the research on metonymy from the lexical and grammatical levels to the textual level, and findings are significant not only to news text analysis but also to our understanding of the organization of written text in general. It provides a cognitive account for text organization from the perspective of metonymy. Although it is not new to apply cognitive methods in discourse studies, to study text organization from the perspective of metonymy is quite a new area.

Methodologically, this study adopts a cognitive-functional approach supported by actual language use, which is another attempt to show how functional and cognitive linguistic approaches can complement each other in discourse studies.

Practically, this research analyzes the organizational patterns of news texts, which is of great importance both for news texts producers and the readers. The analytical framework is also helpful for English learners to have a better understanding of the organizational patterns as well as the interpretation of news texts utilizing metonymy as a cognitive tool.

9.3 Limitations

Although the study has some significant findings, it is by no means perfect. Limitations can be found in the following aspects:

Firstly, the genre of news texts is a complex discourse genre, which can be further divided into many sub-genres (Bell, 1991). Metonymy may have different manifestations in organizing texts of different journalist genres. Besides, online news texts differ from news texts in print in many ways. For instance, print news stories are written in linear order, to be read from beginning to end; online news reports are still written in linear order, but websites provide links to related information from other texts, creating a nonlinear potential for readers to choose whether to finish the reading to the end or start another story for detailed information (Rich, 2009). The present study does not take into account of these differences in its discussion.

Secondly, this research focuses on the functions of metonymy in news text organization. Its functions in other types of genres of written texts as well as spoken texts are also very important to fully revealing metonymy's textual functions. Because of this lack of comparative parameter, it is hard to decide which textual functions of metonymy are particular to the genre of news texts.

Thirdly, the data are collected mostly based on the researcher's own observation. Limited by the researcher's social, cultural as well as academic background, subjectivity both in data collection and analysis is unavoidable.

9.4 Suggestions for Future Study

As a way of structuring our everyday experience, metonymy plays an important part in structuring our language. In view of the limitations discussed in the previous section, the following areas are recommended for future study.

Firstly, to fully reveal the textual functions of metonymy, systematic and thorough investigation into its functions in organizing texts of different genres is strongly recommended. Even within the field of news texts, research can also be carried out to investigate the functions of metonymy in organizing more specific subgenres, such as how metonymy organizes hard news reports, features or news briefings.

Secondly, the principles guiding our selection of vehicles in metonymic expressions are also very important in analyzing news texts. Metonymy is highly culture-dependent and general principles are not the same in all language (Lakoff, 1987). Language users from different cultural background may have different knowledge structures that presuppose linguistic meanings and may structure text organization in different ways. Therefore, comparative studies should be carried out to find out whether metonymy functions differently in organizing texts among users from different speech communities.

On all accounts, the textual functions of metonymy are an area which deserves to be further explored.

References

Abelson, R. P. (1976). Script processing in attitude formation and decision-making. In J. S. Carroll & J. W. Payne, (Eds.), *Cognition and Social Behavior*. (pp. 33-46). Hillsdale, NJ: Lawrence Erlbaum.

Ahrens, K. (2010). *Politics, Gender and Conceptual Metaphors*. Basingstoke: Palgrave Macmillan.

Al-Shabab, O. S. (1988). Organizational and Textual Structuring of Radio News Discourse in English and Arabic. Unpublished doctoral dissertation. Aston University.

Al-Sharafi, A. G. M. (2004). *Textual Metonymy: A Semiotic Approach*. New York: Palgrave Macmillan.

Ariel, M. (1988). Referring and Accessibility. *Journal of Linguistics*, 24, 65-87.

Ariel, M. (1990). *Accessing Antecedents*. London: Routledge.

Ariel, M. (1991). The function of accessibility in a theory of grammar. *Journal of Pragmatics*, 16, 443-463.

Barcelona, A. (2000a). *Metaphor and Metonymy at the Crossroads: A Cognitive Perspective*. Berlin: Mouton de Gruyter.

Barcelona, A. (2000b). Introduction: The cognitive theory of metaphor and metonymy. In A. Barcelona, (Ed.), *Metaphor and Metonymy at the Crossroads: A Cognitive Perspective*. (pp. 1-15). Berlin/New York: Mouton de Gruyter.

Barcelona, A. (2000c). On the plausibility of claiming a metonymic motivation for conceptual metaphor. In A. Barcelona, (Ed.), *Metaphor and Metonymy at the Crossroads: A Cognitive Perspective*. (pp. 31-58). Berlin: Mouton de Gruyter.

Barcelona, A. (2002). Clarifying and applying the notions of metaphor and metonymy within cognitive linguistics: An update. In R. Dirve & R. Pörings, (Eds.), *Metaphor and Metonymy in Comparison and Contrast*. (pp. 207-208). Berlin/ New York: Mouton de Gruyter.

Barcelona, A. (2003). Metonymy in cognitive linguistics: An analysis and a few modest proposals. In H. Cuyckens, T. Berg, R. Dirven, & K. U. Panther, (Eds.), *Motivation in Language: Studies in Honor of Gunter Radden.* (pp. 223-255). Amsterdam/Philadelphia: John Benjamins.

Barcelona, A. (2004). Metonymy behind grammar: The motivation of the seemingly "irregular" grammatical behavior of English paragon names. In G. Radden & K. U. Panther, (Eds.), *Studies in Linguistic Motivation.* (pp. 357-374.) Berlin/New York: Mouton de Gruyter.

Barcelona, A. (2005). The multilevel operation of metonymy in grammar and discourse, with particular attention to metonymic chains. In F. J. Ruiz de Mendoza & M. S. Peña Cervel, (Eds.), *Cognitive Linguistics: Internal Dynamics and Interdisciplinary Interaction.* (pp. 313-352). Berlin/New York: Mouton de Gruyter.

Barcelona, A. (2007). The role of metonymy in meaning construction at discourse level. In G. Radden, K. M. Köpcke, T. Berg & P. Siemund, (Eds.), *Aspects of Meaning Construction.* (pp. 51-69). Amsterdam/Philadelphia: John Benjamins Publishing Company.

Barcelona, A. (2011). Reviewing the properties and prototype structure of metonymy. In R. Benczes, A. Barcelona & F. J. Ruiz de Mendoza, (Eds.), *Defining Metonymy in Cognitive Linguistics: Towards a Consensus View.* (pp. 7-60). Amsterdam/Philadelphia: John Benjamins Publishing Company.

Barnden, J. A. (2010). Metaphor and metonymy: Making their connections more slippery. *Cognitive Linguistics*, 21(1), 1-34.

Basilio, M. (2009). The role of metonymy in word formation. In K. U.

Panther, L. Thornburg & A. Barcelona, (Eds.), *Metonymy and Metaphor in Grammar.* (pp. 99-109). Amsterdam/Philadelphia: John Benjamins Publishing Company.

Bazerman, C. (1994). Systems of genres and the enhancement of social intentions. In A. Freeman & P. Medway, (Eds.), *Genre and New Rhetoric.* (pp. 79-101). London: Taylor and Francis.

Beaugrande R. & Dressler, W. (1981). *Introduction to Text Linguistics.* London: Longman.

Bell, A. (1991). *The Language of News Media.* Oxford: Blackwell.

Berkenkotter, C. & Huckin, T. N. (1995). *Genre Knowledge in Disciplinary Communication—Cognition/Culture/Power.* Hillsdale, NJ: Lawrence Erlbaum Associates.

Bhatia, V. K. (1993). *Analyzing Genre—Language Use in Professional Settings.* London: Longman.

Bhatia, V. K. (2004). *Worlds of Written Discourse.* New York: Continuum.

Bhatia, V. K. (2005). Generic patterns in promotional discourse. In H. Halmari & T. Virtanen, (Eds.), *Persuasion Across Genres.* (pp. 213-225). Amsterdam: Benjamins.

Bierwiaczonek, B. (2007). On formal metonymy. In K. Kosecke, (Ed.), *Perspectives on Metonymy: Proceedings of the International Conference "Perspectives on Metonymy".* (pp. 43-67). Frankfurt/Main: Peter Lang.

Billig, M. (1987). *Arguing and Thinking: A Rhetorical Approach to Social Psychology.* Cambridge: Cambridge University Press.

Billig, M. (2008). The language of critical discourse analysis: The case of nominalization. *Discourse Society*, 19, 783-799.

Billig, M. & Macmillan, K. (2005). Metaphor, idiom and ideology: The search for No Smoking Guns across time. *Discourse & Society*, 16 (4), 459-480.

Bobrow, D. G. & Norman, D. A. (1975). Some principles of memory schemata. In D. G. Bobrow, & A. M. Collins, (Eds.), *Representation and Understanding: Studies in Cognitive Science.* New York: Academic Press.

Bohn, W. (1984). Roman Jakobson's theory of metaphor and metonymy: An annotated bibliography. *Style*, 18, 534-550.

Brdar, M. (2007). Topic-continuity, metonymy and locative adverbials: A cognitive-functional account. *Suvremena Lingvistika*, 63, 13-29.

Brdar, M. & Brdar-Szabó, R. (2003). Metonymic coding of linguistic action in English, Croatian and Hungarian. In K. U. Panther & L. Thornburg, (Eds.), *Metonymy and Pragmatic Inferencing*. (pp. 241-266). Amsterdam/Philadelphia: John Benjamins Publishing Company.

Brdar, M. & Brdar-Szabó, R. (2009). The (non-) metonymic use of place names in English, German, Hungarian, and Croatian. In K. U. Panther, L. Thornburg & A. Barcelona, (Eds.), *Metonymy and Metaphor in Grammar*. (pp. 229-258). Amsterdam/Philadelphia: John Benjamins Publishing Company.

Brdar-Szabó, R. (2007). The role of metonymy in motivating cross-linguistic differences in the exploitation of stand-alone conditionals as indirect directives. In K. Kosecki, (Ed.), *Perspectives on Metonymy: Proceedings of the International Conference "Perspectives on Metonymy"*. (pp. 175-197). Frankfurt am Main: Peter Lang.

Bredin, H. (1984). Metonymy. *Poetics Today*, 5(1), 45-58.

Brown, G. & Yule, G. (1983). *Discourse Analysis*. Cambridge: Cambridge University Press.

Brown, P. & Levinson, S. (1987). *Politeness: Some Universals in Language Usage*. Cambridge: Cambridge University Press.

Bublitz, W. (1996). "I bought a freezer—you've bought a freezer—they've bought a freezer": Repetition as a text-building device. In C. Bazzanella, (Ed.), *Repetition in Dialogue*. (pp. 16-28). Tübingen: Niemeyer.

Buitkiene, J. (2005). Variability of Cohesive Devicesacross Registers. *Studies about Languages*, 7, 17-20.

Butler, C. S. (2003a). *Structure and Function: A Guide to Three Major Structural-functional Theories. Part 1 : Approaches to the Simplex Clause* (*Studies in Language Companion Series*, 63). Amsterdam/Philadelphia: John Benjamins.

Butler, C. S. (2003b). *Structure and Function: A Guide to Three Major Structural-functional Theories. Part 2 : From Clause to Discourse and Beyond* (*Studies in*

Language Companion Series, 64). Amsterdam/Philadelphia: John Benjamins.

Butler, C. S. (2006). Functionalist theories of language. In E. K. Brown, (Ed), *The Encyclopedia of Language and Linguistics* (2nd Edition), Vol. 4. (pp. 696-704). Oxford: Elsevier.

Bybee, J. (2003). *Structure and Function.* Amsterdam/Philadelphia: John Benjamins.

Bybee, J., Perkins, R. & Pagliuca, W. (1994). *The Evolution and the Grammar: Tense, Aspect, and Modality in the Languages of the World.* Chicago: The University of Chicago Press.

Campell, K. S. (1995). *Continuity and Cohesion: Theoretical Foundation of Document Design.* NJ: Lawrence Erlbaum.

Carter, R. & McCarthy, M. (1988). Lexis and discourse: vocabulary in use. In R. Carter & M. McCarthy, (Eds.), *Vocabulary and Language Teaching.* (pp. 201-220). London/New York: Longman.

Chafe, W. (1994). *Discourse, Consciousness, and Time.* Chicago: University of Chicago Press.

Charolles, M. & Kleiber, G. (1999). Associative anaphora and its interpretation. *Journal of Pragmatics*, 31, 307-311.

Charteris-Black, J. (2004). *Corpus Approaches to Critical Metaphor Analysis.* New York: Palgrave.

Chatman, S. (1978). *Story and Discourse: Narrative Structure in Fiction and Film.* Ithaca/London: Cornell University Press.

Chu, C. C. (1998). *A Discourse Grammar of Mandarin Chinese.* New York: Peter Lang Publishing.

Clark, H. H. & Haviland, S. E. (1977). Comprehension and the given-new contract. In R. Freedle, (Ed.), *Discourse Comprehension and Production.* (pp. 1-40). Norwood, NJ: Ablex.

Clark, H. H. (1977). Bridging. In P. N. Johnson-Laird & P. C. Wason, (Eds.), *Thinking: Readings in Cognitive Science.* (pp. 411-420). Cambridge: Cambridge University Press.

Clausner, T. C. & Croft, W. (1999). Domains and image schemas. *Cognitive Linguistics*, 1, 1-31.

Clayman, S. E. (1987). *Generating news: The international organization of news interviews.* Unpublished doctoral dissertation. University of California.

Conrad, S. (2002). Corpus linguistic approaches for discourse analysis. *Annual Review of Applied Linguistics*, 22, 75-95.

Cook, G. (1989). *Discourse.* Oxford: Oxford University Press.

Cornish, F. (1986). *Anaphoric Relations in English and French: A Discourse Perspective.* London: Croom Helm.

Cotter, C. (2001). Discourse and media. In D. Schiffrin, D. Tannen & H. E. Hamilton, (Eds.), *The Handbook of Discourse Analysis.* (pp. 416-436). Oxford: Blackwell.

Coulthard, M. (1985). *An Introduction to Discourse Analysis.* New York: Longman.

Coulthard. M. (1994). *Advances in Written Text Analysis.* London: Routledge.

Croft, W. (1993). The role of domains in the interpretation of metaphors and metonymies. *Cognitive Linguistics*, 4, 335-370.

Croft, W. (1995). Autonomy and functionalist linguistics. *Language*, 71, 490-532.

Croft, W. (2001). *Radical Construction Grammar: Syntactic Theory in Typological Perspective.* Oxford: Oxford University Press.

Croft, W. & Cruse, A. (2004). *Cognitive Linguistics.* Cambridge: Cambridge University Press.

Cruse, D. A. (1986). *Lexical Semantics.* Cambridge: Cambridge University Press.

Crystal, D. (1985). *A Dictionary of Linguistics and Phonetics.* New York: Basil Blackwell.

Crystal, D. & Davy, D. (1979). *Investigating English Style.* London: Longman.

Cuyckens, H., Berg, T., Dirven, R. & Panther, K. U. (2003). *Motivation in Language: Studies in Honor of Gunter Radden.* Amsterdam/Philadelphia: John Benjamins Publishing Company.

Danes, F. (1974). Functional sentence perspective and the organization of the text. In F. Danes, (Ed.), *Papers on Functional Sentence Perspective.* (pp. 106-128). Prague: Academia.

Dickson, S. V., Simmons, D. C. & Kameenui, E. J. (1995). *Text Organization and Its Relation to Reading Comprehension: A Synthesis of the Research (Technical Report*, No. 17). Eugene, OR: National Center to Improve the Tools of Educators.

Dik, S. (1978). *Functional Grammar.* London: Academic Press.

Dik, S. (1977). Inductivegeneralization in semantic change. In P. J. Hopper, (Ed.), *Studies in Descriptive and Historical Linguistics.* (pp. 283-300). Amsterdam/Philadelphia: John Benjamins Publishing Company.

Dik, S. C. (1989). *The Theory of Functional Grammar*, Vol. 1: *The Structure of the Clause.* Dordrecht: Foris.

Dirven, R. (1995). The construal of cause: The case of cause prepositions. In J. R. Taylor & R. E. MacLaury, (Eds.), *Language and the Cognitive Construal of the World.* (pp. 95-118). New York: Mouton de Gruyter.

Dirven, R. (1999). Conversion as a conceptual metonymy of event schemata. In Panther, K. & G. Radden, (Eds.), *Metonymy in Language and Thought.* (pp. 275-287). Amsterdam: John Benjamins Publishing Company.

Dirven, R. (2003). Metonymy and metaphor: Different mental strategies of conceptualization. In R. Dirven & R. Pörings, (Eds.), *Metaphor and Metonymy in Comparison and Contra*st. (pp. 75-111). Berlin/New York: Mouton de Gruyter.

Dirven, R. & Pörings, R. (2003). *Metaphor and Metonymy in Comparison and Contra*st. Berlin/ New York: Mouton de Gruyter.

Dirven, R., Frank, R. & Pütz, M. (2003). (Eds.), *Cognitive Models in Language and Thought: Ideology, Metaphors and Meanings.* Berlin/New York: Mouton de Gruyter.

Dirven, R. & Verspoor, M. (2004). *Cognitive Exploration of Language and Linguistics* (2nd Edition). Amsterdam/Philadelphia: John Benjamins Publishing Company.

Eggins, S. (1994.) *An Introduction to Systemic Functional Linguistics.* London: Continuum.

Eiler, M. A. (1986). Thematic distribution as a heuristic for written discourse function. In B. Couture, (Ed.), *Functional Approaches to Writing Research*

Perspectives. (pp. 49-68). London: Frances Pinter.

Erku, F. & Gundel, J. K. (1987). The pragmatics of indirect anaphors. In J. Verschueren & M. Bertuccelli-Papi, (Eds.), *The Pragmatic Perspective*. (pp. 533-546). Amsterdam: John Benjamins.

Fairclough, N. (1992). *Discourse and Social Change*. Cambridge: Polity Press.

Fairclough, N. (1993). Critical discourse analysis and the commodification of public discourse. *Discourse and Society*, 4(2), 133-168.

Fairclough, N. (1995). *Critical Discourse Analysis: The Critical Study of Language*. London: Longman.

Fairclough, N. (2003). *Analyzing Discourse*. London: Routledge.

Fauconnier, G. (1997). *Mappings in Thought and Language*. Cambridge: Cambridge University Press.

Fauconnier, G. (1998). *Mental Spaces: Aspects of Meaning Construction in Natural Language*. New York: Cambridge University Press.

Fauconnier, G. & Turner, M. (1998). Conceptual integration networks. *Cognitive Science*, 22(2), 133-187.

Fauconnier, G. & Turner, M. (2002). *The Way We Think: Conceptual Blending and the Mind's Hidden Complexities*. New York: Basic Books.

Fawcett, R. (2008). *Invitation to Systemic Functional Linguistics through the Cardiff Grammar: An Extension and Simplification of Halliday's Systemic Functional Grammar*. London: Equinox Publishing Ltd.

Feyaerts, K. (1999). Metonymic hierarchies: The conceptualization of stupidity in German idiomatic expressions. In K. U. Panther & G. Radden, (Eds.), *Metonymy in Language and Thought*. (pp. 309-332). Amsterdam/Philadelphia: John Benjamins Publishing Company.

Feyaerts, K. (2000). Refining the inheritance hypothesis: Interaction between metaphoric and metonymic hierarchies. In A. Barcelona, (Ed.), *Metaphor and Metonymy at the Crossroads: A Cognitive Perspective*. (pp. 59-78). Berlin/New York: Mouton de Gruyter.

Fillmore, C. (1975). Analternative to checklist theories of meaning. In *Proceedings of the 1st Annual Meeting of the Berkeley Linguistics Society*. (pp. 123-131). Berkeley: Berkeley Linguistics Society.

Fillmore, C. (1977). Scenes-and-Frames semantics. In A. Zampolli, (Ed.), *Linguistic Structure Processing*. (pp. 55-81). Amsterdam/Philadelphia: John Benjamins Publishing Company.

Fillmore, C. (1982). Frame semantics. In Linguistic Society of Korea, (Ed.), *Linguistics in the Morning Calm*. (pp. 111-138). Seoul: Hanshin Publishing Company.

Fillmore, C. (1985). Frames and the semantics of understanding. *Quaderni di Semantica*, 6, 222-254.

Fillmore, C. & Atkins, B. T. S. (1992). Towards a frame-based organization of the lexicon: The semantics of RISK and its neighbors. In A. Lehrer & E. Kittay, (Eds.), *Frames, Fields, and Contrast: New Essays in Semantics and Lexical Organization*. (pp. 75-102). Hillsdale, NJ: Lawrence Erlbaum.

Fillmore, C. & Atkins, B. T. S. (1994): Starting where the dictionaries stop: The challenge for computational lexicography. In B. T. S. Atkins & A. Zampolli, (Eds.), *Computational Approaches to the Lexicon*. (pp. 349-393). Oxford: Oxford University Press.

Fletcher, C. R. (1994). Levels of representation in memory for discourse. In M. A. Gernsbacher, (Ed.), *Handbook of Psycholinguistics*. (pp. 589-607). San Diego: Academic Press.

Fowler, R. (1991). *Language in the News: Discourse and Ideology in the Press*. London: Routledge.

Francis, G. (1989). Thematic selection and distribution in written discourse. *Word*, 40(1-2), 201-221.

Fried, M. & Östman, J. O. (2004). *Construction Grammar in a Cross-Language Perspective*. Amsterdam/Philadelphia: John Benjamins Publishing Company.

Fries, P. H. (1983). On the status of theme in English: Arguments from discourse. In J. S. Petofi & E. Sozer, (Eds.), *Micro and Macro Connexity of Texts*. (pp. 116-152). Hamburg: Helmut Baske.

Gee, J. P. (1996). *Social Linguistics and Literacies: Ideology in Discourse*. London: Taylor & Francis.

Gee, J. P. (1999). *An Introduction to Discourse Analysis: Theory and Method*. London/New York: Routledge.

Geeraerts, D. (1997). *Diachronic Prototypes Semantics*. Oxford: Oxford University Press.

Gernsbacher, M. A. & Givón, T. (1995). *Coherence in Spontaneous Text*. Amsterdam/Philadelphia: John Benjamins Publishing Company.

Gibbs, R. W. Jr. (1994a). Figurative thought and language. In M. Gernsbacher, (Ed.), *Handbook of Psycholinguistics*. (pp. 411-466). San Diego: Academic Press.

Gibbs, R. W. Jr. (1994b). *The Poetics of Mind: Figurative Thought, Language and Understanding*. Cambridge: Cambridge University Press.

Gibbs, R. W. Jr. (1999). Speaking and thinking with metonymy. In K. U. Panther & G. Radden, (Eds.), *Metonymy in Language and Thought*. (pp. 61-76). Amsterdam/Philadelphia: John Benjamins Publishing Company.

Gibbs, R. W. Jr. & Colston, H. L. (2006). Figurative Language. In M. J. Traxler & M. A. Gernsbacher, (Eds.), *Handbook of Psycholinguistics* (2nd Edition). (pp. 835-862). Amsterdam/Boston: Elsevier.

Givón, T. (1975). Cause and control: On the semantics of interpersonal manipulation. *Syntax and Semantics*, 4, 59-89.

Givón, T. (1979). From discourse to syntax: Grammar as a processing strategy. In T. Givón, (Ed.), *Syntax and Semantics*, Vol. 12. (pp. 81-112). New York: Academic Press.

Givón, T. (1983). Topic continuity in discourse: An introduction. In T. Givón, (Eds.), *Topic Continuity In Discourse: A Quantitative Cross-Language Study*. (pp. 5-41). Amsterdam/Philadelphia: John Benjamins Publishing Company.

Givón, T. (1992). The grammar of referential coherence as mental processing instructions. *Linguistics*, 30, 5-56.

Givón, T. (1995). Coherence in text vs. coherence in mind. In M. A. Gernsbacher & T. Givón, (Eds.), *Coherence in Spontaneous Text*. (pp. 59-115). Amsterdam/ Philadelphia: John Benjamins Publishing Company.

Givón, T. (2002). *Bio-Linguistics*. Amsterdam: John Benjamins Publishing Company.

Goatly, A. (1997). *The language of Metaphors*. London: Routeledge.

Goldberg, A. E. (1995). *Constructions at Work: The Nature of Generalization in Language.* Oxford: Oxford University Press.

Goldberg, A. E. (2003). Constructions: A new theoretical approach to language. *TRENDS in Cognitive Sciences*, 7(5), 219-224.

Goodin, G. & Perkins, K. (1982). Discourse analysis and the art of coherence. *College English*, 44, 57-63.

Goosens, L. (1990). Metaphtonymy: The interaction of metaphor and metonymy in figurative expressions for linguistic action. *Cognitive Linguistics*, 1, 323-340.

Goosens, L. (1999). Metonymic bridges in modal shifts. In K. U. Panther & G. Radden, (Eds.), *Metonymy in Language and Thought.* (pp. 193-211). Amsterdam/Philadelphia: John Benjamins Publishing Company.

Goosens, L. (2000). Patterns of meaning extension, "parallel chaining", subjectification, and modal shifts. In A. Barcelona, (Ed.), *Metaphor and Metonymy at the Crossroads.* (pp. 149-169). Berlin: Mouton de Gruyter.

Goutsos, D. (1997). *Modeling Discourse Topic: Sequential Relations and Strategies in Expository Text.* Norwood, NJ: Ablex.

Gradečak-Erdeljić, T. & Milić, G. (2011). Metonymy at the crossroads: A case of euphemisms and dysphemisms. In R. Benczes, A. Barcelona & F. J. Ruiz de Mendoza Ibáñez, (Eds.), *Defining Metonymy in Cognitive Linguistics: Towards a Consensus View.* (pp. 147-165). Amsterdam/Philadelphia: John Benjamins Publishing Company.

Grady, J. (1997). Foundations of Meaning: Primary Metaphors and Primary Scenes. Berkeley: University of California.

Graustein, G. & Thiele, W. (1987). *Properties of English Texts.* Leipzig: VEB Verlag Enzyklopädie.

Greatbatch, D. (1986). Aspects of topicalorganization in news interviews: The use of agenda shifting procedures by interviewees. *Media, Culture and Society*, 8, 441-455.

Green, G. M. (1979). *Organization, Goals, and Comprehensibility in Narratives: News Writing, a Case Study* (*Technical Report*, No. 132). University of Illinois: Center for the study of reading.

Grimes, J. (1975). *The Thread of Discourse*. The Hague: Mouton.

Halliday, M. A. K. (1973). *Explorations in the Functions of Language*. London: Edward Arnold.

Halliday, M. A. K. (1978). *Language as Social Semiotic: The Social Interpretation of Language and Meaning*. London: Edward Arnold.

Halliday, M. A. K. (1994). *An Introduction to Functional Grammar* (2nd Edition). London: Edward Arnold.

Halliday, M. A. K. & Hasan, R. (1976). *Cohesion in English*. London: Longman

Halliday, M. A. K. & Hasan, R. (1985). *Language, Context and Text: A Social Semiotic Perspective*. Geelong, Vic.: Deakin University Press.

Halliday, M. A. K. & Matthiessen, C. M. I. M. (1999). *Construing Experience through Meaning: A Language-based Approach to Cognition*. London: Continuum.

Halliday, M. A. K. & Matthiessen, C. M. I. M. (2004). *An Introduction to Functional Grammar* (3rd Edition). London: Edward Arnold.

Hasan, R. (1984). Coherence and cohesive harmony. In J. Flood, (Ed.), *Understanding Reading Comprehension*. (pp. 181-219). Delaware: International Reading Association.

Hawkins, J. (1978). *Definiteness and Indefiniteness: A Study in Reference and Grammaticality Prediction*. London: Croom Helm.

Heine, B. (1995). Agent-oriented vs. epistemic modality: Some observations on German modals. In J. Bybee & S. Fleischman, (Eds.), *Modality and Grammar in Discourse*. (pp. 17-53). Amsterdam: John Benjamins Publishing Company.

Hernandez, L. P. & Ruiz de Mendoza, F. J. I. (2002). Grounding, semantic motivation, and conceptual interaction in indirect directive speech acts. *Journal of Pragmatics*, 34, 259-284.

Heyvaert, L. (2003). *A Cognitive-Functional Approach to Nominalization in English*. Berlin/New York: Mouton de Gruyter.

Hilpert, M. (2006a). Keeping an eye on the data: Metonymies and their patterns. In A. Stefanowitsch & S. T. Gries, (Eds.), *Corpus-based approaches to metaphor and metonymy*. (pp. 123-151). Berlin/New York: Mouton de

Gruyter.

Hilpert, M. (2006b). Chained metonymies. In J. Newman & S. A. Rice, (Eds.), *Experimental and Empirical Methods in Cognitive/Functional Research*. (pp. 1-12). Stanford: CSLI Publications.

Hobbs, J. R. (1979). Coherence and Co-reference. *Cognitive Science*, 3, 67-90.

Hobbs, J. R., M. E. Stickel, D. E. Appelt & P. Martin. (1993). Interpretation as abduction. *Artificial Intelligence*, 63, 69-142.

Hoey, M. P. (1983a). *On the Surface of Discourse*. London: George Allen & Unwin.

Hoey, M. P. (1983b). Three metaphors for examining the semantic organization of monologue. *Analysis: Quaderni di Anglistica*, 1, 27-54.

Hoey, M. P. (1986a). Overlapping patterns of discourse organization and their implications for clause relational analysis in problem-solution texts. In C. R. Cooper & S. Greenbaum, (Eds.), *Studying Writing: Linguistic Approaches* (*Written Communication Annual* 1). (pp. 187-214). Beverly Hills, London, New Delhi: Sage Publications.

Hoey, M. P. (1986b). The discourse colony: A preliminary study of a neglected discourse type. In M. Coulthard, (Ed.), *Talking about Text: Studies Presented to David Brazil on his Retirement*. (pp. 1-26). Birmingham: English Language Research, University of Birmingham.

Hoey, M. P. (1988). Writing to meet the reader's needs: text patterning and reading strategies. *Trondheim Papers in Applied Linguistics*, 4, 51-73.

Hoey, M. P. (1991). *Patterns of Lexis in Text*. Oxford: Oxford University Press.

Hoey, M. P. (2001). *Textual Interaction: An Introduction to Written Discourse Analysis*. London/New York: Routledge.

Horie, K. & Comrie, B. (2000). Introduction. In K. Horie, (Ed.), *Complementation* (*Cognitive and Functional Perspectives*) (*Converging Evidence in Language and Communication Research*, 1). (pp. 1-10). Amsterdam/Philadelphia: John Benjamins Publishing Company.

Huang, Y. (1994). *The Pragmatics of Anaphora*. Cambridge: Cambridge University Press.

Hunston, S. (2001). Colligation, lexis, pattern and text. In M. Scott & G.

Thompson, (Eds.), *Patterns of Text: In Honour of Michael Hoey.* (pp. 13-33). Amsterdam/ Philadelphia: John Benjamins Publishing Company.

Jakobson, R. (2003). The metaphoric and metonymic poles. In R. Dirven & R. Pörings, (Eds.), *Metaphor and Metonymy in Comparison and Contrast.* (pp. 41-48). Berlin/New York: Mouton de Gruyter.

Johnson, M. (1987). *The Body in the Mind: The Bodily Basis of Meaning, Imagination, and Reason.* Chicago: University of Chicago Press.

Katz, A. N., Cacciari, C., Gibbs, R. W. & Turner, M. (1998). *Figurative Language and Thought.* New York: Oxford University Press.

Kintsch, W. (1974). *The Representation of Meaning in Memory.* Hillsdale, NJ: Lawrence Erlbaum.

Kintsch, W. (1988). The Role of Knowledge in Discourse Comprehension: A Construction-Integration Model. *Psychological Review*, 95(2), 163-182.

Kintsch, W. & van Dijk, T. A. (1978). Toward a model of text comprehension and production. *Psychological Review*, 85, 363-394.

Koch, P. (1999). Frame and Contiguity. In K. U. Panther & G. Radden, (Eds.), *Metonymy in Language and Thought.* (pp. 139-167). Amsterdam/ Philadelphia: John Benjamins Publishing Company.

Koch, P. (2001). Metonymy: Unity in diversity. *Journal of Historical Pragmatics*, 2, 201-244.

Koch, P. (2004). Metonymy between pragmatics, reference, and diachrony. *Metaphorik*, 7, 6-54.

Kornetzki, A. (2012). *Contrastive Analysis of News Text Types in Russian, British and American Business Online and Print Media.* Berlin: Frank & Timme.

Kövecses, Z. (2002). *Metaphor: a Practical Introduction.* Oxford/New York: Oxford University Press.

Kövecses, Z. & Radden, G. (1998). Metonymy: Developing a cognitive linguistic view. *Cognitive Linguistics*, 9(1), 37-77.

Kronrod, A. & Engel, O. (2001). Accessibility theory and referring expression in newspaper headlines. *Journal of Pragmatics*, 33, 683-699.

Kwiatknowska, A. (2007). Pre-linguistic and Non-linguistic metonymy. In K. Kosecke, (Ed.), *Perspectives on Metonymy: Proceedings of the International*

Conference "Perspectives on Metonymy". (pp. 297-307). Frankfurt am Main: Peter Lang

Lakoff, G. (1987). *Women, Fire, and Dangerous Things.* Chicago: The University of Chicago Press.

Lakoff, G. (1990). The invariance hypothesis: Is abstract reason based on image-schemas? *Cognitive Linguistics*, 1, 39-74.

Lakoff, G. (1993). The contemporary theory of metaphor. In A. Ortony, (Ed.), *Metaphor and Thought.* (pp. 302-351). Cambridge: Cambridge University Press.

Lakoff, G. (1996). *Moral Politics: What Conservatives Know That Liberals Don't.* Chicago: Chicago University Press.

Lakoff, G. (2002). *Moral Politics: How Liberals and Conservatives Think.* Chicago: The University of Chicago Press.

Lakoff, G. (2004). *Don't Think of an Elephant: Know Your Values and Frame Your Debate.* White River Junction, VT: Chelsea Green.

Lakoff, G. & M. Johnson. (1980). *Metaphors We Live by.* Chicago: University of Chicago Press.

Lakoff, G. & M. Johnson. (1999). *Philosophy in the Flesh: The Embodied Mind and Its Challenge to Western Thought.* New York: Basic Book.

Lakoff, G. & M. Turner, (1989). *More Than Cool Reason: A Field Guide to Poetic Metaphor.* Chicago: University of Chicago Press.

Langacker, R. (1984). Active zones. *Proceedings of the Annual Meeting of the Berkeley Linguistics Society*, 10, 172-188.

Langacker, R. (1987). *Foundations of Cognitive Grammar*, Vol. I: *Theoretical Prerequisites.* Stanford: Stanford University Press.

Langacker, R. (1990). *Concept, Image, Symbol.* Berlin: Mouton de Gruyter.

Langacker, R. W. (1991). *Foundations of Cognitive Grammar*, Vol. II: *Descriptive application.* Stanford: Stanford University Press.

Langacker, R. W. (1993). Reference-point Construction. *Cognitive Linguistics*, 1, 1-38.

Langacker, R. W. (1999). *Grammar and Conceptualization.* Berlin/New York: Moulton de Gruyter.

Langacker, R. W. (2004). Metonymy in Grammar. *Journal of Foreign Languages*, 4, 2-24.

Langacker, R. W. (2009). *Investigations in Cognitive Grammar*. Berlin/New York: Mouton de Gruyter.

Leech, G. (1983). *Principles of Pragmatics*. London: Longman.

Leung, S. K. (2002). *Causation & Causality: Two Mirrors of the Cause*. London: Empiricus Books.

Liebert, W. A., Redeker, G. & Waugh, L. (1997). *Discourse and Perspective in Cognitive Linguistics*. Amsterdam/Philadelphia: John Benjamins Publishing Company.

Lodge, D. (1977). *The Modes of Modern Writing: Metaphor, Metonymy and the Typology of Modern Literature*. London: Edward Arnold.

Longacre, R. E. (1983). *The Grammar of Discourse*. New York: Plenum Press.

Louwerse, M. M., McCarthy, P. M., McNamar, D. S. & Graesser, A. C. (2004). Variation in language and cohesion across written and spoken registers. In K. Forbus, D. Gentner & T. Regier, (Eds.), *Proceedings of the 26th Annual Meeting of the Cognitive Science Society*. (pp. 843-848). Mahwah, NJ: Erlbaum.

Lyons, J. (1981). *Language, Meaning and Context*. London: Penguin.

Lyons, J. (1995). *Linguistics Semantics: An Introduction*. Cambridge: Cambridge University Press.

Mann, W. C. & S. A. Thompson. (1987). Rhetorical structure theory: A theory of text organization. *IPRA Papers in Pragmatics*, 1, 1-21.

Mann, W. C. & S. A. Thompson. (1988). Rhetorical structure theory: Toward a functional theory of text organization. *Text*, 8(3), 243-281.

Martin, J. R. (1985). Process and text: two aspects of human semiosis. In J. D. Benson & W. S. Greaves, (Eds.), *Systemic Perspectives on Discourse: Selected Theoretical Papers from the 9th International Systemic Congress*. (pp. 248-274). Norwood, NJ: Ablex.

Martin, J. R. (1992). *English Text: System and Structure*. Amsterdam/Philadelphia: John Benjamins Publishing Company.

Martin, J. R. (1993). A contextual theory of language. In B. Cope & M.

Kalantzis, (Eds.), *The Powers of Literacy—A Genre Approach to Teaching Writing.* (PP. 116-136). Pittsburgh: University of Pittsburgh Press.

Martin, J. R., Christie, F. & Rothery, J. (1987). Social processes in education: A reply to Sawyer and Watson (and others). In I. Reid, (Ed.), *The Place of Genre in Learning: Current Debates.* (pp. 46-57). Geelong, Australia: Deakin University Press.

Mastui, T. (2000). *Bridging and Relevance.* Amsterdam/ Philadelphia: John Benjamins Publishing Company.

McCarthy, M. (1991). *Discourse Analysis for Language Teachers.* Cambridge: Cambridge University Press.

McEnery, T. & A. Wilson (2001). *Corpus Linguistics: An Introduction.* Edinburgh University Press.

Mencher, M. (2003). *News Reporting and Writing* (9th Edition). New York: McGraw-Hill Education.

Mey, J. (1993). *Pragmatics: An Introduction.* Oxford: Blackwell Publishers Ltd.

Meyer, B. J. F. (1975). *The Organization of Prose and its Effects on Memory.* Amsterdam: North Holland.

Miller, C. R. (1984). Genre as social action. *Quarterly Journal of Speech*, 70, 157-178.

Minsky, M. (1975). A framework for representing knowledge. In P. H. Winston, (Ed.), *The Psychology of Computer Vision.* (pp. 211-277). New York: McGraw Hill.

Nikiforidou, K. (1999). Nominalizations, metonymy, and lexicographic practice. In L. G. Stadler & C. Eyrich, (Eds.), *Issue in Cognitive Linguistics.* (pp. 141-163). Berlin/New York: Mouton de Gruyter.

Norrick, N. R. (1981). *Semiotic Principles in Semantic Theory.* Amsterdam: John Benjamins Publishing Company.

Nunberg, G. (1995). Transfer of meanings. *Journal of Semantics*, 12, 109-132.

Nuyts, J. (2005). Brothers in arms? On the relations between Cognitive and Functional Linguistics. In F. J. Ruiz de Mendoza Ibáñez & M. S. Peña Cervel, (Eds.), *Cognitive Linguistics. Internal Dynamics and Interdisciplinary Interaction.* (pp. 69-100). Berlin/New York: Mouton de Gruyter.

Östman, J. O. & Virtanen, T. (1995). *Discourse analysis.* Amsterdam: John Benjamins Publishing Company.

Panther, K. U. (2005). The role of conceptual metonymy in meaning construction. In F. J. I. Ruiz de Mendoza & M. S. Peña Cervel, (Eds.), *Cognitive Linguistics: Internal Dynamics and Interdisciplinary Interaction.* (pp. 353-386). Berlin/New York: Mouton de Gruyter.

Panther, K. U. & Radden, G. (1999). *Metonymy in Language and Thought.* Amsterdam/Philadelphia: John Benjamins Publishing Company.

Panther, K. U. & Radden, G. (2005). Metonymy. In J. Verschueren & J. O., Östman, (Eds.), *Handbook of Pragmatics.* (pp. 1-14). Amsterdam/Philadelphia: John Benjamins Publishing Company.

Panther, K. U. & Thornburg, L. (1998). A cognitive approach to inferencing in conversation. *Journal of Pragmatics*, 30, 755-769.

Panther, K. U. & Thornburg, L. (1999). The potentiality for actuality metonymy in English and Hungarian. In K. Panther & G. Radden, (Eds.), *Metonymy in Language and Thought.* (pp. 333-357). Amsterdam/Philadelphia: John Benjamins Publishing Company.

Panther, K. U. & Thornburg, L. (2000). The EFFECT FOR CAUSE metonymy in English grammar. In A. Barcelona, (Ed.), *Metaphor and Metonymy at the Crossroads.* (pp. 215-232). Berlin: Mouton de Gruyter.

Panther, K. U. & Thornburg, L. (2001). A conceptual analysis of English *-er* nominals. In M. Pütz, S. Niemeyer & R. Dirven, (Eds.), *Applied Cognitive Linguistics* II: *Language Pedagogy.* (pp. 149-200). Berlin/New York: Mouton de Gruyter.

Panther, K. U. & Thornburg, L. (2002). The roles of metaphor and metonymy in English *-er* nominals. In R. Dirven & R. Pörings, (Eds.), *Metaphor and Metonymy in Comparison and Contrast.* (pp. 279-319). Berlin/New York: Mouton de Gruyter.

Panther, K. U. & Thornburg, L. (2003a). *Metonymy and Pragmatic Inferencing.* Amsterdam/Philadelphia: John Benjamins Publishing Company.

Panther, K. U. & Thornburg, L. (2003b). Introduction: On the nature of conceptual metonymy. In K. U. Panther & L. Thornburg, (Eds.),

Metonymy and Pragmatic Inferencing. (pp. 1-20). Amsterdam/Philadelphia: John Benjamins Publishing Company.

Panther, K. U. & Thornburg, L. (2003c). Metonymies as natural inference and activation schemas. In K. U. Panther & L. Thornburg, (Eds.), *Metonymy and Pragmatic Inferencing*. (pp. 127-147). Amsterdam/Philadelphia: John Benjamins Publishing Company.

Panther, K. U. & Thornburg, L. (2007). Metonymy. In D. Geeraerts & H. Cuyckens, (Eds.), *The Oxford Handbook of Cognitive Linguistics*. (pp. 236-263). Oxford: Oxford University Press.

Panther, K. U., Thornburg, L. & Barcelona, A. (2009). *Metonymy and Metaphor in Grammar*. Amsterdam/Philadelphia: John Benjamins Publishing Company.

Papafragou, A. (1996a). Figurative language and the semantics-pragmatics distinction. *Language and Literature*, 5(1), 179-193.

Papafragou, A. (1996b). On metonymy. *Lingua*, 99, 169-195.

Peirsman, Y. & Geeraerts, D. (2006). Metonymy as a prototypical category. *Cognitive Linguistics*, 3, 269-316.

Pike, K. L. & Pike, E. G. (1977). *Grammatical Analysis*. Dallas: Summer Institute of Linguistics and the University of Texas.

Prince, E. F. (1978). On the function of existential presupposition in discourse. In Farks, D. et al., (Eds.), *Papers from the 14th Regional Meeting of the Chicago Linguistics Society*. (pp. 223-255). Chicago: Chicago Linguistic Society.

Prince, E. F. (1981). On the inferencing of indefinite *this* NP's. In A. K. Joshi, B. L. Webber & I. A. Sag, (Eds.), *Elements of Discourse Understanding*. (pp. 231-250). Cambridge: Cambridge University Press.

Quirk, R. et al. (1985). *A Comprehensive Grammar of the English Language*. London: Longman.

Radden, G. (2000). How metonymic are metaphors? In A. Barcelona, (Ed.), *Metaphor and Metonymy at the Crossroads: A Cognitive Perspective*. (pp. 93-108). Burlin/New York: Mounton de Gruyter.

Radden, G. & Kövecses, Z. (1999). Towards a theory of metonymy. In K. U. Panther & G. Radden, (Eds.), *Metonymy in Language and Thought*. (pp.

17-59). Amsterdam/Philadelphia: John Benjamins Publishing Company.

Reihart, T. (1980). Conditions for text coherence. *Poetics Today*, 1, 161-180.

Reinhart, T. (1983). *Anaphora and Semantic Interpretation.* Chicago: University of Chicago Press.

Renkema, J. (2004/2009). *Introduction to Discourse Studies.* Amsterdam/Philadelphia: John Benjamins Publishing Company.

Rich, C. (2009). *Writing and Reporting News: A Coaching Method (Fifth Edition).* Beijing: China Renmin University Press.

Riffaterre, M. (1990). *Fictional Truth.* Baltimore: John Hopkins University Press.

Ruiz, J. H. (2011). The role of metonymy in complex tropes: Cognitive operations and pragmatic implications. In R. Benczes, A. Barcelona & F. H. I. Ruiz de Mendoza, (Ed.), *Defining Metonymy in Cognitive Linguistics: Towards a Consensus View.* (pp. 167-197). Amsterdam/Philadelphia: John Benjamins Publishing Company.

Ruiz de Mendoza I. F. H. (1997). Cognitive and pragmatic aspects of metonymy. *Cuadernos de Filologia Inglesa*, 612, 161-178.

Ruiz de Mendoza, I. F. H. (2000). The role of mappings and domains in understanding metonymy. In A. Barcelona, (Ed.), *Metaphor and Metonymy at the Crossroads: A Cognitive Perspective.* (pp. 109-132). Berlin/New York: Mouton de Gruyter.

Ruiz de Mendza, I. F. H &J. L. O. Campo. (2002). *Metonymy, Grammar, and Communication*, Granada: Editorial Comares.

Ruiz de Mendoza, I. F. H. & Diez, O. I. V. (2002). Patterns of conceptual interaction. In R. Dirven & R. Pörings, (Eds.), *Metaphor and Metonymy in Comparison and Contrast.* (pp. 489-532). Berlin/New York: Mouton de Gruyter.

Ruiz de MendozaI. F. H. & Hernandez, L. P. (2001). Metonymy and the grammar: Motivation, constraints and interaction. *Language & Communication*, 21, 321-357.

Ruiz de Mendoza I. F. H. & Hernandez, L. P. (2003). Cognitive operations and pragmatic implication. In K. U. Panther & L. Thornburg, (Eds.),

Metonymy and Pragmatic Inferencing. (pp. 23-49). Amsterdam/Philadelphia: John Benjamins Publishing Company.

Ruiz de Mendoza, I. F. J. & Otal, C. J. L. (2002). *Metonymy, Grammar, and Communication.* Granada: Comares.

Saeed, J. I. (1997). *Semantics.* Cambridge/Oxford: Blackwell.

Sanford, A. & Garrod, S. C. (1981). *Understanding Written Language: Exploration in Comprehension beyond the Sentence.* Chichester: John Wiley.

Sanders, T. & Spooren, W. (1999). Communicative intentions and coherence relations. In W. Bublitz, U. Lenk & E. Ventola, (Eds.), *Coherence in Spoken and Written Discourse: How to Create It and How to Describe It.* (pp. 235-250). Amsterdam/Philadelphia: John Benjamins Publishing Company.

Searle, J. R. (1979). *Expression and Meaning.* Cambridge: Cambridge University Press.

Searle, J. R. (1969). *Speech Acts: An Essay in the Philosophy of Language.* Cambridge: Cambridge University Press.

Seto, K. (1999). Distinguishing Metonymy from Synecdoche. In K. U. Panther & G. Radden, (Eds.), *Metonymy in Language and Thought.* (pp. 91-120). Amsterdam/Philadelphia: John Benjamins Publishing Company.

Sinclair, J. (1998). The lexical item. In E. Weigand, (Ed.), *Contrastive Lexical Semantics.* (pp. 1-24). Amsterdam/Philadelphia: John Benjamins Publishing Company.

Sinclair, J. (1991). *Corpus, Concordance, Collocation.* New York: Oxford University Press

Sinclair, J. (2003). *Reading Concordances: An Introduction.* London: Pearson Longman.

Song, N. S. (1997). Metaphor and metonymy. In R. Carston & S. Uchida, (Eds.), *Relevance Theory: Applications and Implications.* (pp. 87-104). Amsterdam/Philadelphia: John Benjamins Publishing Company.

Sperber, D. & Wilson, D. (1995). *Relevance: Communication and Cognition.* Oxford: Blackwell.

Stallard, D. (1993). Two kinds of metonymy. In L. Schnbert, (Ed.), *Proceedings of the 31st Annual Meeting of the Association for Computational Linguistics.*

(pp. 87-94). Columbus, OH: Ohio State University Press.

Steen, G. (1994). *Understanding Metaphor in Literature.* London: Longman.

Steen, G. (2005). Metonymy. In D. Herman, M. Jahn & M. L. Ryan, (Eds.), *Routledge Encyclopedia of Narrative Theory.* (pp. 193-194). London/New York: Routledge.

Stefanowitsch, A. (2003). A construction-based approach to indirect speech acts. In K. U. Panther & L. Thornburg, (Eds.), *Metonymy and Pragmatic Inferencing.* (pp. 105-125). Amsterdam/Philadelphia: John Benjamins Publishing Company.

Stefanowitsch, A. & Gries, S. T. (2006). *Corpus-based Approaches to Metaphor and Metonymy.* Berlin/New York: Mouton de Gruyter.

Stirling, L. (1996). Metonymy and Anaphora. *Belgian Journal of Linguistics*, 10, 69-88.

Stokes, N. (2004). *Applications of Lexical Cohesion Analysis in the Topic Detection and Tracking Domain.* Unpublished doctoral dissertation. University College Dublin.

Stoddard, S. (1991). *Text and Texture: Patterns of Cohesion.* Norwood, NJ: Ablex.

Swales, J. M. (1990). *Genre Analysis: English in Academic and Research Settings.* Cambridge: Cambridge University Press.

Sweetser, E. (1990). *From Etymology to Pragmatics: Metaphorical and Cultural Aspects of Semantic Structure.* Cambridge: Cambridge University Press.

Talmy, L. (1985). Lexicalization patterns. In T. Shopen, (Ed.), *Language Typology and Syntactic Description*, Vol. 3: *Grammatical Categories and the Lexicon.* (pp. 57-149). Cambridge: Cambridge University Press.

Talmy, L. (2000). *Toward a Cognitive Semantics: Concept Structuring Systems.* Cambridge, MA: MIT Press.

Tanskanen, S. K. (2006). *Collaborating towards Coherence: Lexical Cohesion in English Discourse.* Amsterdam/Philadelphia: John Benjamins Publication Company.

Taylor, J. R. (1995). *Linguistic Categorization: Prototypes in Linguistic Theory* (2nd Edition). Oxford: Oxford University Press.

Taylor, J. R. (2002). *Cognitive Grammar.* Oxford: Oxford University Press.

Thompson, G. (1994). Aspects of cohesion in monologue. *Applied Linguistics*, 15

(1), 58-75.

Thompson, G. (2008). *Introducing Functional Grammar*. Beijing: Foreign Language Teaching and Research Press.

Traugott, E. C. (1985). On regularity in semantic change. *Journal of Literary Semantics*, 14, 155-173.

Traugott, E. C. & König, E. (1991). The semantics-pragmatics of grammaticalization revisited. In E. C. Traugott & B. Heine, (Eds.), *Approaches to Grammaticalization*, Vol. 1. (pp. 189-218). Amsterdam: Benjamins.

Tsui, A. B. (1991). Sequencing rules and coherence in discourse. *Journal of Pragmatics*, 15(2), 111-129.

Thornburg, L. & Panther, K. U. (1997). Speech act metonymies. In W. A, Liebert, G. Redeker & L. Waugh, (Eds.), *Discourse and Perspective in Cognitive Linguistics*. (pp. 205-219). Amsterdam/Philadelphia: John Benjamins Publishing Company.

Tomasello, M. (1998). Introduction: A cognitive-functional perspective on language structure. In M. Tomasello, (Ed.), *The New Psychology of Language (Cognitive and Functional Approaches to Language Structure)*, Vol. 1. (pp. vii-xxiii). Mahwah, NJ: Lawrence Erlbaum.

Tomasello, M. (2003). Introduction: Some surprises for psychologists. In M. Tomasello, (Ed.), *The New Psychology of Language (Cognitive and Functional Approaches to Language Structure)*, Vol. 2. (pp. 1-14). Mahwah, NJ: Lawrence Erlbaum.

Turner, M. (1987). *Death Is the Mother of Beauty: Mind, Metaphor, Criticism*. Chicago: University of Chicago Press.

Turner, M. (1996). *The Literary Mind*. Oxford: Oxford University Press.

Turner, M. (2001). *Cognitive Dimensions of Social Science*. Oxford: Oxford University Press.

Truszczyńska, A. (2003). Conceptual metonymy—the problem of boundaries in the light of ICMs. *Poznań Studies in Contemporary Linguistics*, 38, 221-237.

Ullmann, S. (1962). *Semantics: An Introduction to the Science of Meaning*, Oxford/New York: Basil Blackwell.

Ullmann, S. (1963). *The Principles of Semantics.* Oxford/New York: Basil Blackwell.

Ungerer, F. & Schmid, H. J. (1996). *An Introduction to Cognitive Linguistics.* London: Addison Wesley Longman Limited.

van Dijk, T. A. (1972). *Some Aspects of Text Grammars.* The Hague: Mouton.

van Dijk, T. A. (1977a). Semantic macro-structures and knowledge frames in discourse comprehension. In M. A. Just & P. A. Carpenter, (Eds.), *Cognitive Processes in Comprehension.* (pp. 3-32). Hillsdale, NJ: Lawrence Erlbaum Associates.

van Dijk, T. A. (1977b). *Text and Context: Explorations in the Pragmatics of Discourse.* London: Longman.

van Dijk, T. A. (1979). Cognitive Processing of Literary Discourse. *Poetics Today*, 1, 143-159.

van Dijk, T. A. (1980a). *Macrostructures.* Hillsdale, NJ: Lawrence Erlbaum.

van Dijk, T. A. (1980b). The semantics and pragmatics of functional coherence in discourse. *Versus*, 26-27, 49-65.

van Dijk, T. A. (1981). *Studies in the Pragmatics of Discourse.* Berlin/New York: Mouton.

van Dijk, T. A. (1982). Episodes as units of discourse analysis. In D. Tannen, (Ed.), *Analyzing Discourse: Text and Talk.* (pp. 177-195). Washington, DC: Georgetown University Press.

van Dijk, T. A. (1983). Discourse analysis: Its development and application to the structure of news. *Journal of Communication*, 33, 20-43.

van Dijk, T. A. (1985a). *Handbook of Discourse Analysis*, Vol. 2. London: Academic Press.

van Dijk, T. A. (1985b). *Discourse and Communication: New Approach to the Analysis of Mass Media*, Berlin/New York: Walter de Gruter.

van Dijk, T. A. (1985c). Structures of news in the press. In T. A. van Dijk, (Ed.), *Discourse and Communication.* (pp. 69-93). Berlin: de Gruyter.

van Dijk, T. A. (1986). News schemata. In C. R. Cooper & S. Greenbaum, (Eds.), *Studying Writing: Linguistic Approaches.* (pp. 155-185). Beverly Hills: Sage.

van Dijk, T. A. (1988). *News as Discourse*. Hillsdale, NJ: Erlbaum.

van Dijk, T. A. (1989). Mediating racism: The role of the media in the reproduction of racism. In R. Wodak, (Ed.), *Language, Power and Ideology*. (pp. 199-226). Amsterdam: Benjamins.

van Dijk, T. A. (1991). *Racism and the Press*. London/New York: Routledge.

van Dijk, T. A. (1995). Discourse semantics and ideology. *Discourse & Society*, 6 (2), 243-289.

van Dijk, T. A. (1997). *Discourse in Social Interaction*. London: Sage.

van Dijk, T. A. & Kintsch, W. (1977). Cognitive psychology and discourse: recalling and summarising stories. In W. Dressler, (Ed.), *Current Trends in Textlinguistics*. Berlin: Walter de Gruyter.

van Dijk, T. A. & Kintsch, W. (1983). *Strategies of Discourse Comprehension*. New York/London: Academic Press.

Ventola, E. (1987). *The Structure of Social Interaction: A Systemic Approach to the Semiotics of Service Encounter*. London: Frances Pinter.

Verikaite, D. (2005). Variation of conjunctive discourse markers across different genres. *Man and the Word*, 3(7), 68-75.

Voßhagen, C. (1999). Opposition as a metonymic principle. In K. U. Panther & G. Radden, (Eds.), *Metonymy in Language and Thought*. (pp. 289-308). Amsterdam/Philadelphia: John Benjamins Publishing Company.

Warren, B. (2002). An alternative account of the interpretation of referential metonymy and metaphor. In R. Dirven & R. Pörings, (Eds.), *Metaphor and Metonymy in Comparison and Contrast*. (pp. 113-130). Berlin/New York: Mouton de Gruyter.

Warren, B. (2004). Anaphoric pronouns of metonymic expressions. *Metaphorik De*, 7, 105-114.

Werth, P. (1999). *Text Worlds: Representing Conceptual Space in Discourse*. London: Longman.

Widdowson, H. G. (1978). *Teaching Language as Communication*. Oxford: Oxford University Press.

Widdowson, H. G. (2004). *Text, Context, Pretext: Critical issues in Discourse Analysis*. Oxford: Blackwell.

Wierzbicka, A. (1992). *Semantics, Culture, and Cognition.* Oxford: Oxford University Press.

Yankova, D. (2006). Semantic relations in statutory texts: A study of English and Bulgarian. *SKY Journal of Linguistics*, 19, 189-222.

Zwann, R. A. & Radvansky, G. A. (1998). Situation models in language comprehension and memory. *Psychological Bulletin*, 123(2), 162-185.

蔡晖:《转喻思维产生动因的多元思考》,《外语学刊》2006 年第 6 期。

曹道根:《试论标题的转喻性》,《外语与外语教学》2007 年第 10 期。

陈香兰:《转喻与语用推理》,北京师范大学博士学位论文,2006 年。

陈香兰、申丹:《转喻与语篇:伏应与转喻思维》,《外语与外语教学》2009 年第 5 期。

陈香兰、申屠菁:《转喻矩阵域观》,《外国语》2008 年第 2 期。

陈香兰、周流溪:《异形回指和联想回指理解的转喻动机》,《外语与外语教学》2007 年第 2 期。

胡壮麟:《语篇的衔接与连贯》,上海外语教育出版社 1994 年版。

黄国文:《语篇分析概论》, 湖南教育出版社 1988 年版。

江晓红:《认知语用研究:词汇转喻的理解》,中国社会科学出版社 2009 年版。

蒋勇、苏晓军:《从 Thornburg & Panther 的言语行为借代理论看言语的借代功能》,《外国语》2000 年第 4 期。

鞠玉梅:《隐喻报刊体育新闻语体量化研究》,《外语研究》2004 年第 2 期。

蓝纯:《认知语言学与隐喻研究》,外语教学与研究出版社 2005 年版。

李勇忠、方新柱:《理想化认知模型与转喻的语用功能》,《山东外语教学》2003 年第 3 期。

李勇忠:《间接言语行为中的借代》,《解放军外国语学院学报》2003 年第 2 期。

李勇忠:《言语行为转喻与话语的深层连贯》,《外语教学》2004a 年第 3 版。

李勇忠:《语言转喻的认知阐释》,东华大学出版社 2004b 年版。

李勇忠:《语篇建构中的转喻和隐喻》,《外语学刊》2008 年第 2 版。

廖美珍:《隐喻语篇组织功能研究——标题与正文之间的组织关系》,《外语教学与研究》2007 年第 3 期。

卢卫中、路云:《语篇衔接与连贯的认知机制》,《外语教学》2006 年第 1 期。

卢卫中、刘玉华:《小说叙事的转喻机制》,《外语教学与研究》2009 年第 1 期。

苗兴伟:《论衔接与连贯的关系》,《外国语》1998 年第 4 期。

苗兴伟:《关联理论对语篇连贯的解释力》,《外语教学与研究》1999 年第 3 期。

沈家煊:《转指和转喻》,《当代语言学》1999 年第 1 期。

束定芳:《认知语义学》,上海外语教育出版社 2008 年版 a。

束定芳:《隐喻学研究》,上海外语教育出版社 2008 年版 b。

束定芳:《语言的认知研究: 认知语言学论文精选》,上海外语教育出版社 2004 年版。

孙志农:《论语篇连贯的转喻机制》,《天津外国语学院学报》2007 年第 2 期。

王寅:《认知语言学探索》,重庆出版社 2005 年版。

王寅:《认知语言学与语篇连贯研究》,《外语研究》2006 年第 6 期。

王正元:《语篇视点的认知分析》,《四川外语学院学报》2006 年第 2 期。

王佐良、丁往道:《英语文体学引论》,外语教学与研究出版社 1987 年版。

魏在江:《语篇转喻综观》,《外语学刊》2007 年第 3 期 a。

魏在江:《概念转喻与语篇衔接——各派分歧、理论背景及实验支持》,《外国语》2007 年第 2 期 b。

辛斌:《批评语篇分析的社会和认知转向》,《外语研究》2007 年第 6 期。

熊学亮:《话语衔接的认知距离研究》, 朱永生主编:《世纪之交论功能》,上海外语教育出版社 2002 年版。

熊学亮:《认知语用学概论》,上海外语教育出版社 1999 年版。

徐盛桓:《外延内涵传承说——转喻机理新论》,《外国语》2009 年第 3 期。

严世清、董宏乐:《语篇连贯的新视角》,《山东外语教学》1999 年第 3 期。

杨成虎:《语法转喻的认知研究》,上海交通大学出版社 2011 年版。

杨学民:《转喻与小说“空白”——汪曾祺小说的一种现代语言学解读》,《小说评论》2004 年第 2 期。

张德禄:《语篇连贯与语篇的信息结构》,《外语研究》1992 年第 3 期。

张德禄:《语篇连贯研究纵横谈》,《外国语》1999 年第 6 期。

张德禄:《论语篇连贯》,《外语教学与研究》2000 年第 2 期。

张德禄:《衔接力与语篇连贯的程度》,《外语与外语教学》2001 年第 1 期 a。

张德禄:《语篇内部衔接的原则》,《解放军外国语学院学报》2001 年第 6 期 b。

张德禄、刘汝山:《语篇连贯与衔接理论的发展及应用》,上海外语教育出版 2003 年版。

张辉:《汉英情感概念形成和表达的对比研究》,《外国语》2000 年第 5 期。

张辉、孙明智:《概念转喻的本质、分类和认知运作机制》,《外语与外语教学》

2005 年第 3 期。

张辉:《从转喻场景到语用参数和言外 ICM》,《外语学刊》2007 年第 4 期。

张辉、孙明智:《概念转喻的本质、分类和认知运作机制》,《外语与外语教学》2005 年第 3 期。

张辉、周平:《转喻与语用推理图式》,《外国语》2002 年第 4 期。

张辉、卢卫中:《认知转喻》,上海外语教育出版社 2010 年版。

张辉、江龙:《试论认知语言学与批评话语分析的融合》,《外语学刊》2008 年第 5 期。

赵艳芳:《认知语言学概论》,上海外语教育出版社 2001 年版。

朱永生:《试论语篇连贯的内部条件》(上),《现代外语》1996 年第 4 期。

朱永生:《试论语篇连贯的内部条件》(下),《现代外语》1997 年第 1 期。

朱永生、严世清:《系统功能语言学多维思考》,上海外语教育出版社 2001 年版。

朱永生、郑立信、苗兴伟:《英汉语篇衔接手段对比研究》,上海外语教育出版社 2001 年版。